CHAKKA

CHAKKA

*Woman loves animals. Woman takes in orphaned foxes, injured raccoons, half-dead birds, stray dogs, abandoned cats, foster children. What woman really wants is a wolf. Woman acquires wolf pup. Wolf does not eat the foxes, raccoons, birds, dogs, cats, kids, or woman. Wolf **does** turn woman's world upside down. Woman learns to howl.*

Bevie J. Gravlin

STACKPOLE
BOOKS

Copyright © 1993 by Stackpole Books

Published by
STACKPOLE BOOKS
5067 Ritter Road
Mechanicsburg, PA 17055

All rights reserved, including the right to reproduce this book or
portions thereof in any form or by any means, electronic or mechanical,
including photocopying, recording, or by any information storage and
retrieval system, without permission in writing from the publisher.
All inquiries should be addressed to Stackpole Books, 5067 Ritter Road,
Mechanicsburg, PA 17055.

Printed in the United States of America

10 9 8 7 6 5 4 3 2 1

First Edition

Illustrations by Thomas Aubrey

Cover design by Tracy Patterson

Library of Congress Cataloging-in-Publication Data
Gravlin, Bevie J.
    Chakka / Bevie J. Gravlin.
        p.   cm.
    1. Wolves as pets. 2. Wolves—Anecdotes.
    3. Gravlin, Bevie J. I. Title.
SF459.W63G73   1991
636′.974′442—dc20   90-23606
                                                       CIP

ISBN 0-8117-2429-8

To my family—one and all—whose kindness, patience, and love made all this possible

CONTENTS

1	For the Love of Animals	1
2	Furry Balls of Fluff	11
3	Journey Home	29
4	One of the Family	43
5	Have Wolf, Will Travel	59
6	Head Wolf	83
7	In Control	105
8	Wolf Games	121
9	Widget Warmbody	143
10	Spook	169
11	L'Amour	183
12	Fatherhood	205
13	Family Business	225
14	Separations	235
15	Tippy	249
16	Change	261

Welcome to our home,
but remember,
it has survived a wolf.

1

For the Love of Animals

IT WAS A BITTERLY COLD JANUARY NIGHT, and outside the wind was shrieking through the treetops. An occasional snap and ominous thud were heard as the heavy branches of our huge pines dropped or were flung against the house. The forefront of the predicted blizzard had already begun to hammer at the stout sides of our hundred-year-old log cabin home, but I was well prepared. Anyone who lives in northern Michigan learns to lay in supplies when the weatherman even hints at something more than a snow squall.

The fireplace crackled and threw long orange rays across the braided rug. There was food in the pantry, firewood outside the door, and three hundred pounds of dry dog food stashed in the hallway. Bill, my husband, was working in the upper peninsula that month, and the children were all away for the weekend. I knew there was a good chance I would be snowbound for days before the plows worked their way out of town, and even longer than that before our driveway became negotiable. For the moment, I was alone in the house while the wind built up in intensity and the snow plastered itself against the windows, almost obliterating the view of the wildly whipping trees outside.

It was a perfect night to sit down at the typewriter and begin writing about an animal that had taken up most of my waking hours for the previous three years. I poured a large mug of steaming hot coffee, rolled fresh white sheets of paper into the old electric, and poised my fingers over the keys. But before the first word could appear on paper, I was thrown violently forward against the keys and helplessly pinned to the table edge. One hundred and forty pounds of playful wolf had thrust his paws on my shoulders and was peering over the top of my head to see what it was I was doing that so held my interest. It always intrigued him the way I buckled in the middle under one of those unexpected attacks. He quickly lost interest in the typewriter and turned his attention to my unprotected ear. I might still be there if the table hadn't careened away into the wall, dumping wolf and me onto the floor in a heap.

There was nothing Chakka loved better than to find me helpless, and he was prone to take every unfair advantage of the situation. Both my arms were pinned to the floor as he stood on my sweater sleeves with his front paws while sitting on my stomach with his hind end. Grinning at me from his superior height, he proceeded to "groom" my face, a loving gesture on his part but a disaster to makeup. By the time he'd reached my eyebrows, I lay still. I knew exactly what to expect. With his fangs an inch from my eye, and his chisel-edged front teeth clicking rapidly, he proceeded to snick his way happily along the entire eyebrow line, crushing nonexistent fleas and never-been-there burrs. The skin beneath was never touched, but a few loose hairs here and there were expertly removed. I had noticed, over the years, that my eyebrows kept getting thinner—but then, owning a wolf tends to do that to a person. A wolf's motto seems to be "If a stray hair sticketh out, removeth it." To this end, Chakka was diligently applying himself.

I finally managed to roll sideways, dumping him on the carpet next to me. By the time I had gotten to my knees, he was bouncing back and forth in front of my face, ready for more. When a wolf wants to play, you play, or he will allow you no peace until you do. That lesson I had learned very well over the past years, so I growled and lunged to lock my arms around his neck. He was gone before I got to him, behind me, pulling off my shoe. When I protected one area, he attacked another. For ten minutes we tussled and growled at each other ferociously, darting and feinting attacks while the cats peered from behind the security of various chairs. I began to know how a full-grown caribou feels. I seldom saw him in front of me, but the minute I got to my feet he would hit me behind the knees and topple me again. If our fight had been for real, all bets would have been placed on the wolf. As it was, I was playing with an animal that dearly loved me and had never inflicted a bite of any kind, but by the sounds of the growling, I should have been eaten alive.

I remember the looks of anguish we got from people when we told them we were getting a wolf. "It will turn on you," they'd intoned with solemn faces. "They're vicious and can't be trusted." And yet all the dire warnings did not jibe with what I knew of wolves, nor with what I had read. Granted, I had never encountered a wolf in the wilds—they are too shy to ever let that happen—but I did have close contact with a wolf in the zoo during the time I worked with a local veterinarian. If any animal has a tendency toward a contrary nature, it will be amplified by being confined in a cage in a socially sterile atmosphere. The beautiful male wolf we worked on in the zoo was a gentleman who managed to maintain his dignity despite summer seasons of peanut-throwing crowds. I grew to love him and visited him often, gradually earning his trust. His every move was filled with grace and gentleness. We spent hours leaning compatibly into each other or sharing happy grooming times. When he finally died, I felt a great loss and vowed someday to have a wolf of my own.

This may seem an arbitrary decision made impulsively by someone who simply likes wolves and decided to own one. And it most likely would have turned out disastrously had that been the case. No wild animal is easy to raise, nor should a novice attempt it. But in my own circumstances, animals had been an integral part of my life from the moment I'd been born. In fact, they had taken the place of playmates.

We lived in an apartment building, in a large Michigan city, where children were not allowed. Since I was born there a year after the lease was signed, we were permitted to stay as long as it was understood that I was the *only* child who would ever be there. This not only effectively precluded the arrival of any brothers or sisters, but it also made impossible my ever having playmates over. For the first twelve years of my life, my best friends were two canaries and a cat. I remember quite clearly learning to control the tendency to grab, as babies normally do, because my mother was training the two canaries to sit on my finger. Patience and observation were instilled early, and the animals responded with love and trust.

I can't ever remember when animals weren't my avocation and passion. Furred, feathered, or finned, they were all so special that I never missed human companionship. I developed a knack for being able to know what an animal was thinking or feeling just by reading its body language. The rapport was absolute. They knew I wouldn't hurt them, nor was I ever afraid. It used to terrify my mother to see me walk up to a strange, snarling dog and throw my arms around his neck with impunity. To me, he was just another friend.

As I became old enough to go outside and play by myself I found more animal friends. The church next door had huge banks of bridal wreath bushes lining the old brick walls. I spent untold hours crouched under those green canopies, watching the perky city sparrows tend their nests. They became so used to my presence that I could sit with my face a foot from the nest and watch a mother feed her young.

Every old alley cat for blocks around knew me and came for its afternoon handout. By the time I was five, I had learned which meat markets threw out edible scraps and arranged a daily tour to collect leavings for my companions. I fought vacations and weekend trips for fear the animals would miss a meal and think I had let them down. Their comfort was my greatest concern; they were, after all, my best friends. I helped them hide from the dog catcher, protected their litters, and built them castles of cardboard boxes I found behind the shoe store. My days were full and happy.

When anyone asked me what I was going to be when I grew up, my unhesitating answer was always "A veterinarian." Was there any other profession? Any injured animal I found was carried up to our apartment, where Mom and I did our level best to repair the damage. I learned early how to set broken wings and disinfect wounds. We made sure that the patients were able to care for themselves before they were released.

When I was twelve, we bought our first home. Somehow the word soon spread that our house was the place to take stray, injured, or orphaned wildlife, and I took over a steady stream of critters that needed attention.

One of my favorites was a little chipmunk that was brought to us more dead than alive. He arrived at a perfect time, when I was bedridden for a year with rheumatic fever. We nursed his wounds, and I spent days on end holding him gently while I fed him with an eyedropper. He recovered and made the rest of my convalescence pure joy.

He ate from a jar lid set beside my plate on the bed tray, and he wasn't the least bit hesitant about telling me if I was eating something he wanted. He scampered over the covers, came when I called him, and slept in the pocket of my bathrobe, which hung on the bedpost. When I finally recovered, he took bike rides with me, peering out of my jacket pocket at the rushing world. He went to movies, patronized the best restaurants, and visited friends' homes, but no one ever knew he was there. He would not leave my pocket unless I whistled the "all safe."

During this period, Chippie also helped me read every book about caring for animals that I could get my hands on. Mom haunted the libraries for vet manuals, and a kindly local veterinarian gave me a stack of outdated medical magazines. Armed with a good dictionary, I began to understand and learn something new every day. I probably would have learned more if Chippie hadn't made a nest out of thirty-five pages of my dictionary.

6 *CHAKKA*

Over the years, my dedication to animals never wavered, but my plans to attend college never materialized, either. It was the era of the fifties, when "police action" meant war overseas and unrest at home. I had met a handsome young hometown boy, and married him before he left wearing a smart new military uniform. We had barely a year together, little money, and a very small house trailer we had painstakingly built ourselves. The birth of our son took place after my husband was shipped to Germany, and we joined him the following year for a two-year tour of duty. When we returned to the States, we had become strangers. Sadly, we went our separate ways.

Three years later, fortune smiled on Kim and me when I met and married a wonderful man named Bill, whose kind and gentle nature made our family life complete.

I had managed to get a job with a vet, and my knowledge widened considerably. I assisted in surgery, devised special formulas, and paid visits to the zoo when an animal there needed attention. When the vet left to practice in another city, I began taking animals home from the zoo nursery to raise until they were able to stand on their own. A wonderful man at the conservation department brought me injured and orphaned wildlife to be cared for until they could go back to the wilds. I made trips to area schools with animals the children could see, touch, and feed. In the fall, our family took camping trips into protected areas where the animals were given their freedom. We usually lingered ten days to make sure that they adjusted well.

Since my husband worked in television, I was offered a television show of my own, called "Did You Know?" We featured wild animals as well as abandoned pets from the local humane society (of which I was one of the founding members).

After the TV shows, our animal population expanded considerably. We were put in charge of a wide variety of animals not native to Michigan. Of course, we *were* lucky enough to have one small native Michigan animal—our beautiful new daughter, Jenny, born a year and a half later. When Jenny was three years old, we suddenly found ourselves foster parents to two baby chimpanzees straight from Africa. These two chimps were raised with our children until they were two years old and able to be returned to the private animal park for which they had been purchased. At the same time, we were raising a baby harbor seal, as well as agoutis, skunks, deer, raccoons, and other animals too numerous to mention. I treasure pictures of my son sharing his picnic lunch with the chimps and my daughter taking her bath with the seal. My children grew up thinking that anyone who owned only dogs or cats was underprivileged.

There were times when the menagerie was taken so for granted as a part of our lives that we never considered others might find it unusual. When Jenny started kindergarten and the teacher asked the children to talk about their home life for show-and-tell, Jenny blithely described eating breakfast with the chimps, sleeping with her favorite raccoon, and unwinding with the seal. The teacher explained that show-and-tell was for facts, not fairy tales, and asked Jenny to tell a real story. When Jenny insisted, through tears, that hers *was* a real story, the teacher sent her to a corner and forbade her to come back until she could tell the truth. When she came home sobbing from her first day at school and told me what the teacher had done, a mother's righteous wrath was born.

The next day I sent Jenny to school on the bus, but I planned a surprise for the teacher. An hour later, I drove up to the school with a carload of animals for the children to see. When Bill and I walked into the classroom with a chimp on each arm and a menagerie in tow, the teacher took one stunned look at us and said, "Oh, you couldn't be anyone but Jenny's mother!" From that moment on, she was a believer. While the children raced outside to share their swing sets and seesaws with the chimps, or to play in the sandbox with the raccoons, we sat and talked with the teacher. Before we left, the whole school had come to the kindergarten room, and every child had a chance to meet and play with a wild animal. They all left the richer for it, but the teacher did admit she would have difficulty deciding what to believe in show-and-tell sessions in the future.

We always had in mind the fact that most of the wild animals we cared for were to be returned to the wild, so we kept their human contact to a minimum. Sometimes, through frequent hand feedings or regular medical care, they became used to humans anyway. When that happened, we used the time to show them to children in classes like Jenny's kindergarten to promote better understanding of wildlife. When the animals became strong enough to survive on their own, we began weaning them from human contact and eventually released them into carefully selected wild areas.

Our decision to get a wolf, however, did not require planning for its release. A wolf would remain with us for the rest of its life and would take more time and attention than any animal we had ever had. Although we were used to wild animals, a wolf is in a class by itself. Highly intelligent and highly socialized, it is capable of great loyalty but must be worked with constantly. A wolf simply cannot be tied and left out on a chain, nor can it be left alone in a house—as I discovered, much to my chagrin. Wolves are a full-time occupation and commitment that cannot be taken lightly. They are also longer lived than dogs—twenty years and more. Why, I was asked, would we want to make such a commitment? What prompted me to bring a "potential killer" into the midst of our home and family? Those questions had a familiar ring. I had been asked similar questions when we had raised foxes and coyotes. Everyone was sure that we would be eaten alive in our beds some dark night. "A coyote is capable of ripping your throat out when it grows up," I was told. But my coyotes never read that book. Nor did the foxes. They remained loving and affectionate, never once giving us cause for alarm. I had even more confidence in the wolf because of his intelligence and basic good nature. I wasn't sure where these "experts" were getting their information, but I was going to get mine firsthand. The wolf's much-maligned reputation made him the target of every kind of hunter. If he were better understood, there was hope that more people would rise to his defense.

When I talked to Bill about taking on a wolf, he was supportive. If it had been up to him personally, he wouldn't have gotten one, but he knew how much it meant to me. Besides, he said, he had the utmost faith in my ability to handle it. He felt that if I

FOR THE LOVE OF ANIMALS **9**

said it could be raised safely around children, cats, dogs, and assorted other critters, I was undoubtedly right. We certainly were no strangers to wild animals.

For twelve years I waited for an opportunity to buy a wolf. The zoos we contacted promised us that if they had an abandoned pup we would have first choice, but before that time came, wolves were placed on the endangered species list. This should have protected them, but instead it put them in the limelight and further hastened their demise. I was horrified to watch a television documentary showing pictures of wolves being shot from planes, helpless against their pursuers. This "culling-out process" was supposed to reduce their numbers to a manageable level and protect the caribou. In one film, 80 percent of the wolves were targeted to be killed to "balance out nature." It's odd how well nature got along before we arrived.

After seeing the film, I renewed my efforts to purchase a wolf through legal channels, but learned that absolutely no permits were being issued. It seemed my hopes and chances ended there. Wolves could be shot from planes, but they couldn't be kept as pets. Finally, the answer came from a friend who had been in the conservation department for years. According to Michigan law, he said, wolves could be kept as pets if any proof could be presented that somewhere in the ancestry dog genes were present, no matter how infinitesimal. Since man introduced dogs into wolf areas hundreds of years ago, and interbreeding has occurred, there is some professional doubt as to whether a pure wolf strain exists at all in the Western Hemisphere. But for my purposes this was a moot point, since no one could document the proof.

Another problem occurred to me: I didn't want the offspring of some chance or casual mating that was half wolf, half dog. I wanted a wolf. Where would I find a reputable breeder whose animals met my specifications, who bred the most nearly pure wolf line? For two more years we searched, finding and then discarding one possibility after another and getting more discouraged with each mixed-breed litter we saw. Then, an acquaintance in charge of one of the biggest zoos in the country told me of a man who bred the exact combination I was looking for. When I got the man's phone number, I almost jumped for joy. It would seem that my dream was only a dial away. Nothing could have been further from the truth.

Had I been dealing with a man who bred wolves for profit, my contact would have been an easy one. As it was, I ran into a breeder so closely attuned to his animals that he thought of them as his children, and parted with them about as easily. When I phoned with my request, he was abrupt and nearly discourteous. So what if I wanted a wolf, he seemed to be saying. Maybe it didn't want me. I tried to angle the conversation along more friendly lines, insinuating my qualifications, flattering him with his being so highly recommended, and making it clear that I was certain his wolves were exactly what I was looking for. Did he ever ship the pups by air transport? I asked innocently. To which I was told in no uncertain terms that he most assuredly did not. Nor would he guarantee, if I made the two-thousand-mile round trip to his breeding kennels, that I would even get a pup. I was informed that prospective customers were carefully screened for their suitability as wolf owners, and more were turned away than ever got what they sought. By the time our conversation ended, I had him classified as an old curmudgeon, irascible and testy. How could he expect me to make a trip like that, at considerable expense, with the possibility of coming home empty-handed? Besides, his selling price was almost prohibitive, calculated to discourage all but the most serious buyer.

Luckily, I had my family's backing. After hashing out all the pros and cons, we decided I should at least make the trip to talk to the breeder and decide if his wolves met our expectations, and to see if I passed his muster. As Bill pointed out, if I didn't go I would never know the results, and another opportunity might never present itself. Even though our finances were at a low ebb, I took about three seconds to start packing my bag, making reservations for the ferryboat across the Great Lakes. I would undertake the three-day trip to Iowa by myself, armed with sandwiches and coffee, the purchase price for the wolf, and little else except hope.

2
Furry Balls of Fluff

By the time I arrived at the wolf sanctuary, it was past midnight. I had driven into a little country town on rough dirt roads and entered an America I thought had vanished fifty years before. Nothing was open, no electric signs flashed, and, as far as I could see, the town itself consisted of a grain mill and several houses strung along a dusty street.

Way down the road, I spotted a house with lights burning and two people standing outside. Prodding my tired Volkswagen into gear, I rolled down the tree-lined street. Somewhere during the trip, I had blown a hole in my muffler, and on that quiet June night I sounded like a Sherman tank run amok. If no one had been awake before I'd gotten there, I was sure the whole town knew of my arrival then. Over the horrendous noise, the lady just leaving the house graciously tried to give me directions. Finally, she took pity and offered to guide me there, probably out of concern for her sleeping neighbors.

I followed her car as we passed a series of small wooden

homes until her hand pointed out the window to a very small, dark house. I had decided that if no one was awake I would park and sleep until morning. Carefully I cut the engine, coasted into the driveway, and put on the brake. After an asthmatic wheeze, the motor was still . . . and then the car let loose with a gigantic backfire. The upstairs light went on. Fine, I thought. This ought to make me really popular. I cringed in the car until a man's form filled the front door, and I decided to face the music. I left the car and approached with some hesitation.

About the last thing I wanted at that moment was to meet someone who could dash my hopes in an instant. I was so tired from the trip I could barely stand, and any attempt at cheer or ingratiation was clearly beyond me. I staggered across the lawn in an erratic pattern to the open door. The human monolith that dominated the entrance viewed me from its lofty height with crossed arms. I felt like a little kid scuffling her toe in the sand. "I'm truly sorry," I said. "I had no intention of waking you at this hour." The monolith didn't move. I cleared my throat and began again. "Actually, I had intended to find a motel, but I haven't seen one for the last hundred miles. If you could direct me to one, I'll be glad to come back in the morning."

The monolith remained silent. Then it dawned on me. He had absolutely no idea who I was! Although I had told him on the phone that I would arrive the next day, he certainly wasn't expecting me in the middle of the night. I hastily introduced myself and again asked for directions to a motel, explaining that I had been on the road for more than twenty-four hours. The monolith moved down two steps toward me. I still couldn't see because of the house light behind him, but I could feel him staring holes through me. Well, I thought, there goes my wolf. Scratch one dream.

"You say you've been driving twenty-four hours?" I nodded in dumb agreement. "Well," the deep voice said, "There isn't another motel for forty miles, so I guess you might as well come in and at least have a cup of coffee."

I couldn't believe my ears. I stepped across the threshold, glancing furtively into dark corners for a sleeping wolf. Suddenly the kitchen light blazed on, and an ample form in a bathrobe came toward me. "Well, Andy, don't just stand there. Ask her to sit down. She must be dead on her feet." With that remark, I was guided firmly into the kitchen by Andy's wife, Edith, who plunked me down in the nearest chair. Shortly, a cup of hot coffee was in my hand.

In the warm light of the kitchen, these two looked a lot less like ogres than I'd expected. They were a typical Midwest farm couple, hard-working and decent people. While I surreptitiously sized them up, they did the same to me.

Suddenly, Andy's voice boomed across the table, making me slosh my coffee. "What made you drive twenty-four hours nonstop?" he asked. There was only one answer. "If you knew how long I've waited for this moment," I replied honestly, "you'd understand. I wanted to meet you and the wolves as soon as possible." He settled back in his chair with the barest trace of a smile on his face. "What do you know about wolves?" he rumbled. I outlined my background briefly, then added I was here to learn. That loosened the floodgates. Andy leaned across the table, staring at me. "Well, then," he said, "you'd best bring in your suitcase and stay the night. This is going to take a while."

I couldn't believe my luck as I ran out to the car and grabbed my gear. I was over the first hurdle and wide awake now. I returned to the house with my heart in my mouth and my fingers crossed.

We sat for two hours and talked about wolves and Andy's experience raising them. He had a warm and respectful relationship with his animals; they were not some caged beasts waiting to be sold to the highest bidder. I began to feel a kinship with this man. His wolves were family. He talked with obvious love about old Count, the pure white wolf who was limping into his sixteenth year with evidence of heart failure. He was like a man with a large, rambunctious family, carefully cataloging their virtues and grinning at their antics.

Every wolf, like every child, had a distinct personality. Some were subservient, some aggressive, while others were aloof or affectionate. The shape and form of each member began to materialize in my mind, and I wondered what one of these would be like, if indeed I got one.

Andy was careful to evaluate each buyer and then match up a compatible wolf. Many people were turned away as impulse buyers or thrill seekers. I said a silent prayer that he would not relegate me to one of those categories, and wondered what, if I passed muster, he would come up with to match my personality.

Andy had raised wolves for thirty-five years and lived among them long before that in the Great Slave Lake region. He told me of their natural timidity and trusting curiosity about humans. Many times, he said, he would go hunting in the wilds and return with a string of ptarmigan swinging at his side, only to feel a slight nudge as some great animal trotted alongside him and delicately plucked a trailing bird from the string. Never was any overt action directed with malevolence toward him. These beautiful wildlings had not learned that man, with his traps, poisons, and guns was an untrustworthy creature to be feared. Man was rather simply another animal who roamed their territory.

His fascination and respect for these beautiful animals made Andy keenly concerned about their welfare. Many times during the great, unbelievably cold stillness of those bleak winters, he would go out on a hunting foray and shoot game for the starving wolves who kept their snow dens near his cabin. When he returned with meat, he approached their "snow curls"—temporary dens built into the snowbanks and then drifted over with the wolves inside—and gently brushed the snow aside until he could see the animal. He then tossed a chunk of meat to the hungry bundle of fur and bones inside. The wolves returned his kindness with trust and gentle behavior that would put some dogs to shame. Andy walked through the pack with the assurance of one who knows his trust is returned.

One point that impressed him was the basic shyness of wolves. Although they do not seem to fear any animal, man included, they are quite shy about making initial contact. Their natural curiosity, however, soon overcomes the shyness, until they are enticed into closer contact. Many wolves have been killed because of this combination of curiosity and trust. And yet once wolves learn what creatures to be wary of—man, say—they react by simply melting into the background and avoiding the obnoxious beings. Cruel treatment, torture in traps, and indiscriminate hunting by humans, instead of breeding hate and retaliation as it might in the character of some dogs, simply turn the wolf into an elusive creature seldom seen by man.

The higher social order of wolves allows this learned information to be passed from generation to generation. A territory where wolves are hunted is a territory where even the pups are aware that man is not to be trusted. The relationship between wolf and man, which began in caveman days, has steadily deteriorated from one of working-hunting compatibility to one of hunter-hunted animosity. What a shame we have lost our ability to respect and nurture the relationships between animals and man.

Andy told me an interesting story about his first really close encounter with an injured wolf. It illustrates the point that animals know instinctively the difference between a hunter and a benefactor. During his lonely cabin days in the vast, snow-covered north, Andy heard about a wolf that had fallen into an abandoned well and had been there for over a month. The well was almost dry, and Andy, believing there was a good chance the animal might be alive, traveled a long distance into new territory to see for himself.

He found a poor, emaciated, filthy creature that had survived at the bottom of that cold, miserable abyss by digging for frogs and edible debris at the bottom of the shaft, and by finally recycling its own excreta until it was at the end of its food chain and dying. Nonetheless, it was still capable of delivering a death blow to any enemy encroaching on its territory. Andy studied the dying animal before he left to shoot some game.

When he returned, the animal was lying in abject misery, staring up at him with a combination of apathy and resignation. He tossed the game down the well and returned to his camp to consider his resources and devise a plan for lifting the animal from its prison.

When he returned the next day, the animal was on its feet and staggering about, whining softly as it prowled the dark four-foot-wide shaft. Dropping a lasso might result in only strangling the struggling thing before it could be brought to the surface. Besides, it might take days of dangling before a rope could be pulled taut around the wary animal. With more guts than brains, Andy decided that the only way to bring the wolf out would be to go down into the shaft himself. So he dropped a chain down, tied a coil of rope on his shoulder, and proceeded to ease himself into the dark subterranean tunnel.

As Andy approached the bottom, the animal slid quietly to one side, away from his descent. Here the man was, in an area approximately one-quarter the "lunge area" needed by a wolf to fell a full-grown caribou. His chances were nil if he were attacked, and no one was topside to help him, but he continued with soft words to coax and cajole the ravenous animal into a rope sling, which he tightened slowly and carefully. When the wolf was firmly cinched, Andy turned his back to it and gently tightened the straps until the animal was hanging from his shoulders. There were a few struggles, then the wolf lay still, panting, while Andy inched his way up the chain to freedom. He said he remembered a lot of prayers on the way to the top. His fervent mutterings apparently soothed the wolf enough to get them both safely over the edge.

Once they were out of the well, Andy and the wolf lay in a tangle of common misery and fear until he got his breath. Then he slowly released the animal to its freedom. Being a totally committed person, he stayed around the next few days to make sure that the wolf got food enough to survive and begin hunting on his own. An unusual man, but a typical wolf.

During that cool, misty night, Andy and I sat over steaming mugs of strong, black coffee and I listened spellbound to wolf stories. Like humans, there were good and bad, saints and renegades in each pack, but mainly the wolves who contributed to the overall good of the pack were the ones retained in the social order. Renegades were quickly dispatched or forced into exile. More often than not, this resulted in death, because the pack is a working unit and the individual in the wilds is no match for nature.

The leader of the pack is sometimes a male, but more frequently a female. It is up to the leader to hunt new grounds, arbitrate the pack disputes, and act as cohesive agent to the whole. Wolves generally mate for life but usually share in the raising of the young. "Aunts and uncles" baby-sit while the mother of the litter hunts. Raffish, roguish males who would kill another wolf for unseemly behavior will tolerate with stoic aplomb any ear pulling or tail biting their baby-sitting duties expose them to. The return of the mother heralds more than a fresh meat dinner; it signifies the release of the often tattered baby-sitters to their own dens.

Wolf pups are born with rather incomplete stomachs. The acid content within is not strong enough to digest the meat nutrients needed, and so the mother wolf solves this problem by hunting game, eating it, and then returning to the den to regurgitate the catch, including the enzymes and acids from her own stomach, for the pups. In this semi-digested state the proteins are ready for assimilation by her pups who may still be nursing. In addition to the mother, other members of the pack contribute to the feeding of her young until they are ready for small forays of their own to catch a range of snacks from crickets to frogs, mice to birds. Then, again in a community effort, the pups are taken on short hunts by their mothers and other members of the pack. Should a nursing mother die or get killed, the young are raised by other adults of the pack. Seldom are young animals left to starve or fend for themselves. Luckily for the pack, wolves practice a form of natural birth control so that sometimes the only bearing female for that year is the alpha female. Occasionally, one or possibly two more litters are born within the pack, but never enough pups to place an unnatural burden on the hunting members of the pack. In lean years, females may not come into heat at all; or, if they do, refuse to mate.

Since a wolf does not reach adulthood until about two years of age, the learning process is protracted. The female devotes herself to the raising of one litter to adulthood before becoming pregnant again. When her pups have reached the age of self-sustenance, she gradually becomes more aloof and withdrawn, allowing them to take their place as part of the pack while getting ready for her next litter. Occasionally, a pack becomes too large for an area to support, and splinter groups are driven off to become the nucleus of a new pack. But the nucleus of the next unit consists of pups and knowledgeable adults in a ratio consistent with a well-ordered, functional group. Nature takes better care of her own than humans do, and sets a wiser example, had we but the disposition and patience to observe and learn.

How would wolves raised in pens differ from the glorious animals raised in the wilds? I wondered. Would they become the neurotic, high-strung animals frequently seen in show rings, circuses, and zoos? Would they become the inbred, feisty, unmanageable animals that man has managed to ruin with his intervention? Andy discovered that it depends on the breeder. An animal can be as good or as bad as the breeder and his facilities allow. More than anything, the love and care of the animal by the owner makes the long-term difference.

The more I listened to the homilies and basic wisdom from this man who so loved wolves, the more I believed that I had been lucky in the extreme to meet him. And without the good-natured kindness of his wife, Edith, who bottle-fed and raised every wolf pup for placement, I doubt that he could have continued his lifelong work of allowing the civilized world to know and appreciate the glory of wildness.

Because of the necessity of "imprinting" a wolf early in captivity, Andy explained, the cubs are separated from their mother at about ten days of age. Imprinting is the process whereby a young animal learns to associate its bonds with its eventual "master," whether that be human, mother, or lead wolf. It is an extremely crucial period, particularly for the wolf cubs, because they form their initial bonds and impressions for life.

Although the young that were raised by Andy's compassionate wife were likely to form a considerable attachment for her, they were rather flexible until the age of six weeks, when they began to solidify their loyalties in earnest. From that point on, their attitudes tended to become more rigid, and it took considerable effort to reacclimate them to a new owner.

There are many cases on record of wolves forming new attachments, Andy told me, but this cannot be done without continual close contact and an enormous amount of work on the part of the new owner. My wolf—he referred to "my" wolf! Did he mean it?—was four weeks old and had been left with its litter. The only contact these pups had with Edith was when she fed, cleaned, and handled them for a short period three times a day. Consequently, they knew and trusted humans, but tended to associate more closely with litter members. The real imprinting would begin when the pup found its new owner, who would have to devote twenty-four hours a day to the next few crucial weeks of imprinting.

Just how long and lasting the imprinting can be was brought out in an example Andy related to me about a wolf he had sold four years earlier. The buyer obviously adored the animal and treated it well during its imprinting. As Andy told me, there is almost nothing you can do to a wolf in later life that will destroy its basic love and affection for you. But this owner suffered a series of reverses he was unable to handle, and eventually he turned to alcohol. Although he never consciously physically abused the wolf, there were periods when his drinking interfered with the animal's comfort and welfare. It would spend long periods penned up or left alone, but its affectionate greeting of its master never betrayed any emotion other than love.

When Andy learned about the cruel conditions under which the animal lived, he made a trip to the man's home, repaid him his investment, and took the wolf away. He brought it home and settled it in the beautiful pens I was soon to see, fed it properly, and nursed it back to exuberant health. He lavished affection on the animal, and it returned his love and seemed fairly well adjusted among its companions.

Nearly a year went by. One late fall day, Andy was startled to see the man standing at his front door, asking if he could visit with his wolf once more. Whether it was a case of remorse or real love for the animal, Andy couldn't tell, but the man was sober and seemed sincere. Andy agreed to a short visit and took the man back to the pens. The wolf almost broke down the steel-wire fencing trying to lavish wolf love on its errant master. No matter what treatment it had received at his hands, its whole being was directed in love toward the man on whom it placed no blame. It was days before Andy could get the pining animal to eat or respond again. Something vital was missing from its life, and it preferred sharing humiliation and deprivation with the owner to whom it had bonded than living a life of excellent care in its present home. As Andy put it, "First impressions last, and a wolf *never* forgets."

As the clock hands approached the early morning hour of two-thirty, poor Edith had already replenished the steaming mugs several times and was nodding in her chair. I could have sat and listened to wolf stories until dawn, but realizing that they must get up early I suggested that I was tired. They prepared my bed in an upstairs bedroom, and I thanked them for their kindness. As I climbed wearily up the stairs, I asked Andy what time he arose to do the wolf chores, adding sincerely that I would be glad to help him. He answered, "Five-thirty." I asked if he would wake me or set an alarm for me for that time. He answered that it would not be necessary. I took it to mean that he would call me rather than set an alarm.

Sleep eluded me that night. Despite the long hours pounding the highway in my little car and the lack of any rest, my eyes simply would not stay shut. I lay in that strange, dark bedroom straining my ears for the slightest wolf sound, but there was no hint of where the wolf pens were. I knew they were somewhere close to the house, hidden by the veil of heavy summer fog that pressed against the windows. The last time I looked at my watch it was four o'clock. Between then and five-thirty I dozed off, and the next thing I knew I was fairly jolted out of bed by something that electrified me.

At precisely five-thirty, a chorus of thirty wolves ten feet out-side my bedroom window howled in unison as though on command. My hair woke up first. I could feel it standing on end before my feet hit the floor. As I was getting my bearings in the early half-light, I listened to that eerie sound. The voices were unexpectedly soft, full of timbre and vibrato. It was like a well-trained choir, each wolf harmonizing with its neighbor rather than following the same notes. Some voices pitched upward, ending in a soft ululation. Others sank to lower pitches in a softly mellow howl. In unison they sang their early-morning happiness, and then as quickly as it was started, every voice was stilled, leaving an impossible emptiness in the air. I had expected more volume to the song instead of the muted, wild sweetness I heard. It wasn't until much later that I discovered that although soft at close range, the wolf voice carries incredible distances, sometimes sounding as loud across a valley as it does at close range. I stood immobilized a few more seconds and then rushed to get dressed. I now knew what Andy had meant about there being no need to set an alarm.

I stumbled down the stairs into the kitchen to find Edith fixing breakfast for the animals. Coffee was again steaming on the stove, and when Andy came in I could scarcely contain myself while he leisurely spent ten minutes drinking the scalding liquid. Finally he rose and picked up several buckets of prepared food, and we were out the door and headed for the pens.

The wolf pens were constructed in a large U shape that opened up into a central courtyard of fine gravel. All the separate runs were housed under a continuous roof, providing shelter from sun and snow alike. Each wolf run had a plywood floor that sloped gently to the front for easy cleaning and washing down. The front of each pen opened onto an enclosed wire walkway that led to the enclosed courtyard. The pens were immaculate, well constructed for the comfort of the animals, and offered both an open view and an area for seclusion at the rear. As Andy explained, his wolves didn't pace like zoo animals because they had a secure den area in the rear of the pen, safe from prying eyes and affording security. None, however, took the opportunity of disappearing into their dens when we arrived, although most of them retired to the far end of their runs until they had a chance to size up the new stranger in their midst. Then they cautiously and silently padded up to the front of the pens to sniff me and take stock of the situation. When they were assured that I was no threat, their greetings were as different as were their faces and personalities.

In the far pen, I immediately recognized old white Count, with his dark and slender mate. Count came up to the front of the pen to greet Andy, but his mate did not. "Watch this," Andy said. He dampened his fingers in the drinking water and rubbed the front wire of the cage. The female immediately came toward us, sniffed, and urinated a few drops, indicating her willing submission to Andy. He gave her an affectionate rub on the head and proceeded to the next pen.

I stood in awe, watching each great, gentle creature offer him its own particular greeting; some effusive, several sweetly coy, others garrulous and prancing. As each face came forward, I saw a different personality reflected in it. Some eyes slanted in an inscrutable, withdrawn expression. Others were round eyed, mischievous, and abounded in pure hellish glee. Still others were gently sloped and lined in black, giving a soft, doe-eyed look to them. Teeth were bared, not in snarls but genuine smiles, while tails wagged and ears were laid back sleekly against heads in a typical greeting. Each face was as individual and unique as are human faces, perhaps more so. A few licked my fingers gently; others merely sniffed and turned away to something more interesting. None was malicious or aggressive. One great brown male licked my face and then carefully "groomed" my eyelashes with his great front teeth, removing every bit of mascara. I wanted to lift my face to the sky and say, "Look at me, God, *here I am!*" It was one of the happiest days of my life.

As we moved down the line of pens, there was no snarling about who got the food first. A definite, quietly accepted order was in force. There was no shoving; each simply waited its turn. Something I was hard-pressed to accomplish at home in our civilized surroundings the wolves managed: peace at the dining table!

Andy kept up a running commentary about each wolf as we

passed by the pens, explaining its ancestry, origin, and habits as well as personality and quirks. He pointed to a lovely silver-gray male with incredibly long legs and explained he was a timber wolf. Alongside the other wolves, he looked like the coyote in the Roadrunner series, but in the wilds those long legs had served him well when pursuing elusive and swift-footed prey nearly as long legged as himself.

Tundra wolves, more compact, full-bodied, and dark, had eyes without the Oriental quality that showed up plainly in the timber wolf. Each wolf, even within the same species, possessed distinctive markings and a wide variance of color. Soft grays bordering on pearl or white contrasted sharply with near blacks and deep russet browns. Some had full masks adorning their faces; others were gently marked. Ears, too, provided a startling contrast to the features. Some were almost comically large, standing away from the head like great beacons, while others were shorter, delicately rimmed with soft black edgings that ended sharply at the bright pink inner ear. The "language of the ears" was as definite as hand signals in humans. Ears laid low could depict either happiness or readiness for battle, but the rest of the face clearly mirrored the wolf's intentions. They were all beautifully expressive, wonderfully readable. I will never forget those magnificent faces, or the personalities that shone brilliantly through the eyes. It was like looking through centuries of civilized mist to see the clarity of our beginnings.

The last pen we approached contained the six-month-old youngsters, and I chuckled at their clumsiness. All elbows, ears, and feet, they stumbled over each other, chins on the floor, in their haste to greet us. They always got up grinning in silly embarrassment and repeating the act three feet later. Rushing to the pen front with huge pink tongues lolling happily from the corners of their mouths, they planted slurpy kisses on anyone rash enough to place a face near the wires. Not until they were two years old would they gain their full height and girth, and with it some adult aplomb. Until then, they would act like clowns with engaging earnestness.

Finally we were at the end of the open pens, but I still hadn't seen the latest litter. I was able to ask about them when Edith appeared with a pailful of carefully prepared puppy food and motioned me to follow her around the corner. There, in a protected and fully enclosed area, was a floor covered in sawdust and a space larger than most living rooms. Sleeping boxes lined one wall and lights hung from the ceiling at various levels, offering both heat and light when needed. I stared into the room over the half door but didn't see a pup anywhere. As I turned with a puzzled look, Edith smiled and made a soft clucking noise with her tongue. Suddenly there came a small explosion of sawdust in the far corner as a burst of six furry balls barreled toward us, tumbling over each other in their hurry. They rushed to the half door and pummeled it with their feet, woofing and cavorting so boisterously that it was hard to put down the pail without striking one of them on the head. They were anxious for the food, but even more anxious for human attention.

At this age, these round, furry balls of gray fluff showed little evidence of what their adult coloring would be. Only after nearly an hour of observing them was I able to distinguish their individual, almost hidden markings. They were all about twelve inches long, and about as round as they were tall. Their bodies were firmly anchored to the ground by huge feet that constantly got in their way. There was nothing graceful about them, but the humor with which they faced life was contagious to anyone near. While jostling for our attention, they were never too busy to take a playful nip at some other pup's ear or tail, or purposely bowl over a littermate who was not quite as alert. Occasionally, one would leap straight into the air and come crashing down into a tangle of pups nearby, leaving only sawdust and feet visible for a moment. Then the sawdust would settle and two or three would race in a mad chase to the opposite end of the room, only to return barking and nipping at each other on the way. They were flamboyant, comical, absurd. When I felt I couldn't stand on the other side of that door an instant longer, I asked permission to go join them in the room.

If the other pups were fair game for intimidation, I was the

He has never used it to threaten, nor has he growled or otherwise shown his teeth; he doesn't need to. But with Tawny, the opportunity never came up. She simply ignored him. Once, when she was lying in front of the fireplace, Chakka approached and stepped hesitantly over her head, where he stood in his dominant wolf attitude. Tawny snored through the whole routine. Chakka was puzzled; clearly he wasn't getting his point across. He continued staring at her sleeping form another minute or two, then strolled over to one of the wandering cats and placed a paw over its back. The cat sat down and Chakka heaved a sigh of relief. At least someone in the house recognized a king when she saw one!

Tawny remained an enigma to Chakka in his young years. She was far too large for him to even attempt to dominate, so he tried adopting her as his surrogate mother. When she was lying down, he would wriggle engagingly under her chin and roll over to pat her with his feet. Tawny would simply raise her head and stare in some other direction, totally ignoring this worrisome child. Her disregard of his feelings had no effect on his supplications, for he continued, day in and day out, to try for her attention. Ignoring him only escalated his demonstrations. Practically turning himself inside out when she came into the room, he would then follow her slavishly, to no avail, until one day an accident proved to Chakka's little mind that Tawny loved him wolf-style.

I had heard Tawny come downstairs in rather a hurry and head for the back door. As usual, Chakka was Johnny-on-the-spot to go out with her. There is just no delicate way to relate this episode, so I will tell it as it happened—and bear in mind that adult wolf parents regurgitate food for their youngsters. Tawny had just gotten out the door when she became sick and threw up her breakfast. Chakka went into ecstasies, bouncing happily up and down in front of her face, kissing her lavishly. She cared! She cared! He was transported with joy. But before he could accept the offering, I gathered him up and put him back in the house, while Tawny shot ocular daggers at him. The rest of the day Chakka followed Tawny's every move, allowing her no peace. Tawny was so put out that she finally left our company and retreated upstairs, leaving a short-legged wolf pup howling in dismay at the foot. It was weeks before Chakka gave up his helpless love affair with Tawny and transferred his affections to someone more understanding.

5

Have Wolf, Will Travel

WE WERE HOME ONLY TWO DAYS WITH Chakka before it was time to leave on a camping vacation. Normally, I would not have attempted to uproot Chakka from his new surroundings when he was just barely getting used to them, but his availability coincided with plans that had already been set in motion. Rather than miss our chance to get a wolf after all these years of waiting, we decided to go ahead and work out the problems as they arose. It would be confusing to the pup, but as it turned out he adapted beautifully, partly because we took Tawny with us. He spent many hours of happiness curled next to her sleeping form; she was his anchor and security to which he retreated when the world became too confusing.

I had worried that Chakka would be meeting too many new people who would unknowingly force their attentions on him. We resolved before we left that we would pick the most quiet campsites available and do our best to shield Chakka from unwanted advances, no matter how well intentioned. As it was, our fears were groundless, partly because Chakka adapted better than we had hoped, and mostly because he followed goddess Tawny everywhere. It was Tawny's habit to greet everyone as a friend, and when she accepted someone, chubby Chakka followed suit, his idol's stamp of approval being inviolate.

Our vacation that year was one of comparative luxury. Previously, our camp gear had consisted of sleeping bags and little else, and we'd sleep on the ground, good weather or no. Obviously, such arrangements wouldn't have been appropriate with Chakka in chilly or rainy weather. But this year was different; my folks had bought us a used school bus, which we'd spent weeks remodeling. Having taken out all the seats, we'd laid in a heavy plywood floor and covered it with two-inch-thick yellow shag carpeting. If you have never seen an empty school bus carpeted from front to back, you have no idea how truly huge it is—larger by far than the rooms in most modern homes. It was light, airy, and comfortable. We had had neither the money nor the time to build in any furniture, nor to install a bathroom or kitchen, so we decided to leave it totally open and take along folding tables, chairs, camp stoves, and sleeping bags. When we were traveling, our equipment was stored along the sides, leaving the center area for moving around in. We camped at state campgrounds, where sanitation facilities and water were available. It was one of the most enjoyable trips we ever took.

Old Tawny had her own bed, a crib mattress covered with thick cotton carpeting, and her own quilt for cool nights. She went into the bus while we were still working on it and established her nesting area immediately. She was so afraid we would leave without her that she sometimes refused to go in the house when we did, preferring instead to stretch out and wait until we returned. Whenever we were on the move, she would spend the first few minutes sitting up, looking out the window, then lie down happily with a long, soft moan and sleep the remainder of the journey.

The morning we left was Chakka's third day with us, and of course he wasn't yet housebroken. Some sort of confinement had to be arranged for him, both for sleeping and for safety. Bill finally solved the problem by getting a large cardboard refrigerator box, laying it lengthwise, and cutting open the top. Into this went multiple layers of newspaper, a bed, toys, and dishes. When the bus was finally loaded, we carried Chakka out, lowered him into his spacious new quarters, and started our long drive to the Upper Peninsula. What we should have done was get the box early and acclimate Chakka to it before the trip. As it was, he had to adjust to the new bus, the confining box, and the throb of the engine all at once. It overwhelmed him, and he backed into a corner and howled, a repeat of his terror the day I had driven home with him from Andy's compound. Jenny immediately took him out of the box and cradled him while she crooned softly in his ear. Several minutes later he had calmed down enough to start looking out the window. He jumped when telephone poles sped by and nearly went wild when a bridge overpass swallowed our bus whole. Finally, it was just too much for him and he buried his nose under Jenny's arm and fell asleep. For the next few hours, his little body rocked and swayed to the movement of the bus, and when he awoke again it was as if he had been born into these circumstances and none other. The vehicle's shuddering and jolting never bothered him again, but the box remained his nemesis, a thing to be gotten out of as soon as possible and by whatever means available.

We had planned to make our first stop late that afternoon at a favorite little restaurant in the Straits of Mackinac. Denny stopped the bus at a grassy little park before we got to town, so that Chakka and Tawny could be walked. Tawny ambled happily out, and normally Chakka would have followed immediately after her, but the trauma of the trip had unnerved him. We carried him off in our arms and set him on the grass, but he wanted no part of that! He strained and pulled on his leash, crying pitifully to return to the bus. No amount of coaxing or attention could mollify him. He wanted in! After fifteen minutes of struggling, we gave up and let him scramble back to the bus steps. They were too high for his little body to negotiate, and he flipped on his back three times in unsuccessful attempts to mount back up. Finally, Jenny pushed him up the first step and he shot up the rest on his own. I watched the leash disappear out of Jenny's hands as Chakka went flying to the far end of the vehicle, where he immediately squatted and relieved his frustrations in a dime-sized puddle. Soon we were on our way again.

Obviously, we were going to have to begin some sort of housebreaking routine with Chakka, vacation or no vacation! Andy had informed me that housebreaking a wolf is practically impossible, but several observations I had made since we'd gotten Chakka led me to believe that there might be a way. I had kept track of the number of times that Chakka needed to void his bladder, and discovered that it occurred about every forty-five minutes. Armed with this wisdom, we approached his training on a prevention basis. No matter where we were on the road, we stopped the bus about every forty minutes and took Chakka outside. We often found ourselves standing around impatiently for five or ten minutes, but when the proper behavior was forthcoming, we all joined in praising Chakka lavishly. By working on the positive aspect, we seldom had to chastise him for leaving puddles on the carpeting. It might be said that Chakka had us trained, and not vice versa—I personally don't much care how the operation is interpreted. At the end of three weeks, we had Chakka trained to squat when we took him outside, and he had suffered very little trauma in the process.

The second observation I had made proved equally helpful. Wolves are clean animals and have an aversion to fouling their nest area, and since Chakka's cardboard box was used mostly for sleeping, he considered it just that. As long as he was quiet in his box, all was well, but the minute I heard him rustling around or whimpering, I knew the need was urgent. I would immediately pick him up and take him outside, where his actions were again extravagantly praised. It meant some lost time or sleep, but the effort was worth it.

Our third and last observation was that Chakka's digestive system would hold only so much before the tail end activated. Approximately half an hour after a meal of horse meat and dog food, the predictable happened. We established a routine of feeding him three meals a day, and after each one, playing with him for about twenty-five minutes and then walking him outside. The combined bulk in his system and rough exercise always produced the desired results in short order, and he came to accept this as part of his routine. Although we had supplementary dry dog food available for him at all times, he merely picked at it occasionally, preferring to wait for mealtime.

A wolf in the wild is a feast-or-famine animal that can go for days at a time without food while stalking new prey. In nature's marvelous economy, the wolf can retain most if not all of his previous meal in the intestines, where the process of digestion continues, extracting nearly all obtainable nutrients until the next meal necessitates evacuating the remains to make way for the new. The growth pattern, then, in a wild wolf is often sporadic, coinciding with the availability of food. Chakka's meals were frequent and steady, enabling him to grow in a more even pattern. Thus, feeding him three times a day not only made for a healthier wolf, but also helped us to program his housebreaking. An extra bonus was that Chakka looked forward to the praise so much that he tried harder and harder to please. Things couldn't have turned out better.

Finally, after one last stop to answer Chakka's call of nature, we arrived at the restaurant we'd destined for our next meal. Bill opened all the bus windows to catch the breeze from Lake Michigan, and Jenny put Chakka in his box. We stayed in the bus a few minutes with him until he calmed down enough for us to leave. But Chakka would have no part of it. No matter that he could see us standing around the box, he wanted O-U-T! He scrambled wildly and frantically at the sides, working himself into a real dither. His eyes were wide circles of misery, and no amount of soothing talk would placate him. Finally, Jenny lifted him out and sat on the floor, cuddling him. He slowly began to relax and in a few more minutes was fast asleep. I still don't know how we did it, because it never worked again, but somehow we managed to get him back into the box and retreated quietly out of the bus.

The bus was parked approximately fifty feet from the restaurant, where we could keep our eyes on it. Soft music was playing inside while we ate, and I thought to myself how peaceful it seemed after the noise in the bus. Our food was served, and I was just digging in, when Bill leaned forward to say something to me and we heard the strangest sound. He leaned back in puzzlement, but before he could say anything else, the sound returned. My first thought was that something had gone amok with the soothing-music sound system, but it seemed more like a second track playing weird crescendos over the first. Heads in the restaurant swiveled toward the open door. The minute the door closed, the noise abated, but outside in the parking lot people were gathering around our vehicle, pointing and talking. I closed my eyes in resignation. Chakka's baby wolf-howl was in full force, and before he created any more commotion I had to get out there. As I rose to leave, Bill offered to bring out my lunch in a napkin. I glared at him and pointed to my plate containing the specialty of the house—pancakes and maple syrup. Then I hastily made for the door.

Chakka's howls were echoing up and down that tourist-filled street like a siren. Cars slowed up so people could see who was being murdered when I burst in through the bus doors and grabbed Chakka from his box. Outside, angry faces clustered around the bus as fingers pointed accusingly in our direction. Chakka shut up immediately and licked my face, content at his sure-fire way of being liberated from the hated box. I sat on the floor with him, feeling like a traitor—a hungry one—while Chakka amused himself by romping happily around my legs. By the time the family returned, I was tired, hungry, and hot, but Chakka was on a roll. Denny started up the bus and we pulled out quickly. Bill had brought me a hamburger, which I kept trying to get into my mouth as we bounced and jostled down the next leg of our journey. A high point for me it was not.

Late-afternoon shadows slanted through the trees when we finally arrived at Straits Park. Michigan abounds with some of the loveliest parks in the world. This particular one, nestled on the shore of Lake Michigan, catches every cooling breeze that blows across the water. It is woodsy and dense, and at the same time modern and clean. Since all the shoreside campsites were taken, we chose to back the bus into a shady cavern of stately old pines, with picnic table, fire pit, and water hookups right outside the front door. In ten minutes, we had the folding tables and chairs set up, a fire burning merrily in the pit, and supper started. We hooked up our little portable TV to catch the afternoon news. Chakka was on his leash outside, exploring a wonderful world of crickets and sun-dappled sand, and Tawny was stretched out for her daily afternoon nap. After all the excitement, Chakka had finally quieted down to his normal, exuberant self. From other campsites hidden around winding bends in the road we could hear muted sounds of music, laughter, and conversation. Tantalizing aromas of charcoaled steaks and hamburgers began to drift our way, and Chakka's curiosity about his surroundings mounted. Jenny finally took the leash and walked him down toward the sandy lake shore. For the first time, Chakka decided to take the lead, and he tugged happily along the shady paths, investigating any threatening bushes that crossed his path.

When they returned nearly an hour later, supper was ready. Jenny was full of tales about Chakka's first outing. The minute they'd reached the shoreline, Chakka had had his first encounter with an open body of water. The waves had lapped lazily at the shore, leaving him fascinated. With many hesitations and fancy footwork, he managed to get close enough to snap at the incoming waves. Much to his delight, they were not only harmless but cool. Before long, he had managed to wade in up to his tummy, which brought the waves to his chin. That didn't bother him at all, but his first experience of putting his head down to see what was at his feet left him sputtering for a moment. He retreated briefly to the shore and continued his peregrinations along the water's edge, checking occasionally to see if Jenny was still securely tethered to the other end of his leash. Because almost everyone was preparing or eating supper, Jenny and Chakka briefly had the beach to themselves. But suddenly, out of nowhere, a large golden collie trotted toward Chakka.

All dogs in state parks must be leashed, but this one had probably slipped away from its owners when they weren't looking. It made a beeline for Chakka, head held high and tail wagging.

For Chakka it was love at first sight, and after the peremptory canine sniffs, the collie returned the affection. They cavorted and tumbled over the sand and stones until it was time for Chakka and Jenny to leave. At that point, the collie was loath to leave his new friend, so he simply stuck with them on the trip back. Tawny, being a beast of protocol, hauled her great bulk into upright attention as the newcomer strode into view. Chakka raced up to her, his ears flat in greeting, barking the great news of the wonderful acquaintance he had made. He was anxious that she accept this new-found friend. While Tawny tried unsuccessfully to ignore Chakka's leaping and tumbling, she managed a haughty greeting to the collie and shook herself awake. All was going very well indeed, and since supper was almost ready, I suggested that Jenny put Chakka down by his dish so that we could all eat. Animals and humans alike filled their faces contentedly as the last long rays of a warm summer sun settled behind the treetops. When it came time to do dishes, Chakka was sleeping and the collie just polishing off the last of his bone. Jenny picked up the exhausted wolf and put him in the bus in his box. He whuffed a time or two, then curled up to sleep. At about that moment, a worried family appeared around the bend calling for Laddie.

Laddie left his bone and bounced down the road to his people. They walked up to our lot and asked if Laddie had been bothering us. We assured them Laddie had been a welcome guest, and in the usual conviviality of campsites everywhere invited them for a cup of coffee. We all sat around the fire, engaged in good conversation. They couldn't understand, they said, why Laddie had left their campsite. He wasn't used to doing that. Jenny, staunch defender of all animal life, explained that Laddie had followed our wolf home. The moment she said it, she clapped her hand over her mouth. We had agreed before leaving home that we would tell no one that Chakka was a wolf. Indeed, it was still easy at this point to pass him off as a husky-shepherd mix. We all felt that the fear and sensationalism engendered by the word *wolf* would be best avoided as long as possible. Too many fallacies were connected with wolves to convince people of their innate gentleness and good humor. But since the fact was out, we pledged our neighbors to secrecy and proceeded to fill them in on wolf behavior and what we had experienced with our own wolf to date. Needless to say, they were very eager to meet Chakka, and Jenny went to get him.

What followed was not Chakka's most shining moment. The mother, father, and two children trooped in behind Jenny and stood around the box that contained the sleeping Chakka. When he awoke, it was to groping hands and strange faces. In his sleepy confusion, Chakka lowered his head and refused to be picked up, flattening himself against the box floor. Jenny stretched over the edge of the box and managed to get a grip of Chakka's fat tummy. Instantly he turned with a low growl and snapped at the air in front of her hand. Jenny straightened up with the most surprised and hurt expression I have ever seen on her face. The visiting family stood in silence, observing Chakka once again lowered in a threatening pose. By this time I had come in, and, seeing what happened, talked to Chakka for a minute before I reached inside. He allowed himself to be lifted, but he wasn't happy. Sleepy and emotionally drained from his day's experiences, he seemed relieved when we put him back to bed in the gathering twilight. The visitors expressed polite thanks and took their leave. I have often thought what a great pity it was that they saw Chakka in one of the few moments of anger and fear that he exhibited in his life. I'm sure, to this day, that their preconceived notions about wolves were only confirmed. That one moment of misbehavior probably reinforced a fallacy that a whole lifetime of exemplary actions could do nothing to alleviate.

I went outside to find Jenny. By then it was dark and I couldn't see her, so I followed the sounds of soft, choking sobs. After years of dealing with every kind of animal from sparrows to seals, Jenny felt complete defeat from an animal she dearly loved. While she tried to tame her tears I explained what had probably prompted Chakka's actions. To her, she'd only given him total love and he had rejected her. As we sat quietly in the dark, I told her that just because Chakka had snapped didn't mean he didn't love her. He was tired, sleepy, and disoriented. What was the difference, I asked, between Chakka snapping and one of our own dog puppies doing the same in a moment of irritation? The difference was, of course, that with a dog there was no basic fear. You reprimanded the pup, and that was it. Why should Chakka snapping have any more effect on us than that? The answer was that because of years of misconception, a wolf was condemned from the start. A dog was allowed to express itself with snaps or growls, and a human didn't have to feel threatened. But a wolf, by comparison, was condemned for expressing an opinion. "Ah, there it is, the killer instinct!" Chakka, I told her, was only a very tired baby. He had feelings the same as we did, and he could get snappy, as we all do at times, without leaping for the jugular. Jenny dried her eyes and returned to the bus to talk to Chakka, who was awake and howling. I sat under the trees, frankly wondering if we had bitten off more than we could chew.

Chakka's greeting of Jenny when she returned was one of total love. He groomed her eyelashes, kissed her eyes, and apologized a thousandfold for his behavior. In the very few times that Chakka would ever snap or growl, not once would he bite to inflict injury, despite the fact that he could at any time have chosen to rip our hands open with one sure chomp. His snap at bare air was only a last-ditch, gentlemanly warning that he had had enough. All told, Chakka's periods of rare antisocial behavior were shorter than any dog's I have ever known. And unlike many pampered lap dogs who will snap without provocation, his rare tantrums were completely harmless. To this day, after years of experience, I will trust a wolf more than I will any dog.

That evening, a rather subdued Gravlin family tucked in for the night. Chakka had his last period of playtime and then sacked out for the evening. As long as it was dark, he didn't mutter when he was in his box. We left him on the floor while we played cards, took him and Tawny out for their last constitutional, and then tucked him in. Tawny moaned and groaned in happiness beneath her quilt. The night air was chilly for July, so we draped a towel over Chakka. All across the campgrounds, fires were banked, radios squelched, talk subdued. Somewhere in the distance, a group of young people were strumming guitars and singing, but even that faded as our busload of tired travelers snuggled under our blankets for the night.

For me, morning arrives when light dawns, or sometime shortly after that. To Chakka, morning dawns when his bladder reaches uncomfortable proportions. This might occur anywhere from twelve-thirty to three-thirty, depending on the amount of liquid consumed. He sets up a mighty howl when the need arises. I am not the most alert riser, but compared with my family of sleepyheads I'm the only functional human on the planet. During our vacation, Chakka and I were the only ones to see the still, chill parks at midnight, 3:00, and 5:00 A.M. While I shivered in my caftan and slippers, he would take an unconscionable time to find the exact spot for his nightly deposits. Nothing conveniently near the bus would do. Instead, we had to tramp over other people's camp areas, step over smoldering fires, and come so close to tents and trailers that we ran the risk of being arrested as Peeping Toms. When it rained, the scenario was even worse. Then Chakka would relinquish his roaming-far-afield habits and snuffle instead underneath the bus. This left me standing in the drizzle while he spent ten minutes shopping around for an appropriate spot. Invariably, he would return to the bus warm, dry, and relieved, while I huddled in my sleeping bag, thoroughly soaked. This routine didn't work any miracles on my disposition. At forty-two, I had forgotten what it was like to waken with crying babies, and I was having to learn all over again.

We stayed two days at that campsite, partly to let Chakka adjust and partly because we liked the area so much. Many times we took Chakka for walks on his leash—or rather, Chakka took *us* for walks from the end of a people leash. It is simply not possible to steer a wolf. While one may proceed at a relatively good pace in a straight line for some distance, this seldom transpires. At about the time it seems that things are progressing nicely, Chakka will take a hard right or double back between your legs with mind-boggling swiftness. With a young, small-sized wolf, this is not much of a problem, aside from having to untangle the leash umpteen times. But once Chakka got older and heavier, taking a sudden corner at thirty miles an hour could have dire effects on the human holding the leash. We have never succeeded in breaking him of this habit. Any walks taken with him are a study in the art of zigzag mobility, and have a definite detrimental effect on certain joints in the body.

We left for Tequahmenon Falls State Park on the morning of another beautiful, bright, sunny day. After an early breakfast we loaded the bus and headed for the highway. This time Chakka was allowed to run in the bus for a while as a reward for performing properly in the tall grass just before we left.

If it was apparent that Chakka was not the most graceful animal in the world on steady ground, it was twice as obvious in the lurching vehicle. He couldn't take two steps without rolling completely over. This did not deter him in the least; rather, it only seemed to compound his delight. He abruptly sat down on starts, fell on his nose when we stopped, and wobbled like a drunk on the straightaways. He had the merriest time chasing his tennis ball, which seemed to have developed a mind of its own. No one had to throw it for him. He simply had to chase it as it meandered all over the floor. There were times when it went left and he went right, but that just added to the fun. Along with the ball, he found other things to chase, such as flitting sunlight and an occasional moth blown in through the window. The sway and bounce of the floor became customary to him, and the only time he had trouble was when he tried to drink from his dish only to discover the water was capable of coming up and smacking him in the face. He never really understood this, but he tried to cope with it in his own wolf fashion. Approaching the dish on his tummy, he'd lie in wait for a moment, then sneak a peek over the rim. It got him every time. He finally learned to drink up at stoplights.

In a couple of hours we pulled into our second campsite. At the base of the falls, the area was breathtakingly beautiful and very rugged. Pines, oaks, and birch stood in thick clusters, nearly obscuring the steep banks that led to the Tequahmenon

River. The big river itself was a couple of hundred feet down the thickly wooded banks, but several smaller tributaries were within easy reach of our bus. Jenny took Chakka on his leash to explore these crystal-clear streams, while we set up camp. I was just getting things ready when I heard Jenny's voice calling from some distance away. Bill poked his head in the bus and said she wanted me to get the camera. I grabbed it and we all ran down the hillside in the direction of her call.

Jenny was by herself halfway down a steep sand embankment, but Chakka was nowhere in sight. From where I stood, I could see his red leash disappearing into the sandy hillside. We scrambled hastily down the path, and as we rounded the corner I could see that a good-sized cave had been gouged out under some gnarled tree roots extending four feet back into the hill. Inside sat Chakka, immensely pleased with himself. He peered happily out at us from behind the screening roots. We all laughed, and as I bent forward to snap his picture, he turned and began digging. As usual, my mouth was open, so I got a real taste of Tequahmenon sand. We spent at least an hour there, delighting in Chakka's antics. He seemed to think the cave was a fine place, in spite of the rearranging it seemed to need. He chewed roots, bulldozed sand, and darted in and out to check the dimensions. His pudgy little nose frequently sported a patch of sand that stood right between his eyes. He would shake vigorously until sand rained from every pore on his body. It was several days after he left the sand cave for the last time before he could walk anywhere without leaving a gritty trail behind him.

Our fine weather held out all day, but when the sun began to set the wind picked up, and the smell of rain was in the air. Our supper was about ready in the fire pit when the first fat raindrops spattered over the campgrounds. We covered everything and retreated to the bus to eat. Chakka thought that was an excellent idea. Instead of being on the leash, he could bounce under the table and pester our legs until he got some scraps. This was much more to his liking.

We did, and still do, feed our animals scraps from the table. But even our big Danes have been taught to sit quietly and await their turn. Chakka had no such manners. He wanted his supper *now*—that is, he wanted *our* supper now, and no amount of rebuffing would dissuade him. He pranced, bounced, bit, scratched, and squealed around our legs until Bill finally put him in his box. We ate the remainder of our meal listening to outraged wolf-howls. It would be months before we finally had him trained to the point where he would sit and wait patiently. Even then, his eyes followed every move of our forks as they traveled from plate to mouth. If any morsel were dropped, it never hit the floor; a four-footed garbage pail awaited to pounce on it. We had Chakka fairly well trained before he was full grown—a lucky thing, since by then he stood taller than the table and everything was within easy reach. We wouldn't have had enough elbows to keep him in his place!

All night and the next day a raging thunderstorm shook the bus and everything around it. None of this bothered Chakka. He seemed quite pleased to have us all within such easy reach. He pranced happily from one end of the bus to the other, chewing on whatever human happened to be nearest. He amused himself, when we weren't looking, by ripping open a bag of flour in the grocery box and sprinkling the contents over the widest possible area. If you have never tried to sweep up flour from a two-inch shag carpet on a sticky, rainy day, you cannot possibly appreciate my dilemma. It kept me preoccupied for the better part of the afternoon. The activity positively exhilarated Chakka; he had not only myself and the flour to chew on, but also the whisk broom, the dustpan, and everything else in sight. I finally recruited Jenny to rescue me and keep him occupied.

Jenny's method of diverting Chakka was unique, but it created a problem of its own. She sat with him in her lap and blew bubble gum spheres in his face. The first one she blew astonished him so much that he tumbled off her lap and disappeared under the table. Jenny let out a roar of laughter and almost dropped her gum. Finally, she got down on her hands and knees and blew another, smaller bubble under the table for the totally perplexed Chakka. This time he ventured slowly forward to investigate but turned tail when Jenny inhaled the bubble back into her mouth. Twice more she blew a ball of quivering air, and each time Chakka's inquisitiveness got him a little closer. The third time the bubble was still in its formation stage when Chakka reached the front of her face. As if on cue, the bubble burst with a loud pop, and Chakka shot out from under the table with a pink wad of gum dangling from his nose. Before we could catch him, he rolled on the carpet and ground it into everything available, including himself. Since then, the smell of bubble gum has driven him into a corner. But that afternoon, the stuff was everywhere.

I had read somewhere that an easy way to remove gum is to rub chocolate into it and then wash it out. I grabbed a Hershey bar and rubbed it into the carpet and Chakka's fur. By now he was over his fright and delighted in the new game I had devised for him. While I worked, he ate most of the chocolate, the wrapper, and half the washcloth I was using to remove the gooey mess. When I was through, Chakka was reasonably clean, but I was a sight. Bill complained all evening that every time he held Chakka he smelled chocolate and got hungry.

Readying for bed that night, we were all exhausted. Chakka slept quickly, and the rest of us followed his example, praying for a sunny day and good leash weather. The rain had changed from a violent lashing storm that beat against the bus to a steady drizzle, so Bill opened the windows for fresh air while we slept. Sometime shortly before dawn the rain ended, and the mosquitoes, indigenous to river regions, came out in force. I awoke at four in what sounded like a beehive. I have no actual proof, but I'll wager that Tequahmenon mosquitoes are the largest in the world. They don't just bite; they sit on you and chew.

A pearl gray light was about to announce a new day as I struggled out of my sleeping bag and stumbled around the bus, looking for the can of bug spray. While I was searching through the grocery boxes for the can, I didn't notice that Denny had left the radio on as he'd fallen asleep the night before. Since the station had gone off the air at midnight, there was no sound to alert me to this fact. I finally found the aerosol spray, held it aloft, and depressed the button. To my amazement, "The Star

Spangled Banner" blared forth, as at that instant the radio station came on the air. I gazed in astonishment at the can while the rest of the family sleepily peered out of their sleeping bags. It was Denny's guffaw that finally brought me to reality. All I can remember thinking about at the moment were those TV commercials when someone opens a box of margarine and a voice speaks out at them, or someone lifts the lid of an Accent container to the sound of blaring trumpets. By the time our laughter had subsided, we had most likely awakened the entire sleeping park.

There was no sense going to bed after that. We were all wide awake, including Chakka. We put on the coffee pot and watched the dawn pinking the sky. Denny took Chakka out for his morning constitutional, which he claimed took so long that he almost died from anemia and loss of blood to mosquito bites.

Every time Chakka came into the bus, he had to stand on the rug by the door and have his feet wiped. It proved to be one of the most helpful disciplines we taught Chakka. Our dogs are trained to stay on their own rugs until their feet are dry, but Chakka simply won't be restrained that long. If he had been allowed to come straight in with those mud-laden paws of his, the bus would have soon looked like a Conestoga trail in the rainy season. Instead, he knows that part of coming into the house is the "footy-footy" ritual, which involves trying to clean the worst of the material from his paws while he playfully pulls your hair or eats an unprotected ear. It may be hazardous to the keeper, but it sure does wonders for housekeeping.

Hundreds of thousands of people have enjoyed the majesty of Lower Tequahmenon Falls. Two falls, like steps, cascade over solid rock, and although the highest one is only about six feet, the rush of water thunders across the island in a constant reminder of its power. People go there to wade across the river on slippery rock ledges, play under the falls, and sweep gaily into the small riptide pools that dot the river. Many have discovered the little cave behind the water under the falls, and it is not unusual to see the rushing foam pierced by hands reaching out from the cave into the sparkling air beyond. We played for an hour in that beautiful river, and then pushed, exhausted, to the other side.

I had just climbed up the rock escarpment from the water when I gasped. In front of me, on a leash, stood a full-grown gray wolf. I couldn't believe my eyes. The young couple who owned her were there, and we engaged them in conversation. They had gotten their wolf years ago, before wolves were put on the endangered species list. She had been raised from a pup. The more we talked, the more I realized that they were just as impressed with their animal as we were with ours. They'd discovered the same innate gentleness and freedom of spirit already obvious in Chakka's character. Their story did a lot to bolster our morale about what we could expect. Their only problem, they said, was Lady's basic shyness. She took an embarrassingly long time to make friends. We told them how outgoing Chakka was, and they told us that this would change at about three months of age. Although Lady did not greet us or make a fuss while we were there, she did manage a friendly nudge against my hand when we were leaving, after which she returned to lean happily against her master's leg. Her loyalties were unmistakable.

When we got back to the bus, the all-too-familiar wail was wafting over the campgrounds again. Jenny raced ahead and got Chakka out of his box. This was the longest time that he had ever been alone, about an hour and a half. To Chakka, it must have been an eternity. While we were still quite a way down the road, I could see Jenny leave the bus with a gray blur in her arms. Chakka's whole body was quivering with happiness, and he was grooming every spare inch of Jenny's skin that he could reach. As we got closer, we could hear his whimpers and complaints about how badly he had been treated. Jenny turned him around to look down the road in our direction. He froze immediately, and his ears perked, but he pressed against Jenny's arms in uncertainty. His baby eyes could barely make out our forms, and he just wasn't certain. Bill called his name, and the tip of the tail flicked hesitatingly. Bill called again, and suddenly

Chakka recognized us. His feet scrambled wildly when Jenny set him on the ground, and suddenly we were getting an infinitely elaborate, effusive greeting. Chakka bounced from one to the other of us, grooming and kissing while he "related" his entire lonely ordeal. He rubbed against our legs and rolled on our feet to leave his scent and make us his once again. As a finale to his act, he sat on my feet, leaned back against my legs, and howled with happiness. It took him half an hour to work the overwhelming sensations out of his system. During that time he refused a juicy bone, running frantically from one to the other. He was funny and pathetic at the same time, but because he had been so upset, we decided not to leave him alone again. Either we would take him with us or else someone would stay behind with him.

It was interesting to me that Chakka had been so overcome with emotion that he'd set aside his usual reluctance to leave the bus area without much sniffing and hesitation. All his walks before had been cautious and had involved elaborate explorations. This time, however, he'd shot forward like a furry cannonball. It hadn't seemed to bother him that a stray daisy or violet might have been waiting for that particular moment to pounce on him. He ran unhesitatingly past posts and water spigots that had previously taken on great importance.

That evening when we walked up to the camp store, I noticed something about Chakka's investigations that had escaped me before. I had thought he had just been hesitant because he was afraid of "things" along the way. The farther we got from the bus, the more we had to coax him along, and he took exasperatingly long periods to sniff out offending pebbles or leaves. It took us about forty minutes to get to the store, but the way back took only ten. He did not pause to sniff the same areas again, but simply shot forward on a sure path to home. He had been imprinting the trail in his mind, and there was no doubt which way to go. He left puffs of dry sand behind him while his humans struggled to keep up.

We had all gone to get the evening paper, and I stayed under the shade of a tree to wait outside with Chakka for the family to finish the errand. When they came out, Bill was carrying a bag of ice cream on sticks, one for each of us, plus one for Tawny and one for Chakka. This was Chakka's first experience with ice cream. He took a big bite from the corner, sat on his haunches, and opened his mouth until the ice cream slipped off his tongue and into the grass. He sat there for a moment with wide eyes, letting his tongue warm up in the evening sunshine. Finally, he closed his mouth and savored that hint of remaining flavor. It was apparently to his liking, because he bent down and sniffed the creamy blob in front of him. Once again he tried to pick it up, with the same results. He liked the taste, but he sure wasn't happy about the temperature. Time and again he rolled the bite around in his mouth and spat it out until it was half its original size and coated with grass clippings. Perhaps it was the grass that displeased him. He suddenly started pushing small sand mounds with his nose over the morsel until it was completely covered; then he rolled on it. I was to discover later in his life that anything he wanted to save, or even dispose of, would be buried in this manner. He used his nose like a bulldozer to put a good-sized mound of material on top of his treasure. (The only time we ever interfered with this habit was the day he nearly wore his nose off trying to bury a piece of hot dog in an asphalt parking lot.) It was amazing to me that he could return a day or a week later and go immediately to the same spot to see if his treasure was still securely hidden. Although no telltale surface mound was visible, he knew exactly where to go and was horribly unhappy if some dastardly dog had gotten there before him. If that ever happened, he would turn and scratch angrily at the area with his hind feet and then roll in the dirt, apparently leaving a scent reprimand for the creature, should it return.

Chakka's second bit of ice cream came off my bar and seemed to meet with his approval. It just stood to reason that my snack would be a degree and a half warmer than his, and therefore acceptable. He demolished mine and buried his for later.

While I was sitting there watching Chakka eat, Bill suddenly yelled, "Oh, *no!*" He had been holding an ice cream bar by the stick for Tawny to eat, not really paying attention. Before he knew it, Tawny had jerked the delicacy from Bill's hand and gobbled it down, stick and all. Although we rushed over and held her mouth open while I stuck my head in to see where it had gone, there was no trace of the stick, just a normal throat. For the next three days we had some very uneasy moments, waiting to see if it would cause blockage in her stomach or pass through. I fed Tawny half a loaf of bread in an effort to pack bulk around the wooden stick. Each night, when Bill walked Tawny at the end of the day, he would take a stick with him and carefully examine Tawny's efforts for any trace of the ice cream stick. The caper proved embarrassing one night when a flashlight suddenly flicked on from a nearby campsite while Bill was in the process of this chore. The man played the flashlight first on Bill's face, then on the pile, then back to Bill's face. Not a word was spoken, and Bill never explained his mission. He did, however, return to camp and announce that we were leaving the next morning before daylight.

Tawny finally passed the undigested stick on the third day, but of course she couldn't pick some secluded area to do it in. We had driven into town and were parked near an office building with a large, grassy side yard. Bill was in the building and we were waiting in the bus when Tawny let us know the urge had hit—like right now. Denny put her on a leash and hurried out the door to the farthest side of the lawn. There is nothing more ungraceful than a Dane in that particular position anyway, but when you add to it three humans who are standing around cheering her every effort, the situation borders on the ridiculous. By the time Bill returned, we hailed him with the news that Tawny had successfully passed her popsicle stick, totally oblivious to what other people milling about might think. Bill, red faced, rushed us back into the bus for yet another hasty, unexplained departure.

Once again the bus was put in gear, and this time our destination was the very top of Michigan's Upper Peninsula, Muskellunge State Park, one of my very favorites. It is a great, sprawling area of woodlands situated on a spit of land between Lake Superior and Muskellunge Lake. The swimming in the inland lake is delightful, but my favorite area is the wild, wave-beaten shore of Lake Superior, where some of the finest agate hunting in the United States takes place. Professional rock hounds scour these wide, sandy beaches, heads bent in concentration on the stones washed up by the whitecaps. Strange, twisted pieces of driftwood are washed ashore as well and bleached to a white satin sheen by the sun. The wind is always blowing, and one can walk for miles. Chakka found it much to his liking, but made himself rather unwelcome when he insisted on upsetting pails of translucent stones that lapidarists had spent all day collecting. By this time he had learned the meaning of a sharp no, and since he was captive on the end of the leash, he did the next-best thing: He rolled over on his back and wriggled engagingly. It impressed the owner of the bucket and brought a happy response and pettings. In fact, the entire time we were on vacation he perfected this little act shamelessly, and got away with murder. We found it impossible to reprimand him at all in front of people, because they always came to his defense and gave him whatever he wanted, while reprimanding us for speaking sharply to such a dear little animal.

Despite my preference for camping out in the wilds, Muskellunge has always held its own special magic for me, in part because we have met wonderful people there and formed friendships that have lasted years. It is a park of great conviviality, where no one is a stranger. At night we sat around the campfire singing, only to find people filtering in from other sites to join us. Frequently, young people with guitars joined in, and some of the singing was accompanied by very professional string work. We sang through medleys of pop songs, country western tunes, and hand-clapping spirituals. Couples with children and marshmallows in hand sat around our fire, and elderly, prosperous-looking businessmen and their wives joined the singing with as much spirit as the youngest child. As the evening wore on, other campfires flickered through the trees and burned down to embers. It was always late when we got to bed because the music was inspired, the talk exhilarating, and the company perfect. I usually took my sleeping bag outside and sat on it with Chakka on my lap. About dark, he'd poke his nose under my arm and cuddle. When the chill winds whipped in from the great lake, we wrapped ourselves in flannel shirts and sweaters and covered Chakka with beach towels. It was sometimes two or three o'clock before we got to bed. Our day was ended, but Chakka's was only an hour or so away from beginning. We came home from that vacation exhausted.

Our sun-filled days at Muskellunge were happy ones. With regret we packed our bus for the last leg of our journey. By noon of that beautiful summer day, we had reached Wilderness Park, and Chakka once again pranced down the bus steps and found his world outside had changed.

Wilderness sits on low, sandy bluffs at the edge of Lake Superior. It is a national campground, wild and isolated compared with the others we visited. Clean little redwood outhouses, fresh-water spigots, and an endless supply of cut firewood are the only concessions to the camper's comfort. That is still three times what we would have had if we had camped in the wilds as we used to do. Denny pulled the bus into a small clearing under eighty-foot gnarled pines. The minute we set foot outside, a strong wind from the lake whipped at our clothes. Even in 85-degree weather, a sweater or heavy shirt was needed.

For Chakka's comfort, we strung a heavy line between two old trees and snapped his leash onto it. He had much more running room and could explore a wider area. Like any other animal, the minute he reached the tree at the other end of the line, he had to wind himself around it half a dozen times and then howl because he was caught up short. The second we undid him, he'd rush to the opposite end to repeat the performance. It was an exercise in frustration. Finally, Bill suggested we post ourselves around the open grassy area and let Chakka run free for a few minutes with his leash dragging behind him. That way we could easily catch him if he headed for the underbrush.

Once free, I have never seen anything run so fast as that innocent-looking ball of gray fluff. He tore across the level ground and darted under the giant ferns before Denny could catch him. Long-legged Denny made a dive for the undercover, caught the end of the leash, and then screamed in pain. He had slid face-first into a tangle of blackberry branches. We worked gingerly to extricate first Denny, then the exultant wolf. Again we tried, this time more observant and fleet of foot, but it took some fancy stepping to keep Chakka in line. It was his first taste of comparative freedom, and he reveled in it. For an hour he grinned and dodged us, getting within a foot or two of our out-stretched hands and then darting away again. Finally, he sat in the sunlight, rolled on his side, and fell sound asleep. We put his leash back on the line and sat at the picnic table, puffing and drinking our coffee.

Later that afternoon, we took Chakka down to the beach to chase waves. He found all manner of interesting things to investigate. A crayfish, under the edge of a log, nearly got a chunk of Chakka when the wolf poked his nose into Mr. Crayfish's living room. Chakka bounced back in a hurry, pawing and digging at the sand and enlarging the hole. I saw the crayfish depart from the back of the log and scurry away, so I let Chakka dig to his heart's content. He finally managed to dig a hole under the log and clear out the other side. I'm sure he had forgotten by that time what it was that he was chasing, but he had so much fun in the hole that I ended up sitting on top of the log and switching the leash from side to side so he could wriggle back and forth. Finally, the sun dropped down over the water and it got too cold to stay on the beach any longer.

That night it was so cold, even in the bus, that I let Chakka crawl into my sleeping bag with me. I know this wasn't possible, but I'm quite sure that his four-pound body had seven pounds of sand attached to it. I slept in sand, inhaled sand, gritted my teeth with sand. It took me two days to get all those grains out of my life. My comfort notwithstanding, Chakka so thoroughly enjoyed sleeping with me that he set up a real howl the next night when he was put in his own bed. I didn't get much sleep that night either, because I was up and down covering him every time he moved. Much as I loved that vacation, when the final day came to return home, I greeted it with relief. Once home, I foolishly assumed, things would be easier.

6

Head Wolf

IT WAS EVENING THE NEXT DAY BEFORE we finally pulled into our own yard and were given a riotous greeting by the animals that had been left behind. Linda, our critter-sitter while we were gone, came to the door with a cheery greeting. She had a fire crackling in the fireplace, and nothing had ever looked more welcome. Chakka bounced through the door and immediately spotted Scruffy the cat. While he took off in pursuit, we plunked down wearily on the couch.

I noticed Linda craning her neck to see him as he flashed by, but I couldn't understand the look on her face. Finally she turned to me and said, "Do you realize that Chakka is twice the size he was when you left?" Since we'd been with him every day, it was difficult to notice. I didn't believe he had grown at all. Her point was proved when Bill brought out the raccoons to play with Chakka, and the size difference was really apparent. The coons suddenly looked rather small next to him, and Linda insisted that Chakka's facial mask was more pronounced. Over the next six months his growth rate was phenomenal, but we really didn't notice it ourselves until we began comparing photographs of him and asking ourselves if he had ever really been that small.

Our vacation was over, and now our home life with Chakka could begin in earnest. Every day would be a learning process, but Chakka was not about to wait for the next day to begin. That night was to be our first lesson in wolfmanship.

Chakka had barely tolerated the cardboard box during the trip, but for some reason he developed a real hatred for it the minute we got home. Perhaps it was because he had more running freedom in the house, and more animals to play with, that he resented being put to bed. As I tried to lower him into his box, he stiffened in my arms and began wailing. The instant his feet hit the bottom, he scrambled wildly at the sides, and his howls could be heard in Newfoundland.

We tried setting the box next to the stereo in the living room, with the volume turned to low, and shutting off the lights. For half an hour Bill and I sat in the dark while the scratching and wailing continued. I finally gave up, lifted him out, and asked Bill to take the box upstairs next to our bed. After Chakka had calmed down, I went to bed with him in my arms, where he fought sleep as long as he could. I lowered him into the box by my side once again, but I kept my arm draped over the side. He scratched and whined for a minute, then settled down. I spent the whole night with my arm at an awkward angle, my hand gently gnawed at by a wolf.

We fought the box routine for several nights until I decided I would be permanently disabled if I slept one more hour in that position. When Bill took over, he moved the box away from the bed, gave Chakka his half hour of nightly loving, and put him in. The usual protests started immediately, but Bill trudged resolutely to bed. We lay there as long as our ears could take it, and then Bill got up and stomped across the room to the box. He leaned over the side and growled loudly in a menacing manner.

Chakka became quiet in midhowl. As soon as Bill stood up, out of Chakka's line of vision, the howling began again. This charade was repeated several times before Chakka curled into an unhappy ball and went to sleep with the hiccups. From then on, Bill could control Chakka merely by growling. If I, however, tried the same tactics, Chakka bounced around in front of my face and continued whatever he was doing. Clearly, Bill had the better growl.

The box routine was short-lived. Just after we had settled down to sleep on the fourth night, I felt the covers sliding off the bed. I turned over to tell Bill to quit it, but he was sound asleep. On the far edge of the bed I saw two ears, along with a pair of paws working as fast as they could to pull the covers down. Chakka had discovered he could hook his little claws over the box edge and escape. There would be no rest for us after that. I picked him up and went downstairs, where we spent the night on the couch together. It was amazing how well behaved he could be when he got his own way. He chewed my finger and went to sleep immediately.

The next night we taped an extra, foot-high section of cardboard around the top side of the box, put Chakka in, and went to bed. Now Chakka was *really* frustrated, because he knew he had been able to get out of that box before. When he started a howl Bill immediately got out of bed, clumped over to the box, and began a growl. Suddenly a new howl set in—Bill's howl of pain. He had leaned over in the dark, forgetting the box was a foot higher than the night before. Bill and the box connected somewhere across his nose. He disappeared downstairs to put a cold washcloth over his nose, while I dealt with Chakka.

When Bill came back up and I realized that he wasn't seriously injured, I began to laugh. "Gee, honey," I purred sweetly, "now I can tell everyone I gave you a black nose." He walked over to where I was sitting, leaned over me—and growled. I went to bed. A half hour later, Chakka bounded up happily to join us. He had eaten a hole through the side of the box. We threw it out the next morning.

It was obvious we couldn't go on this way, nor could we leave

Chakka loose in the house all night. Not only would he chew the place apart, but his housebreaking routine would also suffer. When he was in the confining box, he asked to go out because he wouldn't dirty his nest area. Besides, his dime-sized puddles had reached the inflationary dollar size. Something had to be done. We finally decided to put gates at both ends of the flagstone hallway downstairs that connected the two wings of the house. That would give Chakka an area about five by ten feet to run in, and also remove the howling from our bedroom.

We spent one morning constructing wooden gates covered with welded wire half the height of the door frame. We attached them with hinges and secured them with slide bolts. Chakka, happily under our feet, played in and out of the porch area as if he belonged there. I had decided we wouldn't put him on his porch until bedtime, and then only after an extra-long play period. We planned the big change carefully, and that night while the family roughhoused with the wolf, I spread papers on the floor of the porch and set down a dish of hot food, a fresh dish of water, two cooked bones, and Chakka's favorite toy, a rapidly disintegrating slipper. He loved that slipper! At last, I thought, all his creature comforts had been taken care of, and it was time for bed. The battle of the box was ended.

Although I sat near Chakka's bed of blankets in the corner of the porch and stroked his head, he knew exactly what was up. He had eaten his supper from the bowl in my lap like a good pup, chewed his bone, and even shaken his slipper with mock vengeance, but no way was he going to let me get anywhere near that gate! If I made the slightest move in that direction, he was immediately underfoot, scrambling for the gate himself.

I told the family to go to bed and shut off all the lights. I stayed another few minutes with Chakka, then left. Not as simple as it sounds, but getting out the gate without the wolf was an act that defies description.

The howls got fainter as I climbed the stairs, but they were still audible. They continued a short while longer, and then blessed silence fell. I was just drifting off to sleep when a hellish noise came from the stairway. It sounded like someone drag-

HEAD WOLF 87

ging a body upstairs. But it was only Chakka dragging his slipper with him. *Chakka!?* His grinning gray muzzle could just be seen struggling over the top of the last stair. I began to wonder if Bill's health insurance would cover a nice, quiet nervous breakdown.

I slid out of bed and tucked Chakka under my arm. When I got downstairs, the gate was in place and the latch securely bolted. I dumped him over the top of the gate and knelt to see if he could somehow have squeezed past the gate. While I was investigating, Chakka expertly hooked his paws through the square holes in the wire and, using the wires like ladder rungs, climbed over the top and landed at my feet. We slept on the couch again.

The next day we constructed a full-length door of welded wire and wood. I stayed away from a solid door because I wanted Chakka to be able to see or hear us and not feel shut out, since the porch would fall into occasional daytime use whenever we found it necessary to restrain him for any reason. I think it is primarily because of the openness of the wire that he hated the porch to a slightly lesser degree than he did the box. Nonetheless, it remained a challenge to be constantly tested, and it took several readjustments before we got it, almost, wolfproof.

That night was the first relatively quiet one we had spent since Chakka had come into our lives. I didn't even mind it when at five-thirty in the morning he scraped his long nails down along the wire door and made the house a sounding board. I even got out of bed with a lilt to my step and managed to greet Chakka with a smile. When I opened the door, he bounded out like a shot, ready for a day of fun. As I straightened up, I looked at the porch. It was a total disaster. He had spilled his food and water dishes and scattered wet paper clear up the wall. His bones and toys were wound in a sodden mass of wet blankets. At that point, it really didn't matter. We'd had our night of sleep, and as I snapped on Chakka's leash for his morning constitutional I was actually whistling.

At about this time in our lives with Chakka, a savior appeared in furry form. Muttley the Magnificent entered our home and our hearts and became Chakka's bosom companion. It started with a phone call at five-thirty in the morning while I stood outside on the other end of Chakka's leash. I slipped the handle of the woven nylon leash over a steel stake and rushed inside to answer.

Muttley's story is typical of the several hundred other animals that come through our door each year, orphaned, abandoned, or injured. We find homes for the domestic animals and release the wild ones as soon as they are able to be on their own. Muttley, however, proved to be an exception to the rule, because the moment Chakka and I saw this dog, we knew Muttley was destined to become one of us.

Muttley had first been seen three days before in a little town near us. He was in the company of three long-haired hitchhikers who were thumbing rides along the highway. Finally, some driver stopped and picked them up but apparently wanted no part of the dog as well. Although Muttley had stood loyally by his masters and waited patiently, they couldn't do the same for him and wait for another ride in which he would be welcome. Instead, as Muttley started to get into the car, they pushed him back. He stood aside patiently, wagging, and sat down. The door slammed in his face and the car sped away. Muttley lay down at the edge of the road and waited for people who would never return.

For three days Muttley kept his vigil, watching each car that slowed down for the corner, and wagging expectantly when he thought it was going to stop. Finally, the gas station owner on the corner decided that Muttley was a nuisance. It irked him that Muttley chose to sleep under the rack of new tires at night and occasionally drank the water from a dripping hose at the side of the station. On the morning my friend called me to see if I would take Muttley, the station owner had a gun and was going to take matters into his own hands. "Bring Muttley right out," I told my friend, not even knowing what kind of dog he was, or what size.

I hadn't been on the phone for more than two minutes when I hung up and went back outside to get Chakka. His leash was

HAVE WOLF, WILL TRAVEL 81

exactly where I had left it, but it was neatly chewed in half, and Chakka was nowhere to be seen.

Panic set in. At best, Chakka could be lost in the cedar swamp behind the woods, or he could be picked up by someone. At the worst, he could be hit by a car on the road by the house. I went flying across the yard in my bathrobe and slippers, calling his name over and over. It was my great fortune that he had not gone far at all. I found him ambling along the fence of the dog run, sniffing at bushes along the way. I caught him with no trouble, because he was more interested in his explorations than he was in me. The lesson learned that day was that his needle-sharp baby teeth could slice through a nylon leash in seconds. Our first purchase, when the stores opened that morning, was some lightweight, welded-link chain and two strong snaps.

I had just returned to the house and begun fixing Chakka's breakfast when my friend drove up with Muttley. Actually, he didn't have a name when he joined us, but after one look, that was simply the only name that would fit.

Muttley's parentage, we later decided, was probably a cross between German shepherd and Airedale. He was large, with fur shading from delicate gray to black that stood out in a wiry, comical pattern, lending a distinctive expression to his gentle face. His most distinguishing feature was his soft brown eyes, which reflected an inner spirit of calm, gentle, unfailing loyalty.

Although he was bone thin, tired, and lonely when he came to us, he entered with the air of a monarch, approached me directly, and offered his paw while his great brown eyes searched my face. People say his homeliness bordered on the cute, but to me he was everything a dog could ever be. Chakka immediately bounced circles around Muttley, trying to get his attention, and finally Muttley rolled on his side and laid his paw over Chakka's back. From then on, it was settled. Muttley was ours. I set to cooking him a hot breakfast.

In retrospect, I don't think it would have been possible to raise Chakka without Muttley. Muttley took on the role of babysitter, protector, companion, and teacher. The load of keeping an eye on Chakka fell from my shoulders to Muttley's. For the first time in weeks, I found I could walk in a straight line without a wolf weaving his way around my ankles and tripping my every third step. Of course, Muttley found his own life somewhat encumbered. He couldn't sit or lie down without first making a body check for the ever-present gray ball of fur that seemed to have become an extension of his own coat.

There was no respite for Muttley. No matter how many hours he played with Chakka, it was never enough. If Muttley rolled on his side for a well-deserved rest, Chakka delighted in attacking the formerly unreachable whiskers and muzzle. Muttley would try, in his own sweet way, to hold Chakka down with a paw, but it never worked for long. In a few seconds, Chakka could wriggle out and attack some other part of Muttley's anatomy. Despite Muttley's unending patience, however, I felt that everyone, even a dog, had a breaking point, and so to provide him some peace and quiet we allowed Muttley to lie on the couch behind a barricade of pillows, out of Chakka's reach. This, I thought, would solve things. As usual, I was wrong.

If there is one thing guaranteed to send a wolf into new patterns of devious behavior, it is an unsolved problem. Chakka tried his usual barking-howling-snuffling, which Muttley ignored with tight-shut eyes. Chakka ranged the entire length of the couch, stiff-legged with indignation. He tried to get up onto the cushions in every way, but his fat little baby legs just couldn't bridge the gap. He attacked the couch, trying to jerk its legs out from under it and reduce it to a more suitable height. When that failed, he went behind it and tried to dig a hole in the floor so the couch would drop down several inches. Needless to say, his tactics were futile, and his rage and frustration grew by leaps and bounds.

Throughout all of this, Muttley would sleep; I could hear his soft snoring punctuated by quavery wolf howls, which carried clearly into the kitchen. I was just at the point of congratulating myself when Chakka, in a fit of pique, came up with his solution.

I don't know if it was an accident or a calculated maneuver, but I do know that once Chakka figured out that he could pull the cushions off to form a ramp to the couch he was triumphant and often repeated this maneuver in the future. I know animal behaviorists argue that animals don't "think" or reason, but I will argue this on the basis of my experience. I have seen Chakka drag pillows clear across the room and pile them near an object that was thwarting his climbing efforts. In fact, a year later when Chakka was first put in his new pen, I saw him use a variation of the pillow solution by pushing his water bucket with his nose until it was close enough to the fence to use as a step stool.

I was just pouring milk into a saucepan when an electrifying scream issued from the living room. I dashed around the corner just in time to see Muttley falling backward off the couch with Chakka firmly attached to his ear. Poor Muttley had been sound asleep when suddenly he'd been seized by ten needle-sharp baby teeth. In his attempt to roll away from the attacker, he found himself falling. Oddly enough, the scream had come from Chakka, not Muttley. What had started as a game with his friend had rapidly deteriorated into a rout. Chakka couldn't let go, nor could he escape. No sooner had Chakka hit the floor than Muttley's full weight came barreling down on him. A muffled thud was followed by another scream of pure terror as Chakka scrambled for footing and tore off across the living room to the safety of his hidey-hole.

A word here about the hidey-hole. Every wolf, like every person, needs a completely safe, private retreat where he can hide and nothing will bother him. Chakka had chosen his when he'd first arrived: the wonderfully dark cave under the blue chair in the corner of the living room. This area was jealously guarded, and we made sure that if Chakka was in there, he was left strictly alone. Within its confines he could heal wounded feelings, readjust his thoughts, and come forth ready to tackle the world again. The safety of the hidey-hole was a balm to his sometimes jangled nerves, and it was to this area that he was retreating as fast as his little fat legs could carry him.

Before Muttley could extricate himself from the pillows and get to his feet, Chakka's quivering gray nose could be seen under the blue chair. I got down on my hands and knees a couple of feet in front of the chair and talked soothingly to Chakka. He pulled his body as far back into the shadows as he could and turned his face resolutely away from me. Finally, he tucked his nose under his tail and heaved a great sigh. Even Muttley's concerned face poking near the opening failed to rouse Chakka, who soon dropped into an exhausted sleep for a half hour. Muttley lay down across the opening and had just drifted off to sleep again himself when a refreshed and jubilant wolf dashed out from under the chair and launched an attack on the same battered ear. The battle was on again.

Muttley's fifty- to sixty-pound size was no deterrent to the barely ten-pound Chakka. In fact, if anything, it spurred him to more ambitious attacks and triggered a very early "dominant" wolf behavior. Anyone who has ever observed wolf cubs at play will realize that, very early in the game, one wolf will begin establishing dominance over the rest of the pack in quite obvious ways. Even at the age of one month, the most aggressive wolf in the pack will make it his business to begin domination of the rest of his littermates through growls, mock battles, and the placement of a paw or chin over the neck of the wolf to be subdued. Muttley seemed unaware that he was being dominated by a ten-pound threat every time he found a wolf paw or chin over his sleeping form. But if it didn't bother Muttley one bit, it made Chakka positively jubilant every time he accomplished such a feat, and he never let an opportunity go by to stand or lean over Muttley's sleeping form and announce to the world that *he* was head wolf.

Chakka applied his dominance routine daily with every animal in the house. If a cat walked into the room, Chakka immediately sauntered over to the feline, draped his head over its neck for three or four seconds, and then gave it a great, slurping kiss. The cats didn't mind the neck routine, but they hated getting the wet kisses afterward. And yet, successful as he was with cats, Chakka's triumph was not complete: Beloved old Tawny had not yet submitted, and his world would not be in order until she did!

She resented him draping his body over her the moment

she tried to lie down, and she most adamantly refused to lie still while he backed up and sat on her nose. Such behavior by Chakka was met with an immediate gesture of rebuke—the snort. Now a snort from anything other than a Great Dane is just noise, but what with a Dane's size and awesome lung capacity, a snort becomes a veritable hurricane of indignation capable of blowing a small wolf into the nearest piece of furniture. Chakka, who wasn't fast enough or large enough to withstand this on-slaught, invariably went applecart over teakettle in an unhappy heap. It seldom deterred him for more than a few minutes, how-ever; he would soon sidle up to Tawny and try again.

Our life may have gone on like that indefinitely if fate hadn't stepped in. Chakka happened to catch Tawny in the deepest of sleeps one day. He laid a paw cautiously over her neck and stared into her ear. Nothing happened. Slightly encouraged, he walked around to her muzzle and sat on it. Tawny did not react. His elation knew no bounds. He was to taste success after all!

Two victories rapidly developed into a veritable orgy of domi-nant behavior. Chakka stood over Tawny's front paws with his tail triumphantly arched over his back. When Tawny went right on snoozing, he tried the ultimate in brazen behavior: walked right up her shoulder and onto her back. Now his exultation was almost overpowering. He stood at rigid attention, a glazed expression in his eyes, and then slowly slid down her side into a heap on the floor. He had conquered at last!

I don't know if Tawny was ignoring him or if she thought it was only one of the cats walking on her back—for they did it all the time, anyway—but I do know she wasn't asleep the whole time. I saw both eyes open into sneaky slits when Chakka slid down her back, and then when she caught me looking she closed them immediately. Perhaps she was just gosh-awful tired of the pestering and decided to put an end to the charade once and for all. The incident worked to Tawny's advantage, too, and Chakka never felt the need to dominate her again.

It became apparent from the first day that Muttley was with us that we couldn't subject him to Chakka's antics without allowing him a place to retreat when he felt the need. Chakka had developed such a dependence on Muttley that any separation was traumatic for the wolf. If Muttley so much as got up to stretch, Chakka was at the ready, leaning lovingly into the great gray side towering over him. If Muttley went outside to perform necessary functions, he was frequently in danger of marking Chakka, not the tree. Although he was patient and tolerant, he deserved some consideration for himself. Also, we wanted to be sure that Chakka identified with us as well as with other animals. Somewhere there had to be a happy medium.

We finally determined that Muttley would have "free" periods during the day for running and playing without wolf distraction. I also decided against putting Muttley on the porch with Chakka at night, not only because both needed sleep but also because Chakka would have to learn that there were limitations to his wolfdom.

Actually, it all worked out better than expected. Of course, Chakka opposed the porch isolation as vigorously as he could, and wailed in particularly agonizing tones about being separated from Muttley, who solved the dilemma in his usual quiet style. He lay down against the wire mesh on the outside while Chakka snuggled as close as he could get on the inside. In a matter of minutes, Chakka was sound asleep on his thick rug, leaving Muttley free to quietly rise and join us in the living room in front of the fire. The rest of the evening was his, without distraction.

Having Chakka on the porch at night presented a problem we hadn't anticipated. Previously, when he had slept in his refrigerator box, he had been close enough for me to hear if he got restless, which always indicated a need to go outside. The porch, however, was too far away from my bed for me to monitor his activities. His nighttime housebreaking began to suffer.

At first I tried getting up in the middle of the night to take Chakka outside. Apparently I didn't get up at the right times, because he had either done the dirty deed or his little system wasn't quite ready to perform. He did, however, enjoy the company immensely and would keep me up as long as I agreed to remain with him while he scampered around my feet in the yard. Clearly, that was not the answer. I was beginning to get discouraged when Bill came up with the solution. If Chakka was loath to "foul the nest," why not spread the nest area over the whole porch? It sounded so simple, it had to be plausible.

The very next night, then, instead of putting Chakka's bed on one end of the porch and his toys and dishes on the other, we spread blankets the whole length of the area. His food and water dishes were placed in a low cardboard box in a corner to define the eating section. If the plan didn't work, I would have a horrendous wash to do in the morning, I thought, as I put him to bed that night with a silent prayer. When Chakka awoke an hour earlier than usual the next morning, he was frantic to get out, but, blessing of blessings, the porch was clean and our problem solved.

At times it was difficult to tell if Chakka had indeed desisted or not, because of his insane desire to rip and shred any available piece of paper to its smallest possible dimensions. I suspect that this was accomplished between the hours of two and four o'clock as a diversion for an otherwise inactive night. Whatever the reason, Chakka was thorough and deliberate in his intent. Paper was so finely shredded that a puff of breeze through the porch was enough to send up a cloud of paper confetti and start the culprit sneezing. I began to worry that perhaps Chakka would poison himself on the newsprint, but that never seemed to be a problem. He did manage, however, to get enough of the black newspaper ink on his paws to paint the walls as high as he could reach. A wash-down of the porch area and disposal of papier-mâché mountains became a morning ritual.

Chakka had several other porch habits that at first seemed totally incongruous. For instance, as soon as I had the porch clean in the morning, supplied with fresh newspapers, bedding, food and water dishes, plus all toys replaced, Chakka would make a beeline for his area the second I let him off his leash and back into the house. It was not his intent to stay on the porch—far from it! But somewhere in the canny recesses of his mind he had devised a plan: He'd dash onto the porch, grab a toy and carry it into the living room, then scurry back, rustle up another toy, and transport it to the living room as well. This went on until every single toy was off the porch and placed somewhere in the living room. Only then would Chakka settle down to play.

His purpose gradually dawned on me. When I put Chakka to bed at night, I carefully replaced all his toys on the porch for his diversion. The ritual signified to him that all was ready for the night. Chakka associated his toys being on the porch with having to stay there. Conversely, if all the toys were *off* the porch, that meant he, too, had been sprung.

One wall of Chakka's porch was floor-to-ceiling glass that looked out onto a screened-in outer porch-greenhouse area. B.C. (before Chakka) I had been able to place my prize ferns, geraniums, and other houseplants on a ledge along the inside log wall, and also along the area at the inside base of the glass wall. Both areas were warm and sunlit, an excellent, natural place for plants. But after Chakka's arrival, it didn't take me long to realize that my houseplants were in mortal danger. Chakka thought the plants had appeared there for his express pleasure. Had he been content to simply nip off a leaf or two, we could have reached an amiable accord. As it was, his idea of horticultural appreciation consisted of pouncing on a plant, breaking it down, devouring the leaves, digging out the root ball, and scattering dirt and what was left of the pot over the widest possible area. It afforded no end of fun for Chakka, but the demise of a faithful geranium that had been flowering for years was a matter of deep regret for me.

I enjoyed having plants on the porch because they were visible from the rest of the house. They were green, inviting, a spot of comfort for the eye. But it was soon obvious I couldn't have plants and Chakka in the same area—or could I? I decided to put all my surviving plants in hanging macrame holders and string them from the ceiling at various levels. They survived both the potting shock and the constant threat that below them, by a bare six inches, lurked a furry murderer, and they began to bloom as if there were no end to the blossoms. Everything was fine until they grew so abundantly they flowed over the sides of the pots. At the time, Chakka himself was growing prodigiously, and soon he was several inches taller and quite capable of once again reaching these tantalizers. My suspicions mounted when two realizations struck me simultaneously: The plants were all neatly trimmed at exactly seven inches below the pot, and Chakka was suddenly producing geranium-scented droppings. I reduced the hanging cords by a foot, assured that any plant life was safe for a few more weeks. But then the last and most irritating porch habit asserted itself.

If Chakka ever heard the expression "walking on water," he decided to vary the act by walking on cast iron. His first performance occurred in the middle of one of the last muggy nights that particular summer was to throw at us. We had all gone to bed feeling slightly out of sorts from the heat and humidity. Chakka seemed relieved to lie down on his cool flagstone, and I was lulled into the expectation that it might be a quiet night. Chakka had other ideas.

Chakka's porch had previously been a storage area for two of my most prized possessions: my plants and my cast-iron cooking utensils. The cast-iron pots and pans, some of which were over a hundred years old, had not, until this particular night, been a problem. They were stored on the tops of several antique cabinets on the porch, and although Chakka could now stretch himself up enough to sniff what was on the cabinets, he had never exhibited any particular interest in cast iron.

We were slumbering fretfully when I was awakened by what sounded like two tanks colliding. Muttley, asleep on my bed, bolted upright so fast and far he appeared to be hanging in midair when I first opened my eyes. Cats flew, terrorized, in every conceivable direction. Bill came alive on the other side of the bed as the sound again reverberated through the house.

Still sleep-befuddled, I careened around the corner at the foot of the stairs and dashed for Chakka's porch. As I came to an abrupt halt at the wire gate, Bill and several of the dogs crashed into the back of me. In the dim light, everything seemed to be normal, but I could see Chakka grinning down at me. *Grinning down at me?* The last time I had taken measurements, I was five-foot-three and Chakka was considerably smaller than that, so what was he doing grinning *down* at me? A flick of the light switch exposed a grim tale.

Chakka, at four in the morning, had discovered his leaping prowess. Previously inaccessible areas were suddenly within his range, and of course the nearest practice point happened to be where my cast-iron collection lay atop the cabinets. Being an essentially clumsy-footed booby, he'd managed to leap to the top of the cabinets only to fall over, into, and through every single kettle resting there. With his customary daintiness, Chakka had proceeded to clear the cabinet top of every object, including a fifty-pound tripod kettle I regarded as only slightly less than family. It lay on the floor, broken as neatly in half as if it had been attacked by a sledgehammer and metal chisel.

I like to think of that night as the occasion of some of my more highly evolved moments. Instead of screaming or committing wolficide, I remained nearly calm. Bill remembers that I said very little, but he claims to this day that as he passed me to go onto the porch I was sinking my teeth into the doorjamb.

Chakka, delighted to have everyone up so very early, bounced in joyous circles through the broken cast iron, while Bill made repeated grabs for his collar. Finally, both wolf and husband disappeared outside and I entered the porch with a sinking heart and a small moan.

Despite Chakka's carefully maintained appearance of innocent stupidity, he can gauge human emotion and play on it like a violin string. He'd discovered early on that if he acted as if nothing were wrong, he could get away with a lot more than usual. Carefully ignoring his porch episode, he greeted the family even more effusively than usual, as in "Let's take the attention away from what I've done and just pretend that you're extremely glad to see me, okay?" My considerably withdrawn and guarded response to his overtures only intensified Chakka's efforts to get me to "forgive" him. He knew exactly what was wrong, and he bent over backward to make things right.

One of Chakka's morning rituals is to wait until I get the mail and open it, and then beg for the empty envelopes. These are a well-loved treat. He can spend half an hour making sure that a standard envelope is torn into enough pieces to cover the living room and half the dining room. He waits expectantly by my chair for his paper treats, and if I am a little slow in my offerings, he gently lays his paw on my lap and gazes at the paper in my hand. That paw can get very heavy if an envelope isn't immediately forthcoming. I have known a standard paw to come to weigh as much as twenty pounds after one full minute of gazing. But on the morning of the porch episode, Chakka sat quietly beside me and then laid his head on my lap and nuzzled gently. When I finally gave him his envelope, he did something unprecedented: He returned the envelope to my lap and gazed up at me. I couldn't take any more. I hugged him and gently bit his ear, and he knew he'd gotten away with it again. His envelope-tearing that morning was especially joyous.

Biting Chakka's ear may have seemed an odd thing to do, but it is one of the few ways possible to discipline a wolf. Although dogs may understand slaps or spankings, a wolf does not. His training and instinct have been bred through centuries. A slap has never been delivered from a dominant wolf. Instead, any infractions are countered by the lead wolf in what looks like an outright brawl. The head of the pack, or someone higher in the social order than the offender, will launch an attack resembling outright murder. The dominant wolf will bowl over the offender in a snarling onslaught, biting the ears for a minor insult or heading for the jugular vein for a more serious offense. At the point where the dominant wolf has grabbed the nose, throat, or ears in a crushing grip, it would seem that the offender has little if any chance of maintaining his life.

Here, once again, the difference between wolf and dog is evident. Dogs will frequently fight to the point of maiming or death when an adversary is down. Wolves do not. The object of the lesson is rebuke, which leaves the guilty party wiser but still able to function in the pack, where he is needed. The moment the offender has submitted through the gesture of screaming or urinating and rolling over, the fight is finished. He is allowed to get up and retreat in dignity, probably never to repeat the offense again. Supremacy has been established. No further action is necessary. In rare cases where the offense has threatened the health and structure of the pack, the offender may be dispatched, but this is the exception rather than the rule.

All this behavior seems to conjure up a problem. How does the human counterpart of a dominant wolf establish his rulership in terms acceptable to both the wolf and human? The answer is surprisingly simple. For serious infractions, the wolf owner must grab the offender by the scruff of the neck, shake vigorously and violently, fling the offender to the floor, and then bite him on the nose or ears until he either screams or urinates, a sure sign of submission. The battle is then over and a new respect has been established.

It may sound simple in context, but small problems tend to arise. For instance, in the midst of a cocktail party or a downtown crowd, how can you administer such rebuke without total incomprehension and gasps of astonishment or horror from onlookers? The answer, again, is simple. When raising a wolf, the owner must ignore outside opinion and relate, one-to-one, to the wolf, not the crowd. And therein lies the success in being the owner of a proud, basically wild animal who has had but a few years to understand the vagaries of human nature. The human must be more adaptable than the wolf.

Lesser wolf offenses, of course, are met with lesser retaliation. Simple rebukes require vigorously shaking the scruff of the neck, but only if the rebuke comes *at the instant* of the offense. Anything even ten seconds afterward cannot be comprehended by the animal.

I tried to train Chakka not to jump on the cabinets, but it was hopeless; he considered it a grand game. Although Chakka's training had progressed rather well in other areas, I was to discover that it was only because Chakka wanted it to progress. When it didn't suit his fancy, he could be the most obtuse, frustrating animal imaginable. Deliberately misinterpreting my scoldings about jumping onto the cabinet, he made a game of it. If I caught him on top, he would jump down immediately and look cute, bouncing so hard I couldn't reach him. In an effort to show him what was wrong, I'd slap the top of the cabinet with my hand and say loudly, "No, *no!*" This was a signal to Chakka to either go get a toy or jump right back up on the cabinet and down again before I could grab him. We went at this particular training program for several days before I finally gave up in disgust and moved my cast-iron collection.

Chakka had effectively used my training efforts to get more attention, and it suited him beautifully. He was willing to play the game as long as I was. As soon as the cast iron was safely out of the way and I quit yelling about the cabinets, Chakka lost interest in them. They were seldom used after that, and then only as a vantage point for some observation.

We had taken so many pictures of Chakka that I had to wait for a decent paycheck to get them processed. Finally, we gathered a couple of months' worth of film rolls together and got them developed. When the photos came back a few days later, we couldn't believe our eyes. Had Chakka ever been that tiny? Because we'd been with him every day, we really hadn't noticed his phenomenal growth rate. In the early pictures he appeared as a round gray fur ball with short legs and a winning expression. In the more recent pictures, an entirely different animal stared into the camera—only the winning expression hadn't changed. Chakka's body had lengthened and filled out, his muzzle had doubled in distance from eyes to tip, and his legs and tail had grown at least four times their original length. Chakka's timber-wolf ancestry showed up clearly in his stride-covering length. Also, his rather comical pup tent ears had suddenly given way to a pair of huge pink triangles that dwarfed the rest of his face.

Chakka's ears were his personal semaphores. Of course they were used to catch sound, but they were also a pair of fur-tipped pink flags that could relay messages quite accurately. Chakka could point them straight forward, indicating interest, or straight back, indicating that he was either extremely pleased or upset. His happiest greeting, reserved for the family, was accomplished with ears laid back on the head and a silly grin plastered all over his face. The grin might look like a snarl to someone un-accustomed to wolves, but it was so clear and engaging to us that it was unmistakable. He usually also cocked his head and ex-posed every tooth on that side. The ears remained sleekly against the head until he received the proper response from his family; then they would pop up immediately.

In most wolves, ears laid back against the head in anger or fear make the face look entirely different. The eyelids, instead of being open and wide, close into narrow slits through which the yellow orbs glint menacingly. The muzzle often ripples with snarls that bare the teeth in a flash of dangerous white. This stance can be maintained for long periods if a situation exists that the animal fears or fails to understand. On the other hand, a sure indication that he is willing to give ground is the barely perceptible flicking of the ear tips. If they come up in the slight-est, the animal is ready to accept a show of retreat, submission, or friendliness. It just can't be pushed too fast, or the advantage is lost.

My theory about the laying of the ears against the head comes from simple observation. When wolves greet each other, even in friendship, there are frequently nips of happiness around the head and throat. When the animals are fighting, again the head and throat are vulnerable. Laying the ears back against the head serves to protect them to some extent from mauling and tear-ing. A cut ear bleeds profusely and is open to infection, which can affect the animal's survival. Protection of the ears seems to be an automatic reflex. Ears are also an easily readable sign from great distances where scent has not yet carried. Whatever the reason, ears are an accurate indicator of a wolf's intent.

Chakka's greeting to either us or Muttley was always prefaced with ears laid down, followed by the submission routine of rolling down either onto one shoulder or completely over onto the back. This showed us that we were viewed as head wolves to whom great respect was rendered. After the preliminaries were over, a full wolf greeting followed, consisting of a repertoire of leaping, leaning, pushing, and pawing. When Chakka was small, the whole process was amusing, but by the end of the first year, when Chakka weighed over a hundred pounds, having something that size lean into you tended to bend the body in unexpected places. More than once over the years we have found ourselves on the floor, much to Chakka's delight. But no matter how exuberant the greeting, we have learned never to refuse. A wolf greeting is an act of total love and must be met in kind, or the animal feels that for some reason you are rejecting him. I have suffered bruised appendages, pulled hair, and mauled clothes in an effort to show Chakka that his love has been returned. Often long-distance loving would have been infinitely safer, but we've continued our close contact, despite the real danger of being loved to death.

7
In Control

THE LAST LONG GOLDEN DAYS OF summer were at their peak when Chakka's size finally nearly equaled Muttley's. Side by side, they were two magnificent gray animals. The difference between dog and wolf, however, was becoming more evident every day. Chakka's beautiful gray puppy fur was just beginning to show definite signs of deeper and more distinct markings. His face was becoming clearly masked, and a fine cape of deep gray fur blended over his shoulders and into a pristine white chest. The very faintest hint of warm buff tones was evident along the outer ear fringes and at the base of the eyes. His baby eyes, which had been a smoky gray blue, were now a beautiful gold flecked with warm brown.

The most telling feature, however, was the expression on Chakka's face. Although it was wild, it absolutely shone with gentleness and intelligence. His every move showed interest tinged with wariness. Pet though he may be, the wildness was still wonderfully integral to him. Without it, he would just have been a pretty dog.

Chakka's relationship with Muttley remained the same, even though Chakka could easily have held his own—or even beaten Muttley—in a fight. Muttley was blithely unaware that his friend was anything more than a friendly pup who was occasionally a nuisance. They had small, nonserious arguments about who got to do what, but beyond that, theirs was a close, affectionate brotherhood. Where you found one, the other was right behind.

Once Chakka was housebroken, I thought the worst of my problems was over. But it seemed the minute one problem was taken care of, another popped up. Chakka was large enough to hoist his frame onto whatever piece of furniture caught his fancy. He loved to crawl onto the couch at night to lie in our laps and watch television. We had allowed him up when he was a pup because this was his "quiet time" with us, and it had helped to settle him down before bedtime. And because he did no harm and since he had been so well-behaved, we allowed the practice to continue. Yet as he grew up and discovered that he needn't wait for us to lift him onto the couch, the privilege suddenly became available all day, not just in the evening. At first it was delightful to see that little gray form stretched out over three-quarters of a cushion, snoring peacefully. Then one day it occurred to me that his little form was stretching over nearly two whole cushions. At night, having his body draped over our laps began to cut off circulation to the feet. It was too late to correct the habit, so it continues to this day—except for one thing. Now when Chakka decides to lie full length on the couch, there is no longer room for us. He takes up nearly all of the four cushions—and the couch is a full eight feet long!

A wolf is an extremely clean animal; otherwise the couch might have become unusable for humans. As it was, Chakka never got it really dirty, nor did he shed nearly as much fur as the other animals in the house—very, very little, in fact.

Fall was rapidly approaching, and with it the occasional chilly showers and accompanying mud. Denny saw what was coming and met the problem head-on. Somehow we had to prevent Chakka from rushing inside directly with muddy feet and jumping all over the couch. Unlike our dogs, who were trained to stay on their rug near the door until their feet were dry, Chakka could not sit still. And so Denny began earnestly training Chakka to the footy-footy routine we'd used on the bus. This involved holding him in one spot long enough to clean each foot off with a soft rag. At first, Chakka thought it great fun. He couldn't wait to outwit Denny, grab the rag and run. Finally Denny got serious about the matter and gave Chakka a wolf scolding. Wised up to the fact that this was going to be a necessary routine to coming in, Chakka bore it with aloof impatience. If he thought he could get away with it, he would certainly try; but if it was inevitable, he would relent and accept it, and then rear across the room like a released spring the second it was over.

If the couch had been Chakka's primary indoor destination, we could have easily lived with that. It was, however, only the beginning. He soon realized that if he stood on the back of the couch and hooked a paw over the cafe curtains, he could catch sight of interesting activities outside. If the curtains got in his way, removing them was a simple matter. All he needed to do was increase pressure on the curtain rod until it buckled. If nothing else, this was guaranteed to bring me on the run and start some fun. Anything else that happened to get in his way was treated in the same cavalier fashion.

Chakka graduated from reclining on the couch to bouncing on chairs and cabinets, and if small things like books, plants, or telephones got in the way, so be it. It began to dawn on me after Chakka had been with us awhile that I was hanging more and more items from the ceiling to keep them safe. This had to stop. I was *not* going to answer my phone perched from the rafters!

Every time Chakka made a leap for a piece of furniture other than the couch, we yelled at him and pushed him off. That game might have gone on indefinitely, for Chakka rather enjoyed it, if it hadn't been for the rearrangement of some furniture. I happened to put the rocking chair in a corner where the easy chair had been. Previously, that particular easy chair had been Chakka's special favorite, as it was heavy enough to withstand his leaping onto its back, turning a neat pivot, and then bounding across the open spaces to the couch. A few hours after I moved the heavy chair and put the rocker in its place, I heard a terrible crash in the living room.

Chakka had made his usual pivotal leap onto the lower back of the chair, where it meets the seat, expecting to sail majestically onto the couch. Instead, the rocker tipped backward under his weight and dumped him in a heap behind it. He was surprised and frightened, but the worst was yet to come. I had a stack of newspapers behind the chair, and every time Chakka tried to stand up, the stack slid beneath his feet, dumping him over yet again.

I came into the room in time to see Chakka's head appear behind the rocker every few seconds with the whites of his eyes showing in great, frightened circles; then he would disappear again. I started toward him just as he finally got his footing and made a panicky leap for freedom. I think his feet must have hit the back of the rockers themselves, because Chakka was just getting airborne when the rocking chair suddenly lurched backward and smacked him in the snout. The backrest pillow unsnapped and flew in the air, covering his face. For one horrible second Chakka seemed suspended, then once again he disappeared from sight, and less than a second later the rocking chair, newspapers, pillows, and Chakka all exploded from the corner at once.

Terrified, he knocked the TV and coffee table flat as he crossed the living room at about thirty miles an hour. I was trying to catch things before they hit the floor when Chakka sailed around the corner and disappeared onto his porch. He had been so frightened that he'd left a streak of urine across the floor, an affront to his normally fastidious nature. This accident accomplished what we probably never would have in a month of Sundays. Chakka never again got on that particular chair. As a matter of fact, he was so wary of it that for several months he passed it with ears laid flat and tail tucked under.

At last the shorter days and the crisp nights produced a burst of color that makes our region unique every fall. The oaks, maples, beeches and other hardwoods were awesome in their reds and golds, accented by the spiky green of the pines. Something about the smell of wood smoke and the special tang of the air makes this and winter my two favorite times of the year. I love running through the whispery, dry leaves and diving into piles of softness that crunch beneath my weight. Chakka loved these excursions outside as much as I did, even if he couldn't run free and had to be kept on a leash. I have heard it said—and it certainly is a fact—that no wolf will ever come on command unless he just happens to be headed your way. I hated having Chakka restricted, but for his own safety there was no other solution. I tried to make up for it by allowing him almost full rein as to where he wanted to go. We sailed across fields, dove through bushes, skirted trees, and generally covered as much territory as leash and feet permitted. Chakka wavered between periods of interest in things far away and moments of intense concentration on an imagined sound or movement beneath a leaf or rock.

Chakka's inborn hunting techniques paralleled wolf behavior in the wilds, proving that it is instinctive. He seemed more interested in mice, moles, and squirrels than he was in the occasional bird we flushed. Actually, birds alarmed him when they rose in flight ahead of us. Chakka took much more interest in the tracks and warrens of mice that crisscrossed the ground. He pushed his nose as far into the turf as he could and sniffed energetically. Twice a startled mouse broke for cover, and the ever-vigilant Chakka nearly tore my arm from the socket chasing after it. He also found hours of pleasure in digging down burrows that I'm sure were vacated the instant he laid a paw to the opening.

That fall was Chakka's first real experience in hunting. Indifferent hunter, he'd devote as much time trying to catch a cricket as he would a mouse. It was simply something to do, a survival instinct practiced whether necessary or not. I had some qualms about whether he would treat our house pets any differently after he learned to hunt. He apparently made no connection between a four-footed animal that might be food and those we had roaming the house. The exception was any of the small rodent family.

Chakka's method of hunting anything moving was in the time-honored wolf tradition of the pounce. The first time I observed this was when I happened to check on Chakka while he was outside on his leash that fall. I had just come out the door and noticed him crouched about halfway down, his head and neck extended in an unnatural pose. I watched him for a few seconds, unsure exactly what was wrong with him. When he didn't move, I began walking toward him. Just as I approached, he leaped straight into the air and came down with all four feet aimed at an area less than six inches in diameter. An instant before he hit, I saw a mouse that had been unfortunate enough to try to cross our backyard on its way to the woods. The mouse never knew what hit it, and a scant second later it was lodged firmly in Chakka's stomach. I was rather surprised that he'd eaten it, since he refused any raw meat under ordinary circumstances. As I considered this behavior, Chakka regurgitated the mouse on the ground and nosed it over thoroughly. I tried to retrieve it before he could down it again, but I wasn't quick enough. I forced his jaws apart, but the mouse was gone. We repeated this performance twice before I finally grabbed what was left of the mouse and disposed of it. Chakka didn't seem to care about his loss.

It was Chakka's affinity for the rodent family that led to our first real dispute. Since I have written and illustrated children's stories for years, I have kept many caged creatures to observe for my drawings. One of my very favorite animals is the North American deer mouse. This beautiful, tiny creature is as different from a regular mouse as hummingbirds are from sparrows. A deer mouse is exquisite in every detail, from its beautiful fawn-and-white coloring to its exceptionally large, shiny black eyes. A very shy animal, it is seldom seen, so the only way to really observe it is in a cage with artificial lighting and visible nesting and eating areas. I had built a cage to meet these requirements, and with it I was able to observe the mice through a full-fronted glass area, as well as several smaller glass areas on the side so I could see them in their nest boxes. The cage was lit from inside so that I could sit in a darkened room and watch the mice without their being disturbed by my presence. The first time Chakka saw the cage lit up, he was as interested in them as I was, but where I appreciated them for their beauty, he clearly saw them as four-footed supper.

Chakka's discovery of the cage was strictly an accident. It was usually kept in an area inaccessible to him—the dining room table, where I had just finished a monthly cleaning. The room lights were off and the cage lit when I heard the door to the living room open. I was unaware that Bill had brought Chakka in with him when suddenly, from behind me, came a spurt of movement, and Chakka shot across the table and smashed his front paws into the glass front of the cage. The glass didn't break, but the force threw the cage across the table to where it rested against the wall. Before I could reach the cage, Chakka had charged again and had the lid of the cage in his jaws. Chakka barely had time to think before I backed him off the table. His feet hardly hit the floor when he came back, determination in every line of his face.

He grabbed the cage and began pulling it off the table while I fought to hold it together. I finally wrenched it away from him and held it behind me while keeping him under the table.

I had committed several errors. My actions had been sudden and seemingly, to Chakka, without reason. Second, I had actually struck him in the process of getting the cage away from him; and third, I had cornered him under the table in what to him was a safety area. His reaction was swift and predictable, had I only had the time to anticipate it. When I leaned down to look under the table, there in the dark Chakka and I were face to face, his teeth bared to the fullest. His growls shook the whole table. Less than a foot separated my face from his fangs, but he was more frightened than angry. Had his only reaction been anger, my chances would have been better; I could simply have waited until he cooled down. But this was different. If I have learned anything from dealing with wild animals, it's that injury to the caregiver is a hundred times more likely when an animal is frightened. I had few options. Backing away was unacceptable, because I never wanted Chakka to get the feeling that he had the upper hand. I had only one choice left.

I could feel the heat from Chakka's throat wash over my face with each growl. I began talking, and the talking only served to make him growl louder, as if trying to drown me out. Nonetheless, I persisted. Bill had turned on the overhead light and could just barely see us in the shadows under the table. Somehow the light seemed to normalize things slightly, and Chakka suddenly realized that it was only me he was facing. He was, however, backed into a corner and still badly frightened. The ugly wrinkles still surrounded his muzzle, and his eyes were pinpoints. Slowly I raised my hand so he could see it, and while I continued to talk I brought it near his face. One false move and we would both suffer.

My voice took on a different tone. I tried to sound simultaneously lofty and stern, telling Chakka that this was no way to behave, and wasn't he ashamed of himself. I raised one finger and tapped him lightly on the nose, telling him all the while that it was really rude to growl at a friend. Each tap on the nose made the growls louder, but I had detected a slight twitch in the tips of his laid-back ears. Gradually he quieted, still growling softly and defensively. Eventually I was able to pet his head and then reach for his collar and pull him gently into my lap. He began shaking and hiccupping. The battle was over. We had both preserved dignity and neither had forced the other into overt action. He apologized effusively, licking my face and hands, and I held him close. Behind me Bill let out a shuddering breath of relief.

Actually, the encounter was less serious than it seemed. The elements of surprise and fear were the real problem. Moreover, under the circumstances I couldn't allow the precedent of Chakka threatening me and getting away with it. My task, therefore, had been to maintain the status quo. We both came away from the incident with a healthier respect for each other, but with mutual love undiminished.

IN CONTROL **113**

Some authorities may argue that I should have backed off from the encounter with Chakka rather than risk a real danger to us both. After all, what is one small battle won or lost? If it had been any other wild animal—a raccoon, for example, which has no need to show dominance—I would have allowed more latitude. But a wolf is like no other wild animal. His whole instinct is grounded in superiority and testing. In a wild, well-ordered pack, the head wolf constantly reasserts his dominance with firmness and kindness, laced at times with well-controlled anger. When the head wolf becomes too old, disabled, or uncertain of his actions, the time has come for the next-strongest animal to take over. Any signs of weakness are transmitted to the whole pack, and the restlessness is unrelieved until a firm control has once again been established.

To Chakka, I was not a human being; I was his lead wolf. A good leader keeps the world in line with a steadying influence. While a wolf will scarcely ever turn on its owner, it *will* play on his weaknesses until the results can be uncomfortable and downright antagonistic. Only the strongest are fit to lead, and I will not allow *myself* to be led by a *wolf*. In forcing the battle to its conclusion, I showed Chakka I loved him enough to maintain control. One slip on my part would have revealed a weakness he'd have felt obligated to play upon until the confrontation was once again enjoined. Why not settle it the first time around?

This incident has an instructive purpose, of course. I would have people understand not only the wolf but other wild animals, and in turn love them. But how can anyone really know or love an animal if he can't accept its behavior? Neither humans nor animals may be perfect, but animals are a whole lot more predictable. Anyone who contemplates getting a beautiful proud creature such as a wolf had better think twice. It is both a privilege and a heartache to own one, and if you can't take both, don't try it; the animal is far better off without you.

An animal can sense fear immediately, and for some strange reason this increases its own fear. The cause-and-effect spiral persists until someone gets hurt, and invariably it is the animal that suffers from the encounter, no matter whose fault it is. I have felt caution with wild animals many times, but I can honestly say I have never felt fear. I panic at the sight of a dentist's needle, but animal fangs bring out in me a healthy respect. It is this reaction on my part that I am sure has saved me many times from serious injury. It has also enabled me to forgive and love the animal in question instead of backing away, all trust and affection gone. Chakka and I were as close ten minutes after the encounter as we had been before, perhaps more so.

The long, lazy days of autumn worked strange magic on Chakka. His throat and chest area expanded daily as the thick pelage, the underfur, filled out for winter temperatures. Even though he was a house pet, his system was preparing him for the rigors of the Arctic. His attitude, usually devilish, became more contemplative. Of course he was getting older, but that wasn't it. It seemed he knew that winter demanded more of him than the carefree, lethargic days of summer and autumn. He began to put on weight at a much faster rate.

By November, when he was six months old, his face had already lost most of its puppy look, and he'd gone from the four and a half pounds he weighed when I got him to seventy. His body was like a teenager's, all feet and elbows, gawky, and sometimes uncontrollable. The graceful, fluid movements of an adult wolf had not come to him yet, but changes were evident.

From about three to seven or eight months, Chakka's attitude had undergone an amazing change where strangers were concerned. At first it really puzzled me, but I have since learned this is typical of a wolf. From lovable, friendly, and fairly outgoing animals, they become wary, shy, withdrawn pups. When Chakka had previously met strangers with at least curiosity, he now retired to the point at which he refused to be in the same room with anyone who hadn't been about for several hours. Even then, he approached stiff-legged, snuffling, and snorting, stretching forward but keeping his hind feet well back in a safety position. The slightest movement or attempt to encourage him to join a stranger only resulted in a hasty retreat. People he had known earlier were now suspect. He began to act like an animal that has been beaten and trusts no one. I slightly despaired that he should react in this way, but I decided it was a phase and was determined to wait patiently for him to outgrow it. And it turned out that it was just a phase. If we had made more of it, it might possibly have become a real problem.

I remembered Andy's advice of letting the wolf make all overtures and never allowing anyone to force attentions on him. Although I might at times try to talk Chakka into entering the room with someone new, I never forced him to act against his will. He was free to make his own choices. During this period he seldom bestowed his presence on anyone other than family, although there were a couple of notable exceptions.

I knew a woman in her sixties who had once owned and loved a wolf, and whose daughter had worked with wild animals. Whenever they visited our home, he greeted them as if they were old friends. I was caught off guard by his immediate acceptance. During an evening's visit, he relaxed on the floor in front of them and extended his chin on each of their laps for a head rub. I sat with my mouth open. How many friends of mine would have thrilled to similar behavior and been ecstatic over it! To other people, who were truly interested in Chakka, he was always coldly distant, or at best barely tolerant of their presence. Somehow, he knew the elderly lady and her daughter were wolf people and accepted them.

On the other hand, he totally embarrassed me with some of my very closest friends. One man had been a dear friend for twenty years. He was large, gruff, blustery, and yet as generous to me and my family as if we were part of his own family. We had been so close for so long that it seemed we actually were related. It never occurred to me that Chakka would feel differently. Perhaps the size of the man was intimidating. Maybe it was his deep voice. Whatever, Chakka simply would not warm to him. My friend pretended not to notice, but I felt somehow let down. I wanted everyone to love Chakka, and vice versa. These two were dear to me, but the chemistry simply was not there. I was hurt and disappointed. Bill told me to be patient, that Chakka was still a baby and later he would change.

Chakka never did warm to the man, and over the next two years our paths drifted further apart. Interests, jobs, and goals all came between our families, and although there were no quarrels or disagreements, we saw less and less of each other. To this day, the sadness that he and Chakka never really knew each other still exists.

One other person who was part of Chakka's life during his "difficult period" was accepted immediately, and still remains a friend. In fact, Becky, a delightful young woman in her twenties, loved Chakka so much that she ended up being a parent to one of Chakka's crossbreed pups. When she first met Chakka, she got right down on the floor with him, which delighted him no end. He made a few desultory passes at her and then leapt in to dominate her. The action erupted into a free-for-all, and Chakka was in seventh heaven. Even today, his greetings to her have a special warmth, and he showers attendance on her the whole time she is with us.

The rest of the world did not fare as well with Chakka. He steadfastly refused to make friends with anyone new and barely tolerated people who were guests for three or four days at a time. My parents once stayed with us for nearly two weeks. They were ignored for the first few days, tolerated for several more, and then finally accepted, although grudgingly at first. Chakka probably would have taken to my father sooner, had it not been for a slight misunderstanding between them.

My parents had been with us for four days, and Chakka was just beginning to nose around them when they weren't expecting it. A golden opportunity presented itself when Dad relaxed in the chair in front of the fire and fell asleep. Mom and I were on the couch talking when I happened to spot Chakka creeping cautiously around the corner of the chair, sniffing the air in front of Dad's feet. Very slowly Chakka inched up for a closer look, but ready at any moment to bolt. The closer he got, the more encouraged he became. He was at the point at which he was sniffing Dad's hands and probably deciding that maybe he wasn't so bad after all, when Dad's head shifted and he let out a loud, cross sound somewhere between a snore and a cough.

Chakka went straight up in the air, turned, and bolted from the room. Dad was never even aware that Chakka had been close to him, but the occasion was so frightening to Chakka that although he finally did make up to Dad later, he never completely relaxed in his presence.

Mom had an easier time of it. Both my parents love animals, and of course animals know this. Chakka, however, is prone to play on emotions, and if he thinks someone loves him but isn't quite strong enough to stand up to his antics, he will push the matter as far as he dares.

Mom was reading on the couch when Chakka jumped up and stepped across her lap. Mom waited a moment for Chakka to move. Finally she reached up and scratched his side and then gently pushed him on across to the other end of the couch. Chakka turned, looked at her, and then got down. A moment later he was back on the couch, walking over Mom's lap again. Mom admonished him gently and gave him another push.

I could see the light dawn in Chakka's eyes as he got down, padded around to the end of the couch, and jumped up to Mom's lap yet again. There he stood, towering over her and grinning from ear to ear. What a great game he had devised! Mom caught on immediately. She roughed up the fur around his face, told him he was a goof, and pushed him down. He was back on the couch before his hind feet were completely off it, but Mom was waiting. Mom balled up her fist and pushed right up against Chakka's nose at the same time as she was asking him if he wanted a "wolf-beating." This was a favorite threat of ours when Chakka really got rambunctious, and he knew that. Coming from us, it was a harmless, empty threat. He really wasn't sure about Mom, though. He got a rather uneasy look and then did what he does best. He ignored her and stared out the window over her shoulder as if something very interesting was going on in the yard. After a whuff or two at whatever it was he supposedly saw, he jumped down and went to terrorize Muttley. Mom had won that battle.

Although Chakka never bit in anger or to hurt, there were a couple of times he inflicted minor damage to someone. Usually it happened if we were playing rough-and-tumble with him. I always played with him barehanded, and he learned to be careful of my hands no matter how active the play. He never clamped his jaws down on me with anything more than the slightest pressure, only "mouthing" me to show mock ferocity. On the other side, I have been bruised many times when my hands or arm hit his open mouth and struck his teeth. Then the fault was mine, not his, though it hurt all the same. If Chakka ever realized I was injured, the play would stop immediately and he'd be all concern and love.

Denny used the opposite approach with Chakka, donning a pair of heavy leather gloves when playing with him. In this way, Chakka soon knew what to expect when he saw the gloves (ah, rapture!), and he'd be able to play harder and work off more energy besides. He loved these nightly battles, and if Denny was slow in getting the gloves down from the tall cabinet, Chakka stretched his body as far in the air as he could and tried to sniff them down. The minute Denny reached for them, Chakka bounced back and forth in a frenzy, hardly able to contain himself until they were on so he could attack. Although Chakka could and did bite the gloves, he never bit anywhere else. He seemed to know that Denny was protected in the glove area, and he made the conscious distinction that saved Denny from injury elsewhere.

Only twice have I seen Chakka deliberately nip anyone, and it was only nipping, not biting. Both times it was the same person and, I presume, for the same reason. Fortunately, the young woman in question was and is a good friend of the family, but that doesn't make it less inexcusable.

Chakka seemed to like Claire quite well, but the circumstances that caused the nips were somewhat akin to waving a red flag in front of a bull. Claire was extremely short and had a weight problem. Much of her excess weight was carried in her posterior, and for some reason that fascinated Chakka. She was safe as long as she faced him, but if Claire turned her back, she was in trouble. The first time it happened, he sneaked forward and nipped right where the target was the largest. The squeal that resulted was both frightening and invigorating to Chakka. He knew immediately he had done the wrong thing, but he looked as if it had been worth it. He was punished, and the episode nearly forgotten.

The second occurrence was several weeks later. We were all outside with Chakka, and Claire and I had fallen into conversation. Out of the corner of my eye, I saw Chakka slink downward and circle in from behind. His ears were down, and the expression on his face was one of pure devilry. I was about to shout a warning when he pranced sideways and leaped in for the attack. There was another squeal of outrage, and Chakka beat a hasty retreat, all the while doing his best to look engaging.

I wrestled him to the ground and bit his nose hard. It was the first time in months that he had been chastised, and he was shocked. It also alerted me to yet another facet of our changing circumstances: Administering a wolf reprimand was getting much more difficult than it had been. Luckily, Claire once more forgave Chakka, but she never again turned her back on him. And I suspect that if Chakka were ever presented with that target again, the results would be the same. He has never done this to anyone else, but he couldn't seem to resist the urge with the lady in question.

Actually, these "attacks" on a human were not of a harmful or nasty nature, and were the only errant behavior Chakka ever exhibited. We felt completely at ease when we took him into a grade school and let him roam free in a room of first and second graders. Chakka loved children, and he was in his element when allowed to sniff, push, and otherwise associate freely with a gathering of them.

Wild animals are especially patient with the young of any species, and baby animals can do things with impunity that would net an adult animal a severe reprimand. Kids could hold, cuddle, and pet Chakka—or even pull his ears—in safety. It wasn't until he discovered the cabinet area, however, that his audience roared with laughter and became his forever.

He had amused them by poking his nose behind stacks of books and pushing them to the floor. Then, suddenly, his attention turned to the low counter area, just the right height for Chakka, where a faucet, sink, and mirror were located. As he ambled over and sniffed the faucet, I turned the water on in a slow stream, and the children watched Chakka drink daintily from the spigot. Then he put his feet up on the cabinet and poked his face at the mirror. I'm sure Chakka must have looked in the mirrors at home many times. Perhaps in the context of the home, seeing another wolf was not too bad, but seeing one in that little square above the sink at the school startled him so badly that he lost his footing on the slippery floor and fell sideways. The children shrieked with laughter, and Chakka immediately got himself back on his feet again. He shook his fur, lowered his head, and stalked cautiously up on the mirror. Ever so slowly, he inched up on it and then thrust his head before it.

Yup! There was that wolf again! Chakka whuffed and scrambled away, while the kids went wild. The second time must have seemed like fun to Chakka, for he bounced around the floor with his front shoulders and head lowered, his tail wagging furiously. Even the teacher laughed so hard that tears streamed down her cheeks.

Then Chakka made a third assault. He crept up to the mirror and gave a mighty heave. The mirror spun outward on its wire and banged smartly back against the wall, making a loud clap. Chakka's feet moved so fast they blurred as he tore between desks toward the back of the room. The classroom was in an uproar, but Chakka was scared to death. I went back to try to calm him, but he was through for the day. He could put up with kids for hours, but that other wolf was just too much. Reluctantly, we took Chakka back to the car. The children were sorry to see him go, and he was the topic of discussion for weeks afterward.

Gradually, Chakka outgrew his hesitation with strangers, although he was still very selective. At least he didn't disappear every time someone came through the door. He might not always seem especially glad for the visitors, but he could afford to ignore them now. Things settled down as fall came and went, and one morning Chakka awoke to find something new to conquer. Snow.

8

Wolf Games

NOTHING IN CHAKKA'S EXPERIENCE prepared him for the sight that greeted him that morning in October. He had just bounded off his porch toward the door, ready to go outside for his morning ritual, when he looked through the glass in the door and stopped dead in his tracks. The night before, his world outside had been familiar. Now suddenly something had changed. It was all white, and he wasn't about to set foot outside! I had him by his collar, ready to attach it to the leash right outside the door, when he anchored all four feet and adamantly refused to budge. No amount of coaxing helped. I wondered, briefly, what wolves in the wild do on their first snow. Do they anchor themselves in the den opening, waiting for mother wolf to push them outdoors? At that point, pushing Chakka was more than I could manage. I decided if he wouldn't go out to see what snow was, I would bring it in to him.

When I returned with a handful, he backed into a corner against the wall, thoroughly frightened. Deciding that forcing the white stuff on him wasn't going to work, I put the snow down on the carpet before him. He remained in the corner, sniffing the air suspiciously. I closed the front door and sat on the couch to await the outcome. Gradually, Chakka lowered himself to the floor and cautiously stretched toward the mound of snow. It took him quite a little while before he decided the stuff didn't qualify as a bona fide wolf-killer. As the snow melted, Chakka became more emboldened. Finally he conquered his fear enough to grind the last of the snow crystals into the carpet with his nose. The time had come to try the outdoors again.

But Chakka wouldn't be hurried. He stood in the open door, while I shivered and shook in my robe. Finally, one cautious paw reached out and touched the ground. Gradually, we inched our way out the door, where I attached the outside leash to his collar. I hurried back inside, closed the door, then stood at the door and watched him through the glass window.

Every movement was a deliberation, as though the ground might lash out and bite him if he moved too fast. Each step, however, brought more confidence, and soon he was moving at half speed. He lifted each paw high in the air, then placed it gingerly ahead of him like a wolf doing the goose step. He nearly jumped out of his hide when a load of wet, heavy snow dropped from the pine branch overhead and crashed down beside him. That required at least ten minutes of investigation. Ever so slowly, his confidence returned, and finally he decided he really liked the stuff. Within a half hour he was rolling in it and having a grand time. When I brought him back inside he shook and sprayed half the house with wet, icy chunks.

By midmorning, when he was ready to go out again, the snow had melted. I opened the door and he stood there confused. With a look of reproach he picked his way outside in stiff-legged disapproval. Over the next few weeks he waited eagerly for every snowfall. By November, he had more of it than he could have imagined.

It was an especially hard winter that year. Snow came early, built up heavily, and was a long time on the ground. Six- to ten-foot drifts were usual, and Chakka, a fervent convert to the stuff, was in his element. Instead of walking out the door he'd bolt in a tremendous leap and roll immediately in the fresh snow. If his leash happened to be attached at that point, no harm was done. If, however, I still had my hand firmly attached to his collar when he bounded and rolled, the two of us got a snow bath that was a real eye-opener, especially in the early morning when I was seldom dressed in anything more than a robe and slippers. Bill could tell from the frequency and severity of my gasps when I returned whether or not Chakka had rolled me.

Chakka loved having someone to play with in the mounds of cold white. He would crouch and leap, knocking whoever was playing with him into the nearest drift. He was also quite adept at burying you before you could get to your feet.

At first he thought it a wonderful game to catch the snowballs we tossed at him, but the extreme cold made his teeth ache, so he began butting the snowballs with his head, rather than catching them.

He soon discovered that snow did another strange thing, transforming, for instance, meaty, cooked bones into chunks of ice and iron-hard material. Far from deterring him, that seemed to make chewing an even greater adventure. I have often wondered how he was able to chew on a frozen bone for hours without it bothering his teeth, while the snowballs he caught apparently did. Perhaps it was not the teeth themselves that were tender, but the soft palate and tongue instead. I have seen him chew icicles for several minutes with apparent gusto, then stand with his head down and mouth open, saliva running down his tongue. Bill claims he probably had an "ice-cream headache." Whatever the problem, it didn't apply to the bone department, for we could both hear and feel the tremendous crunching clear inside the house when he was demolishing a bone outside. It was a forceful reminder that he possessed awesome crushing capacity in those jaws.

The larger Chakka grew, the more restraining his leash became. We took him for long walks and played with him in the open as much as possible, but he needed an unrestricted leaping and running area. Much as we might have wished to let him run in the fenced part of the yard, we didn't dare. Not only was he now able to leap over the four-foot enclosure with no difficulty whatsoever, but he could also burrow down to astounding depths in the sandy soil. He had once built himself a "cave" with a tunnel entrance that was large enough for me to crawl into, all in less than two hours. We made up our minds that come spring, a large, fenced kennel area would have to be built for Chakka. Most of the time, however, he would remain in the house with us.

In the meantime, Chakka devised several games to play that worked off energy for himself and usually someone else as well. One of my good friends, a woman who loved Chakka, frequently brought other people over to meet him. She was fascinated by his personality and laughed at his antics. Chakka, in turn, would often do something to purposely amuse her. I am sure this must have been in his mind the afternoon he decided to take her for an unexpected ride and roll in the snow as she gripped his collar to put him on the leash.

I hadn't noticed that she was preparing to take Chakka outside, or I would have warned her. She really hadn't had to restrain him physically since he'd been a small pup, and the unbelievable difference of strength between then and now caught her by surprise. All I saw of the action was a truly astonishing picture of her heels disappearing out the door. I heard a muffled scream from outside and raced to the open door just in time to see a flurry of snow as Chakka rolled her expertly. I yelled at her to hold on, fearful that Chakka would break loose and we'd never catch him again.

Before I could get outside, Chakka was upright and racing down the path with my grim and determined friend holding resolutely to his collar and pushing up great mounds of snow with her nose as he dragged her prostrate body along behind him. I sprinted down the path as fast as I could go and just barely managed to reach Chakka before her grip on the collar broke. She claimed later that she lost her grip only because I'd run up along her back to grab Chakka. She also claims I left her buried and helpless while I put Chakka on his leash and spent a very long time telling him how sorry I was that our friend couldn't play with him. It took a large glass of wine in front of a roaring fire to mollify my companion, and she still maintains one arm is longer than the other as a result of the escapade.

If Chakka couldn't enlist any person or animal to play with him in the house, he resorted to a game he could play by himself. First, he'd walk around for several minutes in bored frustration, looking for something to get into. Then, somehow, his meandering took the form of ever tighter circles, until finally his tail came into view. Then the game was on. Sometimes it took repeated attempts before he'd manage to grab the end of it. After that, the only way to go was in circles. Round and round he would go, banging into furniture, scattering cats, and alarming dogs who happened to be in his way. Nothing deterred him. Rugs would fly out from under his feet, spilling him, but somehow he managed to maintain a grip on his appendage. Occasionally, he'd hit a wall so hard that he was momentarily stunned, and the tail would flop back where it belonged. The second his rattled senses returned, the chase would resume until the tail was caught and he was running in circles again. I might see him keep this up for fifteen minutes at a time, and when he'd finally stop he'd still be upright, though glassy eyed and wobble legged. I put the blame on the fact that he was still a pup and perhaps not too bright at times, but the truth is to this day he plays his circle game if there is nothing else to do.

Anything that Chakka was not supposed to do was exactly what he would spend hours trying to accomplish. Part of the strategy was to get my attention. He seldom failed in that endeavor. If he did something once and found that I yelled or acted upset about it, the project became infinitely more interesting. It was information to be filed away and repeated when things got boring. One thing that really irked Chakka and spurred him to unacceptable behavior was my answering the telephone. He loved to hear me talk, but when it gradually dawned on him that my attention was directed to something besides himself, he would resort to naughty tricks to get my attention.

One of his least destructive ploys was to amble nonchalantly into the bathroom and wait to see if I noticed. If my conversation continued in the living room, he would push open the shower door and step in. A large array of forbidden objects waited within easy reach—soap, creme rinse, shampoo, brushes, washcloths and towels, a back brush, a hand-held shower hose. He rather liked to start with the soap. Instead of chewing it, as might be expected, he would deposit the bar on the carpeted floor and then roll and rub his neck and shoulders in it. No doubt the scent pleased him, for he wasn't satisfied until his neck fur was spikey with caked soap, the bar of course now useless, coated in wolf fur that took hours to clean off.

Next he tackled the shower hose, gripping it firmly until he'd wrenched it from its attachments. Then he chewed both ends in delight. Over a period of time, our shower hose became so badly mauled that in order to use it you had to nearly squat in the tub so enough hose was available for rinsing your hair. After the hose came the shampoo and creme rinse. These were usually in plastic containers that exploded if bitten hard enough. Chakka knew that once they were punctured they became slippery and would scoot across the floor when pounced upon. All manner of games could be played with such toys, but the pièces de résistance were the back brush and towels.

Before Chakka was a year old, his diet consisted of seven-tenths dog food, three-tenths back brush. Dessert was bath towels and washcloths, both of which he rolled on, chewed, and shredded into tatters. Bathtub activities were sure-fire attention-grabbers once the lady on the phone picked up on the suspicious silence.

The only truly harmless bathroom activity that amused Chakka—and which I allowed—was his game of catching the drips under the faucet in the tub. He would wait in all sorts of postures for the water to drop, and then make a lunge for it. When he was small, he could maneuver from the back of the tub area, but as he grew his body filled the whole tub, and the only thing he could move with any ease was his head. His teeth clacked against the porcelain as he attacked each drop. Once in a great while he would attempt something more energetic, but both the size and slipperiness of the tub not only hindered him but posed a health problem as well. He would emerge from these forays thoroughly soaked and happy.

As messy as the tub fiascoes were, they were absolutely nothing compared with what Chakka could do to the fireplace. If it was not in use, and I wasn't at hand, Chakka couldn't wait to dive into those cold ashy depths and wreak as much havoc as possible before he was asphyxiated. He adored dragging out charred logs and chewing them with relish. They crunched wonderfully well, sweetened the breath, and left a fine black mess all over the carpet. The real test, however, was the act of getting as much of his body into the fireplace as possible and then digging with a backward motion, which shot ashes clear across the room. Very little breathing was done during this maneuver, and the object of the game was to time things so that just as the mistress of the house was rounding the corner, the largest possible cloud of ashes was blanketing the room. I can remember, vividly, that my first (but not last) real case of tears was when I saw my living room shrouded in at least fifteen pounds of powdery gray ash. Even the walls and curtains were gray. I worked for days to clean up that mess, and before I was finished, the phantom had struck again. It's a good thing I control my first instincts, or Chakka would have expired many times over.

The lowest point in our relationship occurred the day he ate our bed. It had started out as a perfectly normal day. And then company arrived.

It was company we hadn't seen for some time, and they didn't know Chakka. The first hour or so of their visit was spent admiring him and making a fuss over every darling little trick. Chakka basked in the limelight while pretending to ignore his audience, but he hammed it up atrociously. He was becoming more extroverted as long as *he* set the rules. Eventually, we all trooped into the dining room for coffee. Chakka came right along, filched his usual treats, and lay down under the table. As we all sat around reminiscing, for an hour or more, it occurred to me that Chakka was no longer under my feet. Our guests were leaving and we had a lengthy good-bye. As soon as the door was closed, I went in search of Chakka. He was nowhere downstairs, so I headed up the stairway. Suddenly I noticed it was snowing . . . inside. I stopped climbing the stairs and looked up at the ceiling. Flakes and shreds of something white were sticking all over the walls and ceiling, dropping in quiet spirals to the floor. I had no idea what this stuff was until I cleared the top of the stairs and saw our bed, or what was left of it. And Chakka.

He was sitting in a welter of bedding all wadded into unusual shapes and pieces, but despite the fact that he was sitting on a heap of material, he appeared to be lower than the mattress itself. His muzzle and fur were flecked with the same white material that hung from the ceiling and was festooned over the room. When I approached the bed, I could see why Chakka was sitting so low. Only the outer edges and four corners of our extra-thick foam rubber mattress were intact. The rest of the mattress had been attacked with such unholy glee that shreds of foam rubber were strewn all over. Static electricity made it stick wherever it landed, ceiling or floor. A gaping hole clear down and into the innersprings underneath allowed clear vision to the floor beneath the bed. Chakka was balancing as best he could on the remnants of our crushed velvet bedspread and a few tattered pieces of sheeting.

They say demented people don't remember their actions. My mind is a merciful blank regarding any overt action I took at that point. Denny says that Chakka came barreling downstairs and headed directly for his hidey-hole with ears laid back and tail tucked under his body. Unfortunately for Chakka, he hadn't used that hidey-hole under the chair for weeks, and unbeknownst to him, he had outgrown it. However, speed and determination managed to catapult him full tilt in the right direction, and he didn't stop until he was wedged in so badly that Denny had to lift the chair to release him. By this time, my outrage upstairs was hysterically mounting, and as Chakka heard my descending footsteps he made a dive for his porch and actually cowered in the comer, baring his fangs in real terror. I didn't dare touch him for fear I would do real damage to our relationship. Murder has been known to do that.

There were times in Chakka's life when he knew he had done something wrong, and he more or less accepted his reprimand. There were even a couple of times when he dared to argue the point, at least a little bit. But I have never, before or since, known Chakka to be so unsure, frightened, and ashamed that he voluntarily went to bed at four in the afternoon and didn't ask to be let off his porch until the next morning. We did not hear one single peep out of him all night—and believe me, it's not hard to waken someone sleeping on bare springs.

It never occurred to me, before Chakka, that our home was small. We have raised Great Danes, the largest of which was 220 pounds, and even they didn't seem to dwarf our living quarters the way Chakka did. That's because Chakka was not particularly well behaved when it came to keeping his nose out of things. His natural curiosity, coupled with his flair for getting into mischief, made everything in the house a potential hazard. Cooking in the kitchen was one example.

When Chakka was small and couldn't reach the countertops or stove, he contented himself with scratching my leg or foot until he got his tidbits. I would not allow demands any more forceful than this, because it could have been dangerous for both of us. Thank goodness Chakka never learned to leap up and grab what he wanted while I was working. He begged like a gentleman and took the offering sweetly. That is, until he got old enough to walk up to a counter and discover that it fit right under his chin, without any stretching on his part. Even so, as long as I was there he was pretty darn good about keeping his wolfie nose out of things. Perhaps his brush with the pressure cooker helped.

To steam all of Chakka's bones, we used a commercial-grade pressure cooker, which held fifty or sixty pounds of extra-large bones, fat, and meat scraps. After an hour of cooking at a pressure of 20 pounds per square inch, the bones were juicy, and the broth enriched dog food dinners for several days. Chakka soon learned to associate the sounds and smells of the cooker with treats. Consequently, the minute he had any inkling that the cooker was in use, he was there also, waiting impatiently for the finished product.

Chakka knew that the cooking was a lengthy process, and he learned to develop some degree of patience, but not much. By the time I released the steam from the kettle, Chakka's last shred of control gave way to outright food lust. Since the bones were much too hot to eat when first removed, I'd scoop the rich, meaty broth from the cooker, pour it over a huge container of dog food, and cool it down with warm water. At that point Chakka could eat.

One afternoon, Chakka was just a little too impatient for his own good. He saw me fixing his big dish of food, but he wanted one of the bones. I saw his muzzle sniffing the steamy vapors from the kettle, but I wasn't worried that he would jump up at it. It never dawned on me that he would dare to press his nose against the side of the kettle until I heard a sizzle and anguished yelp from Chakka. Where his nose touched the metal, he left a print of scalded tissue. He ran for his hidey-hole, and I went right after him. The nose on a wolf is exceptionally tender, and Chakka was pawing at his and crying. Feeling acutely sorry for him, I held him for quite a while, and then returned to the kitchen. When I brought him a dish of goodies and a bone, he turned his head away and refused them. He really did hurt.

I almost underestimated the shock to Chakka's system. Although we immediately cooled his nose with ice and put Nupercainal on it for the pain, he went into shock. Animals from the wilds, even those as tame as Chakka, can die of shock in very short order. Sometimes it stems from fright rather than injury, but whatever the cause, the effect can be disastrous.

When I realized how upset Chakka was, I pulled him up on the couch and laid his head in my lap. He was shivering from nose to toes and panting. His heart beat so fast it was fluttering the fur over his ribs. Jenny got an afghan and we threw it over Chakka's body and covered his head so he felt safe. Bill started a large fire in the fireplace in front of the couch, and I sat petting and talking to Chakka until late in the evening. Color finally returned to his lips and gum line, indicating the worst of the shock was over, and he fell into an unnaturally deep sleep. By bedtime his breathing was deep and regular, and he had taken some liquids. It had been a close call, and over such a seemingly small oversight, but it made me aware that Chakka's welfare required constant vigilance.

Although he learned his lesson and never touched the kettle again, his adjustment was peculiar. Instead of acting frightened about it, the way I thought he might, he ignored the kettle totally. To my knowledge, he never again even glanced at it, although he still got excited about the bones and broth I placed in his dishes. It was strange to see him sitting in the kitchen, waiting for supper, his back turned to the kettle. At the sound of the steam being released, he would trot to his dish, but he refused to look at the stove. The memory, it seemed, was literally too painful.

At about this time in Chakka's life I noticed he seemed to be chewing on everything a good deal more than usual. There was a steady increase in the number of rounded corners on furniture, for example. Previously, Chakka hadn't really chewed anything simply for the sake of chewing; it was a byproduct of his search-and-destroy behavior. But now he seemed to be chewing with an almost distant expression in his eyes, as if he had his mind on other things. When I retrieved my slipper from his jaws one morning, I noticed a sharp white object lodged in the leather of the toe. Chakka was teething.

Over the next few weeks, we found his baby teeth in strange places. I knew his teeth were bothering him because he would roll and rub his jaws vigorously against the carpet. One day, when he yawned near my face, I saw many gaps where those needle-sharp baby teeth had been, and one loose tooth barely hanging on. I tried to reach in his mouth for it, but Chakka thought I was playing and bounced all over the room. Holding him still by myself was hopeless, so I had almost resigned myself to waiting for Bill or Denny to help when the solution struck me. I remembered that when I was small and had a tooth ready to come out, my mother would give me a caramel. With the first good chew, the tooth usually popped out painlessly. I decided to give it a try.

Chakka was delighted with the idea. Nothing pleased him more than chewing on something, no matter what it was, and he could hardly wait until I had the cellophane off before he grabbed the sweet. As was his style, he ran off a little way, set the candy on the floor, and sniffed it over thoroughly. This was just ritual. If it passed inspection, it was returned to his mouth and gnawed. The caramel was not on the carpet for long before Chakka was mouthing it in obvious joy.

It didn't take more than a few chews for the candy to begin softening. Somehow, before he was quite aware of what was happening, Chakka found that he had less control over the candy than it had over him. He began to open his mouth wider with each bite, curling his tongue out in protest. The caramel stuck to his teeth, and Chakka began backing up and pawing at the air with each opening of his mouth. Nothing was going to dislodge that gooey mass, so he applied the only method he knew to expel it: He gagged. I have seen Chakka gag before, but never deliberately. He was literally gagging himself as hard as he could. I knew if I didn't reach him in another second or two, we would have a caramel *and* his supper all over the floor. I was just in time to reach in and snatch the candy from his jaws on the biggest gag of all. Chakka closed his mouth, licked around a little, and then sat down and stared straight at me. It was impossible to read his expression. He was probably just plain puzzled. He didn't know if I had played a dirty trick on him, or if the candy was dangerous, or if something had gone wrong. He watched as I put it into a paper towel and threw it in the wastebasket. An hour later, he had retrieved the offending morsel and was rolling on it to leave his scent. He may not have wanted to eat it, but it was his, and he was leaving his message on the sticky stuff.

Eventually, Chakka's baby teeth all dropped out and his second teeth came in so fast that it seemed he was never without a full set. The new teeth kept growing and growing, until finally the fangs were clearly visible when he opened his mouth even to the slightest degree. We lifted his muzzle on both sides over the fangs and told him, "Smile!" Very soon he realized that we all laughed when we did this, and he learned to show off his brand-new teeth to any admirer. He also did much more yawning than necessary, creating as it did such a stir with company. People always wanted to see his huge fangs, and were always impressed with their size and fearsome qualities. As far as I'm concerned, his grown-up set weren't half as dangerous as those sharp baby teeth. They might be large and powerful, but at least they didn't slice a finger if it so much as passed over them.

With his new teeth, Chakka's grooming ceremony became a little more hazardous for us. Chakka loved to groom us with his front teeth as a sign of affection. He used the small teeth across the front, between his large canines, or fangs. These little front teeth would go a mile a minute across skin and hair, clacking happily as he removed any offending debris from us that he could find. "Offending debris" included makeup, stray hairs, and even moles. Anything that was to his mind unwolfish was removed from the unwary. I once had a hangnail nipped so close to the cuticle so quickly that I hardly knew what had hit me. Yet there was no bleeding or discomfort. The only time Chakka ever hurt was when he first got his adult teeth and wasn't used to their broader, more chisel-like action. He could nip threads from clothing with the efficiency of a pair of scissors. Any irregularity in the weaving of cloth was given a thorough going over and grooming. Seams and buttonholes were fair game, but Denny and Bill drew the line when it came to zippers.

Chakka amused himself for hours at night in his daily grooming of the family as we watched TV. It was one of his most contented times of the day. He seemed to be taking comfort in being part of a pack, and taking rather good care of them at that.

I tried to respond to Chakka's grooming in a way that he would understand. Clearly, he saw grooming as a loving obligation, and he took his duties seriously. How could I groom Chakka in return so that he knew he was loved and cared for? Nipping at him with my front teeth was a little beyond me, even though I still occasionally used my teeth on a muzzle or ear for a wolf lesson. I finally decided I'd comb him, and see how he reacted. He took to it as if it was the most natural thing in the world. The minute he spotted the comb, he would flatten out on his back and stretch, waiting like a monarch for his homage. Occasionally, when the comb was near his muzzle, he mouthed it and nipped it affectionately. If I forgot or was a bit slow in this routine, Chakka knocked the comb off the table and rolled onto it.

Chakka's fur, as thick as it was, remained devoid of mats, even when he was shedding. Actually, when he did shed, the hair came out in huge chunks, but never snarled or matted. The fact that Chakka was not running in weeds helped, but I have seen house dogs that have never been near a field look like one solid mat of hair. Wolf fur is much less likely to mat. Also, wolves spend many hours grooming themselves and each other. Whatever the reason, Chakka's fur was always glistening and clean. To be sure, there were times he rolled in something less than divine, but it seldom remained on his coat for long. In a matter of minutes, he could clean himself completely—which was a great advantage, since one can never bathe a wolf. Bathing removes the essential oils, and the fur loses its elasticity and waterproofing, thereby making the tender skin underneath vulnerable to a myriad of problems. Wolves can and do go swimming. Shampoos, creme rinses, or soap can damage their fur.

As Thanksgiving passed and Christmas approached, Chakka began to look more and more like an adult. He was nowhere near his full size, but he made even the largest German shepherd look small. We noticed that his growth was now more sporadic. Sometimes his weight gain and height accelerated so rapidly that people noticed a difference from one week to the next, after which he'd seem to reach a plateau.

However, as Chakka's size increased, some of his puppy-ploys began to make a larger-than-life impression on his humans. For example, Chakka used his flank approach for two reasons. Number one was to protect himself from nips or scratches if he was unsure of an animal he was approaching. He would back into the situation, offering his thickly padded hindquarters first, testing the waters. If everything was safe, he extended the flank attack to sitting on the object of his attention. Dogs, cats, and low-slung animals were easy, but humans were a slightly larger challenge. The flank attack had to be escalated. To begin with, he must find someone lying down, or at least sitting. The next step in the game was to back into them and sit perched on their shoulder as though they were giant footstools.

Strangely, Chakka used only his flank approach in loving the family. With us, his motto (like the Fonz's) seemed to be "Sit on it," but this is proclaimed with love. He wouldn't bother to impress a stranger with his behavior. It's only the Gravlins who walk around with one shoulder permanently lower than the other.

Evenings were special for Chakka, because he had the family together in a relaxed atmosphere. During the day we'd all be too busy for the undivided attention he sought. But after supper, with everyone lounging in front of the fire or TV, it would be virtually impossible for us to ignore him. He had us, of course, at a lower level than usual, and we were more likely to be receptive to his advances since it is extremely difficult to see anything when one's eyes are being tenderly groomed by a long, pink tongue, or when a matched set of ribs are being ground into one's face. And it would have offended Chakka terribly if we'd failed to respond. After all, he was only performing his wolf-duty to his pack.

Denny instituted a ritual in the evening that became Chakka's special treat. I had taken three pairs of panty hose and braided them together for a tug-a-dog toy. Although its original intent had been to amuse the dogs and possibly Chakka, the end result was a toy made expressly for tug-a-wolf evenings. No night was over until Denny and Chakka had demolished the living room in their growling, scrambling battles over who would drag whom the farthest.

Many times, while Denny dragged mightily on his end of the toy and Chakka pranced and pulled on his half, somewhere in the middle another one or more of the Gravlin dogs would leap into the battle. Most of the time they were left hanging in the air, gripping the stretched material firmly in their teeth and being jerked wildly from side to side. Their growls, added to the usual pandemonium, made watching TV impossible.

Chakka dearly loved this nightly endeavor. If we forgot it, he brought out the toy and placed it in our laps, nudging hopefully. He so loved that stretchy nylon piece that it was months before I could pull on a pair of panty hose without being dragged across the bedroom by a happy wolf who thought I was playing.

Pulling is second nature to a wolf—notwithstanding the fact that I'm convinced it's part obstinacy, part rebellion. If a wolf on a leash is going in one direction and the person on the other end decides to let the wolf go in that direction, the fun is over. The minute a wolf finds that you are following him, he changes tactics so that he can pull. If he can find the direction you don't want to go, he is happy: he can pull to his heart's content.

No one in his right mind ever takes a wolf for a walk on a leash anyway. It is dangerous to traffic patterns, ego, and anatomy; everything suffers but the wolf. There have been times when Denny and I had a double leash on Chakka, and I still don't remember hitting the ground more than every third step. Chakka can change directions so fast that a north-bound person on the end of the leash can find his compass rearranged in a flash. It was this distressing habit that almost ended in tragedy for Chakka and his family.

In late November, when the sky was heavy with threats from winter and temperatures were plummeting, Chakka decided to enter into the spirit of the holidays. Now, I am a winter/Christmas person; no time of the year makes me more exuberant. Chakka sensed this and chose a beautiful, snow-swirled evening to go for a walk. I didn't mind a bit—in fact, I couldn't wait to bundle up, snap on Chakka's leash, and head out into that lovely black night, where Chakka and I could sail down our rural roads past homes where yellow lights sparkled on the snow. As we were leaving the house, Denny decided to join us and Chakka bounced in happiness. We left the yard with shouts of laughter and high spirits.

How we sailed down the road! Chakka was feeling superior, exalting in being able to drag his people in whatever direction he chose. Denny had the leash, and I soon realized I couldn't hope to keep up with them and was quickly left behind. I heard Chakka's excited panting and Denny's laughter echoing from the edges of the dark woods and black bay shores. Occasionally they'd shoot back past me and disappear on the other side of a hill. In that black, snow-blanketed night, I felt a communion with Chakka's soul. There was a wildness, an unfettered swift rushing of exhilaration, that defied description. Chakka obviously sensed it. When he wore Denny out, I took the leash for a while and knew how Mercury felt, on winged heels. We sailed and soared, oblivious to obstacles. Chakka plowed and roared into the deepening drifts, while I simply fought to stay upright.

By the time Chakka once again led me toward the road, I was gasping for air, just able to reach Denny before my grip on the leash gave out. The two of us skidded behind Chakka on the icy road, whooping with delight. It took the two of us to control Chakka's heft and happiness until we reached home, weak-legged with exhaustion. Chakka, still fired up, was unwilling to go in. We put him on the leash and went inside.

Outside, Chakka lifted his muzzle to the snowy skies and howled with joy. Inside, we sat before the fire and listened. I knew we were lucky to be able to share the glory of raising such an animal, and I reflected on how wonderful he was. There was no fear between us, only love and respect. We had each tested the other's mettle and come away with a feeling that no matter what passed, we each understood the other. His wildness was the most beautiful part of him. I hated the necessity of chaining and restricting him, even if it was for his own good. In every other way, we determined to make it up to Chakka that freedom was not an option, much as we might like it to be. For the restrictions we imposed, we bent over backward to make him happy. It was in this mellow, reflective mood that I sat lost in thought when Jenny suggested we bring Chakka inside. The temperature was dropping rapidly, and she felt that after his run he might get chilled. She opened the door to an empty backyard.

Of all the horrifying experiences one may encounter in raising a wolf, a runaway is the most dreaded. I had no fear that Chakka would attack anyone; far from it. Shy as he was, he was unlikely to confront anyone anywhere who he might otherwise avoid. Nor was I afraid Chakka would abuse any animals he might meet, at least not at this age. As a friend once remarked, she could picture Chakka chasing a moose, but only if he knew it very well. My fears did not concern themselves with what damage Chakka might do as much as what horrors people might inflict upon him should they find him running loose. Simply the whispered word *wolf* was enough to cause guns to be taken from racks and oiled in readiness. At this point my neighbors were unaware that Chakka was a wolf, but had they been, their attitude would have been one of alarm—despite the fact that they thought Chakka was just fine, passing as he did for a shepherd-husky mix. I prayed fervently that no one would realize what he was before we got him back.

Denny and Bill both dashed for their cars and took off to search along the roads. Jenny donned her heaviest jacket and set out for the woods and cedar swamp behind us. In between putting on boots and going out the back door, I took the time to call my friends at the sheriff's department. I had worked there as a dispatcher for a couple of years and knew all the patrolmen well. They loved Chakka and came to visit him often, well aware of his true origins. As soon as I reached them, they were concerned enough for Chakka's safety to send two squad cars into the area. By that time, it was pitch black outside, and a heavy snow was falling. Our search seemed hopeless.

We covered every inch of territory we thought Chakka might be in, but saw nothing, not even a track. The wind was beginning to howl off the bay, cutting visibility down to almost nothing. With the deepest possible discouragement, I called a halt to the search at midnight, and we returned home to warm up and plan our next move. I knew Chakka was enjoying his freedom to

WOLF GAMES   139

the limit. I could imagine him loping happily along, oblivious to any possible dangers. If he was lucky enough to escape anyone seeing him in the storm, he was in peril from other sources. The highway curved along the bay less than a quarter of a mile behind us. Suppose he got in the way of traffic? Or what if he got as far as the bay itself and fell in? Even a wolf would be hard-pressed to survive the steadily dropping temperature if his coat got soaked. And last but not least was the fear that he might easily get lost, this being his first foray into unknown territory. Our chances of getting Chakka back were diminishing every minute.

The sheriff's department called to advise us that there was still no sign of Chakka and that the incoming shift of deputies would be notified of the search. As fate would have it, however, the new shift never got the message, and piled into their squad cars unaware that a wolf was on the loose.

We decided the only thing to do was warm up, grab a few hours of sleep, and be back hunting for Chakka slightly before dawn broke. Our hope was that by that time he might be tired enough to slow down and perhaps be seen through the trees. I knew that even if we caught sight of him the battle would be far from over. A wolf simply will not come when called. In fact, he considers it a great challenge to maneuver as much as possible to outrun his humans. The game could well cost Chakka his life. It was on that dispirited note that I finally kicked off my boots and curled up in the chair to await dawn. I sat on the chair nearest the door, hoping that Chakka might double back to the house and I would hear him. I was just beginning to doze when the phone rang.

The new dispatcher on duty at the sheriff's department asked in a slightly awed voice if I might happen to have a wolf loose. One of the deputies had been traveling along the bay behind our house when a large gray animal streaked across the road. Its shape and manner of running made the deputy slow down for another look. As he cautiously turned the car around, the gray form hurtled across the road again and stood panting at the edge of the woods. This man, who is an especially good friend of mine and Chakka's and one of the first to realize that Chakka was not a dog, had always followed Chakka's escapades with great interest. As soon as he saw Chakka in the headlights, he called the office and asked them to telephone me.

While he sat in the car, waiting for an answer, his partner stared at Chakka's size. Despite my friend's assurances that Chakka was loving and gentle, the other deputy elected to stay in his seat while we rushed to the scene from home. It took us less than four minutes to reach the area where the headlights were spotting a tired Chakka.

I had Muttley with me on a leash. The minute he spied Chakka he strained to join his friend, and when he found he couldn't reach him, he barked. Chakka's head snapped toward us as he stared through the glare of the headlights. Suddenly, he seemed to disappear right before our eyes. In fact, he'd dropped down along the side of a culvert and silently raced its length, away from us and toward the woods. I watched him run away with a sinking heart. With true wolf instinct, he was departing with the intent of circling back and investigating us at a distance more advantageous to him. He had heard Muttley's bark, but he also knew strangers were in the area. He was going to be a bit cagier than they were!

Seeing Chakka run, Denny doubled back up the road, running frantically to keep our elusive friend in sight. I waited quietly, hardly daring to move. The stillness was unearthly. Suddenly, I heard a snort of greeting somewhere just beyond our circle of light. I am not sure who grabbed Chakka, whether it was Denny or myself, but I do know that by some miracle his gray form was suddenly attached to a leash and he was giving us warm and loving wolf greetings, knocking Muttley to the ground in his exuberance. I sank to my knees in the snow, weak with gratitude. We had so nearly lost him, and it struck me anew just how much a part of our lives he had become. Obviously, we were going to have to find a more secure method of controlling Chakka. Although the chain that had tethered him in the garden had been made to restrain cows, he had snapped it with ease, springing the heavy cast-iron latch in two places. I wished fervently that we had built a pen for his outdoor outings, but it was impossible to build one during the long Michigan winter.

After the scare of almost losing Chakka, we rigged a "double-safe" chain and latch arrangement, which I hoped would hold him until spring. Actually, improving on the chain arrangement wasn't the whole answer. We still had the problem of getting him outside and on the leash without losing a grip on his collar. This was becoming increasingly difficult for me. Bill and Denny found themselves pressed into service more and more, and even they were having problems. Finally, because I was so afraid he could break out of my hands, I got an extra-long welded-link chain that reached from the tree outside into the house. That way, I could bring in the end of the leash from outside, snap it onto Chakka's collar, then throw open the door and release him, thereby eliminating the dangerous middle step. Content, I thought Chakka couldn't get loose.

But Chakka didn't like being thwarted. To him, going outside and giving us a snow bath was part of the deal. The way things were arranged now, he didn't stand a chance, so he proceeded to come up with ways of frustrating us. The first time I saw him work around this restriction I couldn't believe my eyes.

I had been sitting on the couch with my back to the door when I thought I heard someone coming into the house. My first reaction was to make a grab for Chakka and hold him until the door was safely closed again. The problem was, I couldn't find Chakka.

I turned to the door to warn whoever was coming in to be careful. But no one was coming into the house. Chakka was trying to get outside. He had his mouth around the doorknob and was gently turning his head from side to side to get the thing open. If the doorknob had been anything other than smooth and round, Chakka would have succeeded in opening the door easily. Of course we had never taught him to open the door. It was strictly Chakka's power of observation and intelligent use of senses that came into play. Many times after that he worked on the knob, for as long as fifteen or twenty minutes, trying for success. Eventually he gave up, satisfied that only humans could master that particular technique.

9

Widget Warmbody

WINTER WAS UPON US AND CHRISTMAS only two weeks away when Chakka began to sense a heightened state of excitement in the household. Preparations were in full swing for company, due to arrive in a day or two. New and exciting decorations began to appear, which intrigued Chakka no end. We strung garlands of piney swags across the mantelpiece and wound strings of "grain of wheat" lights about the house, their flashing colors holding Chakka's attention once he discovered they were harmless. At first he had viewed them with alarm, since every time he sneaked up on the becalmed lights they'd flicker on the instant his nose hit the garland. Eventually, he realized putting his nose on them had nothing to do with their flickering, and he was content to simply watch them. Finally, however, they lost their appeal because they never "did" anything, didn't even smell.

We had planned to introduce the decorations in easy stages so that Chakka would have time to investigate each and learn

143

that its destruction would be frowned upon. I didn't want Christmas to be traumatic for Chakka, but on the other hand, I didn't want the house in a shambles, either. We decided the decorations should be thoroughly investigated by Chakka before they were put up, and perhaps in that way we could prevent him from tearing them down in his enthusiasm to discover their innermost nature. The plan worked fairly well. Chakka sniffed and snorted at crystal snowflakes for the windows and was uninterested in them until they were hung on the window. He discovered that if he got up close and exhaled on them, they'd clatter against the glass in a most satisfying way. Diligence was the key word on my part. If I heard telltale clatter from another part of the house, I'd dash into the living room and reprimand Chakka. When he found he could get my attention that way, things became very lively. He refused to accept the fact that I was serious, and treated the snowflake rattling as a joke. In fact, he got quite coy about it. When I rushed about yelling my head off, I'd find Chakka sitting nonchalantly, gazing innocently into the fireplace. Sometimes he would heave a tremendous sigh and flop down as if the whole incident were just too boring to contemplate. His air of disdain didn't fool me one bit as I'd find the snowflakes still swaying back and forth at the windows. I began to wonder, if Chakka wreaked that much havoc over a few ornaments, how in heaven's name would he react to the Christmas tree?

We considered giving up a tree that year, but we couldn't bear the thought. Christmas at our house is a great event, and the entire family was gathering for the holidays. I just couldn't picture my parents and our children and grandchildren trooping into a house without a Christmas tree. Somehow we had to devise a way of having our tree and keeping it safe from Chakka.

Someone proposed a very small tree, about three inches high, and hanging it from the rafters in the living room. I wasn't sure, even then, that Chakka wouldn't get it with ease. We toyed with the idea of a small table tree, but it didn't fit with our concept of Christmas. Finally we decided we would have our usual large tree, complete with all ornaments except the handmade and the antique ones. Somehow, we would keep Chakka away from it.

Jenny suggested bringing in the tree early, putting it up with lights, and then adding the ornaments later so Chakka could get used to it gradually. It made more sense than anything else we'd considered, so we tried it. To this day I still can't believe it worked so well.

Chakka ate a few branch tips the first day. He got under the tree and almost knocked it over the next day. Other than that, he really wasn't interested. Since he still wasn't old enough to lift his leg when he wet, we didn't even have that worry.

We decided we would not put presents under the tree as they arrived. They went into closets until Christmas Eve, when they could be placed under the tree while Chakka was on his porch for the night. Luckily, as members of the family began arriving from various parts of the country with gifts, Chakka was more interested in the people than the packages.

By that time, Chakka was reacting more positively toward people, so Christmas would be the supreme test for him. Not only would he meet many strangers, but they would also be living in his house! We discussed how he might adjust and decided he would behave beautifully. The only danger would be if Chakka knocked over one of the grandchildren in a fit of exuberance, or maybe scratched someone in the face as he leaped up to give his loving wolf greeting. Such possibilities would bear watching, but otherwise we felt confident all would go well. Since Chakka had outgrown the chair in the living room he had used as his hidey-hole, he had taken over his bedding on the porch as his safety area. I insisted that this place be inviolate for when things got rough or else he got tired of people; he had to have a quiet place to go to renew himself. And indeed, there were moments during those next two weeks when I was more than envious of Chakka's haven on the porch. I wanted one of my own!

With the greatest wolf dignity possible, Chakka breezed through the hectic holiday times as if he were used to a houseful of twelve people, three of them very small and a lot of fun to tease. Charmed that humans could come in such a convenient size, he loved staring eyeball to eyeball with our grandsons, Chrissie and Shawn. Another handy point about small humans was that if they had anything edible in their hands, it was at the right level to share with a wolf. After all, an ice-cream cone can be licked from both sides just as well as one. During that Christmas Chakka found he'd never had so many cookies at once, and so cheerfully given! Life was rather pleasant in a full house.

Two incidents with the children slightly marred the holidays, neither one serious. The first caused much laughter on our part and a tiny screaming rage for Chrissie.

Chakka followed the children all over, preferring their company to that of adults. Best was when he could corral both kids in one area, but if they happened to go in different directions at once, Chakka had a problem. Since Chrissie was a toddler, Chakka had more trouble keeping him in sight than he did Shawn, who was just crawling, so Chakka would stand in front of Chrissie, blocking his way, while Chrissie would stoop down slightly and walk right under him. This disconcerted Chakka, until he came up with a solution. As Chrissie was walking away from him for the umpteenth time, Chakka reached out and grabbed the seat of his disposable diapers and pulled them down around the toddler's ankles. Chrissie did his best to walk away and pull up his pants at the same time, but whenever he got anywhere near accomplishing the feat, Chakka would grab the diapers and pull them down again. After four or five repetitions, Chrissie's rage was matched only by our helpless mirth. As for Chakka, he was mightily pleased with himself. My foster daughter-in-law Linda finally rescued her son and replaced the plastic tatters he was wearing. From that moment on, Chakka delighted in catching a child in diapers. He never so much as touched the skin, but it still thrilled him. And although we did our best to discourage him, the moment a child was untended, down came the modesty.

Chakka's second unpopular move was one that scared my other daughter-in-law, Kim's wife, Bev. Grandson Shawn had crawled over to where Chakka was sleeping and fallen into Chakka's midsection, grinding his tiny knee into a vital part of the male physique. Chakka's reaction was swift. He woke with a start, rolled onto his stomach, and wheeled his head around with a tremendous growl and bared teeth. In a flash, Chakka's mouth was at Shawn's shoulder area. Had Chakka been anything other than the magnificent animal he is, my grandson could have been seriously hurt. As it was, Chakka saw instantly that it was one of the children and pulled away, scrambling to his feet and streaking for his hidey-hole. There wasn't a mark on Shawn. He probably would not have been as lucky with a domestic dog jolted awake in such a manner. The situation did serve, however, to remind us all that there are limits to what any animal (or human, for that matter) can take. I am sure that if Shawn had been bitten, many people would have felt it was just another case of a wild animal "turning" on its people. The wolf would have had no defense. As it turned out, Chakka and Shawn were playing together half an hour later, neither realizing the danger they had been through, but from that moment on we were all more watchful.

At about this time, Chakka was beginning to think the whole world was made up of negatives. He couldn't pull down diapers, he wasn't allowed to eat the Christmas tree, he was told he couldn't play window tattoo with the crystal snowflakes, and he was scolded if he put his nose on the table where all manner of wonderful edibles were arrayed. A couple of times I caught him slinking out of the room with a dejected air of defeat and I began to worry. Were we inhibiting him too much? Were we expecting too much from him? Was the effectiveness of the word *no* going to pall if it was used too often? More and more, the frequent censoring drove Chakka to slink back to his hidey-hole. Wolves are proud.

Unlike a dog, who will take such experiences in stride, a wolf has to keep his ego intact. And at this point in his life, Chakka's ego was suffering a rout. Somehow, some way, I had to make it up to Chakka and let him know his world was something more than just restrictions. I couldn't turn his home into a prison.

One thing that always made Chakka feel good was a howl. When the world was either depressing or very happy, a howl vented emotions very satisfactorily. Almost any occasion could inspire a howl: a train passing through the countryside, a siren, another dog, or a biscuit orgy. Now *there* was something Chakka loved! We decided to increase the number of biscuit howls from one in the evening to several during the day for an added boost.

It always started with Tawny deciding to go into the kitchen and stare through the glass oven door to see if the box of biscuits inside was still intact. If no one paid attention to her, she began muttering softly under her breath, moaning and mumbling until someone took notice. Usually about five seconds of muttering was enough to attract the attention of the rest of the household, and everyone trooped into the kitchen to see the performance.

Exuberant Muttley would give out with a few barks, and that did it. Chakka was off on a howl, joined by every dog in the house. Since there are usually eight or ten dogs in our home at a time, this activity could get a little loud. Chakka was especially pleased if I dropped what I was doing, sat on the floor next to him, and placed my head against his. We would howl together, harmonizing and congratulating each other with short yips. After two or three minutes surrounded by howls, I would raise my arms and yell, "Enough !" That was the signal for the howl to end and the biscuit orgy to begin. Out came the box of treats, with wolf and dogs lining up to await their treat. Sometimes a whole box of biscuits would disappear, and still they'd be lined up with expectant looks on their faces. In an attempt to boost Chakka's morale, we spent a minor fortune on treats over the holidays, and when they were over, Chakka had no intention of giving up this new-found bonanza. I suspect it cost me fifty dollars to get him through to the new year.

Eventually, Christmas Eve arrived, and with it the air of expectancy so special to that holiday. Chakka wasn't sure what was going on, but he was almost dancing on his toes. He cavorted and rolled, acted goofy, and generally joined in the fun as much as he could. He ate an ornament or two that night, and I sat there and let him. He was so happy and had really been so well behaved, I considered the ornaments an early present to him.

The children were put to bed, stockings were hung on the mantel, and a few hours remained before the big occasion. We were all in high spirits.

Bill brought out armfuls of packages, and we made a respectable mound of them under the tree. Chakka's curiosity could not be contained. He had to sniff every gift. I thought he was checking the scents, but on Christmas morning I discovered he had neatly snipped off half a dozen tags, leaving us hard-put to guess whose package was which. Finally, when all was in readiness, we dimmed the lights and sat in front of a blazing fire for a few minutes before going to bed. Chakka was put outside for his evening constitutional. When I left him on his porch for the night, his eyes glittered with devilry. It was almost as if he knew something special would happen in the morning.

One would think with a houseful of children that they would be the first to wake up in the morning. Not so. At five-thirty my irrepressible foster daughter-in-law, Linda, was singing "Jingle Bells" to the accompaniment of hoarse protests to lie down and go to sleep.

Chakka, delighted to have people up so early, raked his long nails up and down the wire doors to the porch. Trying to sleep through that is like trying to live at the base of a very active harp. Everything in the house resonated. In two minutes, the kids were up and lights were on. Chakka was put outside on his leash with a bone treat. We decided that trying to open packages with him in the house would be impossible. He was to remain outside until the festivities were over and then let in for his own special treat. We saved all the wrappings and ribbons for him to play with when we were through.

I am sure that Chakka waited outside with increasing expectancy. Even though he had his bone, he knew something better was going on inside. Finally, all our packages were unwrapped, everything admired, and the moment of truth for Chakka arrived. Smack in the middle of the living room floor was a veritable mountain of wrapping paper, dotted liberally with ribbons, sticky tape, cards, and bows. This was Chakka's Christmas present.

Bill opened the door and let Chakka in. For an instant Chakka surveyed the situation. If there was one thing in life Chakka truly loved, it was a piece of paper he could shred. There, right in front of him, was enough to keep his wolfie heart in ecstasy for hours. In one gigantic leap, he sailed through the air onto the top of the heap and sank in over his head. Papers flew everywhere. Then the volcano erupted and Chakka roared out, scattering wrappings and ribbons clear to the ceiling. Amid shouts of laughter, he dived back into the heap, and the mountain-sides slowly gave way in a shuddering slither of paper. Again, papers exploded as he tore out the other side, with a jaunty bow stuck to his shoulder. When he had bounced on the paper mound so often it was almost flattened, he proceeded to roll on it, snorting and blowing shreds of tissue paper all over. We laughed and applauded his antics for the better part of an hour before he collapsed with his head in Jenny's lap in a surfeit of pleasure. He fell asleep nestled against her new bathrobe, one paw flung over her knee. He certainly looked fetching in pink and lace—as he still does.

While Chakka slept, we burned the debris in the fireplace and prepared Christmas breakfast. By the time we were ready to eat, he was awake again, looking for his papers. Having anticipated that, we had a diversion ready. Chakka celebrated with his first ham bone that morning. While we munched toast, ham, and eggs, Chakka crunched his way through four inches of solid bone. We all finished at about the same time.

My daughter-in-law Bev brought in the youngest member of the family, granddaughter Brandy. Only a couple of months old, Brandy had been asleep during the confusion, but was now awake and gurgling happily. Chakka had seen her before but had not been allowed to kiss her or groom her, and this left a small, unsatisfied need in his heart. Bev was sitting at the table with the baby in her lap when I noticed Chakka slithering quietly between the chairs. I signaled Bev and she turned her head just as Chakka put his warm nose against the baby's feet and snorted. Brandy laughed out loud and Chakka looked up and grinned at her. We decided he would be allowed to take a close look at her as long as he didn't lick. He gave her a thorough going over and, satisfied, lay down by Bev's chair.

Half an hour later, while I was talking to Bev, I noticed Brandy's black curly hair slowly sink farther and farther into the blankets. Bev stared down in astonishment as the baby slid nearly out of sight. From the other end of the blankets, Chakka tenderly pulled at the end of Brandy's nightgown. In another minute he would have had her on the floor, where he could love her to his heart's content. Bev's cry of outrage set Chakka back on his haunches and caused his ears to stand straight up in surprise. Obviously, Bev was unaware that wolf fathers do as much of the grooming and cleaning of the young as the mothers do, so what was all the fuss about? Bev let loose with a string of epithets I have never heard her use before or since. Chakka, abashed at this display, retreated to the living room with offended dignity on every wrinkle of his face. Young mothers were so peculiar!

Eventually the holidays ended, and our family began drifting back to their own homes. After the hectic preparations, the mass confusion, and all the excitement, it suddenly seemed unnaturally quiet in the house. We had taken down the tree and decorations on New Year's Day and put the tree out in the backyard, strung with suet for the birds. I had offered Chakka the tree to chew on, but without its ornaments and lights it held little fascination for him. Chakka, in a postholiday letdown, became listless. He gave a desultory chase to a cat or two, but his heart wasn't in it. He had gotten used to all the hubbub, and now he missed it. We might have had a real problem keeping him amused if fate hadn't once again stepped in. At that lull in our lives, Widget Warmbody appeared.

A friend had a young pup that she couldn't keep. The pup's parentage was a matter of some conjecture, but she certainly had to have been mostly Chihuahua. As a pup, she could sit in the palm of my hand with ease, and at full-grown size she weighed barely four pounds. But instead of having the delicate Chihuahua build, she was short-legged and stocky, like a well-stuffed sausage. She had more personality per square inch than any other dog I have ever encountered. The instant Chakka saw her, she became the ultimate love of his life and he her devoted slave. In a strange way, perhaps it was just as well she didn't live long enough to have her first heat period, because I'm sure it would have left poor Chakka a quivering mass of frustration.

The day I brought Widget home, I was concerned for her safety with Chakka. I was sure he would realize she was a dog, but if he tried to play with her like one, he'd be liable to flatten her before he realized what he had done. Consequently, the first time Chakka saw Widget, I held her in my hands and called him over to sniff at her. I had expected her to cower or cry when that large muzzle came near, but to my amazement she stood up, raised her hackles, and growled! Chakka tipped his head to one side quizzically. Then he edged in closer for his first sniff. Before I could prevent it, that tiny blond bundle shot out of my hand and attached itself to Chakka's tender nose. The wolf, more surprised than I, sat abruptly on his haunches and shook his head. Widget flew off, and I jumped up to see if she was hurt. Before I could even reach her, she had recovered and shot back across the carpet and attacked Chakka's feet in a growling fury. Chakka's ears were standing at the alert as he lifted the paw she was attacking and stared down at her. Undaunted, she attacked the other paw, forcing Chakka to sit up with both front feet off the ground. Widget then raced in under Chakka's chest and launched an attack on his hind feet! That was too much. The poor wolf scrambled backward into a corner and held his front feet up while he did a fancy dance to keep the back feet clear of those little teeth. I reached in and grabbed Widget before she could devour my expensive wolf.

It was Widget's total lack of fear that entranced Chakka. In his world, it was either dominate or submit, and it had been his experience so far that animals smaller than himself submitted nicely, with no back talk. That was as things should be. But his meeting with Widget Warmbody taught him that not everything in the world goes as planned. He was absolutely mystified that she could so easily turn the tables on him. It obviously never occurred to him (thank God) that she might make a lovely mouthful. He just took her antics in stride. It is a strange sight indeed to see a hundred-pound wolf roll over and submit to a dog weighing just a little over a pound.

After rescuing Chakka at least half a dozen times the first day, I got disgusted and gave up. He obviously wasn't going to hurt her, and I didn't think that she could do too much damage with those tiny teeth, so I let nature take its course. Besides, it disgusted me to see Chakka roll over the minute she came into the room. The whites of his eyes showed clearly as he silently begged her not to punish him too soundly. Widget, who thought this great fun, made him submit at least once each hour. I grabbed my camera—no way would anyone ever believe what was happening without proof positive.

The first day was a testing ground for both animals. By the second day they were inseparable. If Chakka lay down for a snooze, Widget stretched herself full length under his chin and slept also. In puppyhood, she was barely as long as his muzzle, and even full grown she was much smaller than his head. But despite the size difference, Widget appointed herself Chakka's protector. While he slept the heavy sleep of an innocent wolf, she relaxed but was ever watchful. If another animal came too close, a tiny, threatening growl issued from her throat as she stood protectively across his nose and defied the world to bother her wolf. It was an unbelievable combination, and people who saw it couldn't credit their eyes.

It was because of Widget that Chakka finally adjusted to the quiet, long winter months. She kept him constantly occupied with some new mischief of her devising. One of their favorite games was tug-a-dog on the braided nylon rope. Chakka would grasp his end firmly in his teeth and lower his head to the floor. Usually his hindquarters were stuck up in the air and his front legs and head flat on the floor. Widget would grab the other end of the toy and away they went, growling in mock ferocity while they tugged and stretched the braid. Of course, when Widget shook her end of the toy, it didn't faze Chakka because of his immense size, but when he shook the toy, Widget had a tiger by the tail. It didn't bother her one bit. She held on for dear life and growled all the harder. The minute her feet hit the floor again, she did her best to drag that large gray form clear across the room. They would play until they fell into an exhausted, sleepy heap. Half an hour later the living room would erupt in another battle of tug-a-dog.

Chakka and Widget reminded me of a shark and its tiny companion fish, the remora. While other fish get eaten, the little remora nestles against the side of the shark in complete safety and even shares its food. The shark would be lost without its companion, because remoras clean parasites and food scraps from the shark. It is a strange symbiotic combination, but it answers a need in both creatures. So it was with Chakka and Widget. Where one went, so did the other. They became inseparable. If I took Widget for a ride in the car, Chakka threw a fit and tore great chunks of frozen turf out of the yard until we returned. Widget was always delighted to go on a ride, but when we had been gone for any length of time, she grew restless. On the way home she watched out the window, quivering in anticipation and hardly able to control herself until we were in the yard and she saw Chakka again. Their greetings were always a rough-and-tumble, exuberant affair. You would have thought they had been separated for years.

Widget could do no wrong, as far as Chakka was concerned. There were times, however, when her behavior perplexed him. Just after Widget arrived, Chakka was lying on the floor, yawning. Widget walked right straight through his mouth and out the other side. Chakka's eyes watered, and he gagged before closing his mouth. His reaction pleased Widget so much she never lost an opportunity to take advantage of similar circumstances and reprise the move. I'd see her step onto his tongue, walk to the back of his throat, and stare in fascination down that huge tunnel. His gagging would usually deposit her in a hurry somewhere outside that large mouth. Why that antic held such interest for her, I'll never know, but I'd see her rush clear across the room to run into Chakka's mouth before he could complete his yawn. It became such a habit that Chakka took to sneaking yawns behind chairs and in unobserved corners.

Chakka's attachment for Widget was no greater than hers for him. I know of nothing in the wolf wilds that compares with it, or sets a precedent. I think it was just unique with those two, and a very cherished part of their existence. Of course, Muttley was still an important part of Chakka's life, but Widget took great care to see that he wasn't too important. She would tolerate some play between the two animals, but if Chakka was getting the worst of the battle, she would rush to his defense. Of the terrible twosome, I would rather have tackled Chakka any day.

Gradually, Muttley allowed himself to be usurped. I think he actually enjoyed the rest and peace it afforded him. As Chakka had grown in size, it became harder and harder for Muttley to match his stamina. I began to suspect Muttley was older than we had originally thought. However, until his death several years later, Muttley was a valued part of Chakka's pack.

Chakka and Widget taught each other many things, not all of them commendable. Widget showed Chakka how to eat my potted plants (again) when they could be reached, and she also taught him that empty shoes and socks could provide a whale of a good time. Her favorite trick was to undo the laces from shoes. She could carefully work at the cords until they were completely free from the shoe eyelets, then she'd dash off and bury the string somewhere. Chakka's approach had been a little less precise. He simply grabbed the laces in his mouth and jerked until they snapped free, occasionally with small pieces of shoe attached. After being trained by Widget, however, Chakka became so good at undoing laces that he could remove them from a shoe while it was still on the foot, frequently leaving the wearer unaware of the problem until he walked right out of his shoes.

Chakka had several tricks that he, in turn, taught Widget. His most distinctive was the howl. Widget would sit at Chakka's feet, gazing up into his face while he howled. She would turn and tip her own little head back, clearly puzzled by the meaning and function of this maneuver, but if it was one that her friend considered worthwhile, she would learn it.

The first time she howled, Chakka stopped in midnote and looked down at her. Indeed, alongside his magnificent deep-throated melody, her piping screech was as puny as it was funny. Practice, however, improved her technique, so that she eventually could hold a note even longer than he did. Chakka carefully harmonized with her, giving his best basso profundo to her high A. If they were into a really good howl, Chakka would sink slowly on his haunches until he had lowered his head to her level. While they vocalized in unison, Widget leaned her tiny frame hard against Chakka's face and howled lovingly into his ear. He sometimes bore a strained expression, but it never deterred his music.

Another trick Chakka taught Widget was how to dig a den. During the extremely hard winter we had that year, when the ground was frozen solid, the going was a little rough. Widget didn't mind helping dig "snow-curls," but she refused to lie down in them unless she could perch jauntily in Chakka's recumbent side. She didn't have his hardy constitution for the outdoors, but she shared his enthusiasm for the physical activity of digging. When it came to trying to tunnel in the frozen earth, however, she was little help. She found, in short order, that she didn't have the feet or muscle to make a dent in the soil. She contented herself with helping, assembly-line style. While Chakka tore at the frozen dirt, wrenching chunks of it loose with his huge paws, Widget positioned herself between his front legs and slightly to the rear. As the chunks flew, she would push them farther on their way with as much determination as if she had done all the digging herself. The two of them made a splendid team. Together, they turned my yard into foxhole alley.

Chakka considered Widget part of his pack, but she considered him her private and personal possession. She loved us, to be sure, but her prime reason for living was Chakka. Without him, she was lost and incomplete. If she left the house to go anywhere with us, her return greeting to Chakka was exuberant and loving in the extreme. If Chakka left to go anywhere, however, she always came along. She might not be able to match his mile-eating strides on their runs, but she was never far behind. Luckily for her, Chakka was slowed down considerably by the human who was attached to the other end of his leash. On one occasion we took Chakka somewhere without Widget, for some reason. When we got home and opened the door, Widget flew out and thoroughly cleaned Chakka's clock for abandoning her. He submitted repeatedly, but she wasn't satisfied until she had actually worn herself down. It wasn't poor Chakka's fault, but he bore the brunt of her fury. After that, she was adamant in her insistence that where he went, so did she.

Winter winds howled and tore at Michigan that year. The weather took its toll of wildlings outside, because of both the extremely heavy snow and the subzero temperatures. Chakka had no real worries since he was in the house, but he seemed fascinated by the screeching winds and crackling of frozen tree branches. In the worst possible storms he would ask to go out and then stand with his nose turned to the fury of the weather. Somehow he seemed to welcome the challenge. Widget, of course, went right out with him, but her close-coated fur could tolerate only a few moments at best of the frigid blasts. Usually, she could walk on top of the fresh-swirled drifts, but once in a while she fell through and Chakka would dig frantically until he had her freed. If she eventually had to admit defeat and return before Chakka was ready, she spent the time inside staring out the window at her friend. When Chakka finally came back, she would assist him in nibbling the ice chunks from the pads of his feet. After the grooming was finished, they'd both commandeer the couch and stretch out in luxury. It was a life saved from tedium by the love and caring between them. There was always something to do, and whatever amusement one didn't think of, the other did.

The more it howled that winter, the better I loved it. A fire blazed in the fireplace all the time, and a pot of coffee bubbled on the antique wood-burning kitchen range in the west wing. There were days when everyone was snowed in and electric lines were down. We were lucky because of the wood heat that kept us warm. As far as preserving foods without a refrigerator, we had the world's largest refrigerator right outside our door. It made life a little difficult for Bill, however, because he had to try to get to work in town in all that white stuff. Sometimes the car would make it, sometimes not.

One night, when the car had quit before he'd gotten all the way home, he came in the back door absolutely purple with cold and shaking from head to foot. While I quickly poured some hot coffee and helped him off with his stiff clothes, he eyed Chakka and Widget sleeping cozily on the couch in front of the fire. He ran a finger through Chakka's thick, warm fur and got a decidedly wicked gleam in his eye. When I asked what he was thinking, he simply explained that if he had a jacket lined with fur like that, he probably would never feel the cold. I drew in my breath in mock horror. "Then, on the other hand," he mused, "I would probably have to bite it on the ear every time I wanted to hang it on a hook and have it stay there." Chakka slept through the whole conversation, oblivious to everything but his own creature comforts.

It is unfortunate for Chakka that at this crucial time in his development Bill's radio and television directing took him to the Upper Peninsula, too far from home to make it back very often. Although Chakka always greeted Bill effusively, Bill's "upper hand" began to suffer from lack of use. Since Bill was no longer there to take part in the discipline, Denny became the "head wolf," and Bill's authority slipped unnoticed. Chakka still tested me and Jenny every chance he got, and we reprimanded him as needed, but his chief disciplinarian became Denny. I didn't realize this until signs of spring began showing timid traces on the landscape.

It was the last of April, and the snow had changed to sleet and hail. Somehow, it felt colder than it had before. Chakka, attuned to every change around him, grew restless and more than a little high-spirited. He and Widget raced around the house like demons, knocking over furniture, so that I wished anew for a large pen so they could run outside and work off some of that steam, if only for a few hours each day. As the wolf had grown larger, the house had shrunk in size. It was during one of Chakka's more energetic days that Bill returned home and was nearly flattened by a charging mountain of gray fur chasing

Widget. While we tried to talk and bring each other up on the latest news, Chakka repeatedly knocked over suitcases and grabbed mittens. Bill had spoken sharply to him several times, but Chakka had not taken him seriously. Finally, he made the unforgivable error of snatching Bill's fur hat from his head and leaping onto the couch with it. Bill stopped in midsentence and strode purposely toward Chakka, intent on retrieving his hat before it found its way into the nearest stomach. Chakka still had his new toy in his mouth when Bill reached for it. Chakka turned his head several times, successfully evading the outstretched hand. Having traveled a long way in difficult weather, Bill was in no mood for play, so when he finally managed to grab the hat, he rapped Chakka on the nose with it. The mood changed instantly. Chakka's hackles rose, making him appear twice his size, and he bared his teeth and emitted an ominous growl. Bill, more surprised than frightened, without thinking did the very thing he should not have done: He backed Chakka into a corner. At this point Chakka recognized Bill but didn't view him as an authoritative figure. When Bill closed in on him, the growl became so loud that it shook the windows. I shouted for Bill to stop before something terrible happened, and luckily his anger passed and he backed away. Chakka still growled defensively, but more from fright than anything else.

I am sure that if Bill had continued, he could have been bitten. Perhaps not seriously, but who can say? As it was, it was several minutes before Chakka came to himself and once again approached Bill, this time with a forgiving and happy smile. Bill, who is big enough to admit that he can make a mistake, gave Chakka a friendly roughing up that was enjoyed immensely. It was, however, enough to make us realize that the problem of discipline should be left to those closest and in most constant contact with Chakka. He might accept even strangers as friends, but he was getting old enough to resent discipline from all but a very few. We didn't physically punish Chakka for that breach of etiquette, but I did scold him roundly, and he was rather quiet the rest of the hour until Widget induced him to play again.

Bill was home for two days and then gone again. During his

stay, Chakka seemed to be apologizing. Several times he approached Bill quietly and laid his head on his lap. I think he knew exactly what he had done wrong and was sorry for it. It was something that should not have happened, but it made me wonder anew just how much we could expect from Chakka without making his life so restricted that he resented it. In reality, I worried more than was necessary, for Chakka never again repeated such actions. We were, however, careful to be sure that no one except Jenny, Denny, or I ever punished Chakka for anything. It was unfair to ask him to be a dog. He was not a dog, but a beautiful wild animal with distinct likes and dislikes, and a mind of his own.

Four times since that incident, Chakka has been struck by someone other than ourselves, but each incident was accidental. Chakka's instant reaction, even when taken by surprise, was one of disbelief, then wariness, but never retaliation. All four times he merely backed away from the offender. Once, he was accidentally hit so hard on the head with a two-by-four that I was afraid he had been knocked out. I know the pain must have been almost blinding for a moment, because the board fell from quite a height and was caught just an instant before it hit him. He hadn't seen it coming; he only saw the stranger with it in his hand a second after it hit him. And yet he never growled or acted aggressive. He seemed more than willing to forgive anything from a stranger the first time.

Just as suddenly as winter came that year, it left, and in its wake was a whole world of wet, sticky mud. Every time we let Chakka and Widget out the door, they came back in several pounds heavier and more than several shades darker.

I don't know what it is about mud that makes animals roll in it, but the attraction is inevitable. What was amazing was that Chakka could be plastered with the stuff one minute, and clean as a new day the next. He spent hours grooming himself and Widget, making sure that all imaginary fleas were removed as well.

One day, as he groomed his flank, I was startled to see him

wrench a plate-sized piece of hide from his thigh. I let out a scream and dove toward him to prevent further mutilation. It was with the greatest relief that I found he was still in one piece. He had simply started pulling out his thick winter coat, which because of its density was coming out in large pieces—downy thick, soft, incredibly light material that was nearly totally waterproof. I tested it by submerging it in a pan of water, then shaking it out. It was nearly dry to the touch. When I tossed a portion of it into the fireplace, it sizzled and burned, then formed a hard, dark material more like plastic than fur. This nugget of material finally burned down like a piece of soft coal. Dog fur, on the other hand, flared and burned up in a matter of seconds. I am sure a chemist could explain the difference, but to me it just proved that wolves are made of superior material.

Now that the weather had finally broken and green things were beginning to poke through the soil, Chakka was more restless than ever. Taking him for walks was an exercise in how to stay upright and smile while your arm was being torn from its socket. He could be straining to the right one second, and then make a leap onto an unsuspecting violet straight to the left. Arms don't bend that way within a second—at least not normally. Which made it all the more imperative that we construct a pen for him. I wasn't so much concerned with his exercise as I was with keeping my own body whole.

We mulled over the plans for the pen time and again. I remembered that Andy's pens had plywood floors because he didn't believe in raising animals on cement, which was hard on their joints and footpads. I felt, however, that we would have to go with a cement floor because of the large 16-by-35-foot pen we were contemplating (too many plywood seams to chew). Also, he would only use it several hours each day. If we were to prevent him from digging his way out, it would have to be cement floored.

Heavy-duty woven wire fencing eight feet high was another must. Chakka could clear the four-foot dog fence without exerting himself. We also decided to construct a double doghouse with a central porch area where he could escape the elements or relax in the shade. The house resembled two very large dog-houses facing each other, with a roofed and floored runway in between. By having the doghouse doors open onto the runway, we were assured that drafts would be cut down and privacy maintained. Every conceivable comfort was considered for Chakka, including pouring the cement run around an existing pine tree so that he could enjoy its shade, as well as other benefits obvious to a male animal. It seems we had considered everything but the cost. Despite the fact that I nearly had to sell my soul to do it, work on the pen began within a few short weeks.

Chakka was alert to everything going on, and the pen fascinated him. While construction continued, we took him out with us to watch. I wanted him used to it before he was put in, so that it didn't frighten him.

He casually watched us putting in framing for the cement, and then watched it being poured and leveled. It took fourteen hours of dirty, back-breaking, hot, miserable work to get it in. Chakka's interest really perked the day the steel mesh fencing arrived and was put up in sections. When the gates were finally attached and secured, we decided to test it. We let him inside to play while we spent the next several days building the doghouse. That would give him lots of time to run, enjoy us, and feel familiar with his new play-exercise area. It also gave him plenty of time to snatch hammers, scatter staples, and rip open bags of nails. I had an upsetting accident when I placed a long board across two sawhorses and proceeded to cut the end with a Skil saw. Chakka chose that moment to leap on the other end, and the board, the saw, and I all went sailing. Luckily, the electric plug was pulled out during the fray and the only thing hurt was my dignity.

We had thought of everything. The doghouse had a roof pitched so steeply that Chakka couldn't jump on it for extra leverage to leap over the fence. The day before he was to be put in the pen alone with his dog companions, we filled the dog-houses with fresh, clean straw two feet thick. I never admitted it to anyone before, but after the straw was in place, I crawled into both sides of the house and sat in each for an hour to leave my scent for Chakka. Actually, it was kind of nice in there—though I convinced myself that the exercise was entirely in Chakka's best interest. Finally, the big day arrived.

We put the dogs in the pen, took Chakka and Widget for a run, and then brought them back to the pen gate. I opened it while Denny led them in and unsnapped Chakka's leash. He ran all over, chasing dogs, yipping with delight, crashing into the fence, and knocking over the watering pail. Finally, he spied the finished doghouse and raced inside. There was a great thudding and clamor from inside, as bits of golden straw were hurled through the door. Chakka's grinning face would appear for a second and then disappear again to the tune of more thudding. We crawled into the porch and stuck our heads inside, choking on the flying straw. Chakka was buried up to his shoulders in it. Suddenly, he leaped forward, hurling mounds of it over his back; then he dove into it all over again.

Somewhere in the straw we heard the muffled barking of Widget, who'd been buried completely. I called her and she popped up, banged Chakka in the nose, and disappeared back under the straw. They were having the time of their lives.

Chakka finally tired of racing from one side to the house on the other side and he tore back out through the porch door. We watched him race the dogs from one end of the pen to the other. As we smiled and congratulated ourselves on a job well done, Chakka charged the full length of the pen, leaped up on the doghouse roof, and let his momentum carry him to the top of it, which was nearly level with the top of the fence. I stared in horror as he balanced a moment, apparently contemplating whether or not to jump over. Despite the extra-steep pitch to the roof, he had found a way to the top, and we had to do something immediately.

I yelled, and he ignored me; Widget barked, and Chakka jumped back down. The crisis had passed, but we had a problem. While I led a reluctant Chakka out of the pen toward the house, Denny collected the tools and materials to remedy the situation.

Two hours later, Chakka's house had a smooth, slippery roof

covered in aluminum sheeting. We decided to try again. This time when we let Chakka loose, he made two swift turns around the pen and a long run for the roof. I held my breath. It had seemed impossible that he could even have made it the first time, so I wasn't taking any bets. When he was about eight feet from the roof, he leaped. He hit the aluminum with a thud and started scrambling to get to the top as he had before. But this attempt had decidedly different results. His momentum had in fact carried him about halfway up, but that was where he stopped. His toenails screeched against the metal, his ears were laid back, and his feet were going a mile a minute. Suddenly, all four paws lost traction, and Chakka's chin bounced about three times as he slid backward off the roof and hit the pavement. I have never seen a more startled wolf. He just couldn't figure out what had happened. Finally, he stood on his hind legs and sniffed the roof cautiously. That didn't answer his questions. I'm not sure what crossed his mind, but eventually he decided to have a go at the slippery thing again, and he renewed his run with a vengeance. His leap carried him to the same spot, but he didn't land as squarely. He never quite got his feet under him before he was flipped on his side and the thrust of his jump carried him toward the center of the roof in an upside-down position. What goes up must come down. Newton, or somebody, said so, but no one had to tell Chakka. As his upward movement stopped, he began sliding backward down the roof again. The dogs, who had been watching from below, scattered in all directions while Chakka, ears laid flat and all four feet scrambling wildly at the air, sailed, backside first, off the slope. In an instant he'd recovered and disappeared into the doghouse, refusing to come out for over an hour.

I would like to say that was Chakka's last attempt at roof jumping, but such was not the case. Over the next few weeks he managed a coup of sorts. He finally got the timing and forward thrust coordinated to a point where he could leap onto the roof, actually make it to the top for a second or two, and then race down again before he fell. He could even make it look as if he just didn't want to stay up there for long and was coming down of his own accord. It was a study in coordination, and I was amazed at his success. The only time I saw him miss was when he tried his act right after a rainfall. He learned to avoid that in a hurry. At any rate, he never got to stay at the peak long enough to get his feet under him for a jump over the fence.

Over the next few weeks, I felt completely safe in assuming that I could leave Chakka outside to play without having to worry about him getting loose. It really relieved the strain of having him race through the house to get exercise. It also gave him a good chance to cavort with the dogs in a rough-and-tumble way. Chakka himself called the signals as to when it was time to go out and time to come in again. He so thoroughly enjoyed this new form of domination over me that he tended to abuse it and had me running back and forth ten times a day. I finally put my foot down and established a schedule, of sorts.

One afternoon, about a month later, it was hot and muggy for the first time that year. Chakka still had some of his winter coat, and I could tell he was uncomfortable by the way he stretched out on the pavement. When I called him to come in, he raised his head and stared at me. He was satisfied where he was, thank you. For some reason, Widget elected to return to the house with me, leaving Chakka alone. He didn't seem to mind. When I checked on him periodically, he seemed quite content, so I left him in the pen.

About ten that evening as I sat down on the couch, the most terrible crash shook the whole house. It was in the vicinity of the back door, and the dogs and I rushed toward it at the same time. The light from the living room reflected on the screen, so I shielded my eyes and leaned up close to look outside. The air had already turned cool, but what was rushing past my face was warm and somehow familiar smelling. It took a second to realize that I was peering right down Chakka's grinning throat!

I have no idea how long he had been out of the pen, but I'm sure the fact that Widget was inside kept him close to home. When I opened the door, he bounced in happily and settled on the couch. I went outside to the pen to check the gates. I couldn't imagine how else he'd gotten out. A few minutes later I returned to the house, more mystified than ever. The gates were securely locked, and the dogs were inside. The only possible answer was that Chakka had gone over the fence. But how?

The next morning, the four of us took Chakka back to the pen first thing, then waited for him to repeat his escape. Since Chakka loves an audience, he cavorted and played in his most endearing style, but he did not attempt to go over the fence. After more than an hour of waiting, we gave up and trooped back inside. Chakka watched us go and waited a moment or two to be sure we weren't coming back. I could see him through the living room window, but he couldn't see me against the glare of the sun. Finally, he got bored and began to pace. I was sure his next move would be to jump onto the doghouse, but I still didn't see how he could get over the fence. As I watched, his strides got longer and longer, a sure prelude to flight, but I wasn't prepared for his next move. I had just told Jenny and Denny to be ready when Chakka suddenly took a gigantic leap and vaulted to the top of the fence where it made a corner. We were all out the door in a flash as Chakka hooked his front feet over the top, gave a push with his hind feet, and sailed on over. He had hardly hit the dirt when six hands pinned him to the ground. Before he could escape, he was wearing that hated leash again.

I was truly discouraged at this point. After all our work and expense, we were no further ahead than we had been before. We discussed all sorts of remedies to the situation, but most were either too expensive or dangerous. I didn't like the idea of barbed wire, nor could we afford to cover the whole top of the pen with screening. Jenny finally suggested we run a single strand of wire around the top and attach it to a fence shocker, a method we'd used to deter her horse from jumping its fence. I was sure the idea would work. It might not be pleasant for Chakka to get jolted when he tried fence jumping, but it wouldn't hurt him. That afternoon, with our family sixty dollars poorer and one electric fence richer, the pen was once again fixed.

We put Chakka in and observed him. He thought that was just

grand, but refused to even attempt the jumping routine while we were present. Obviously, nothing was going to happen while we were around, so we returned to the house and watched him from the window. This time the sun was right so that Chakka could see us inside, and he watched right back, ears pricked up at a jaunty angle, outstaring us! I began to feel awfully dumb. After making sure that Widget was in the house with us, I told everyone to get away from the windows.

Occasionally, we sneaked a glance, but things were normal in the pen area. While supper was being prepared, I kept craning my neck around the corner but saw nothing unusual. Perhaps this wasn't going to be tested for a day or two, since Chakka was leery of anything new. We would just have to wait and see. Besides, Denny had pointed out that the shocker was set on alternate charge, which meant that instead of electricity going through it all the time, it was pulsed through. A faintly audible click could be heard, and this made Chakka more cautious than ever.

We had just started eating supper when we heard *"Ff-faaaoooooo!"* from the pen area. Chakka had obviously met up with the fence with less than comfortable results. As we peeked through the window, we could see him backing up and snorting as he faced the fence. His hackles were up and his ears were laid back. If that fence made one false move, it was dead! Chakka was clearly quite frightened by the jolt he received, and I ran out to bring him in. It took several minutes to calm him, and a whole lot of coaxing to get him to go through the gate past the wire sides. I think he thought it was out to get him, and he was going to be ready. Whatever his feelings, it wasn't until a week later that he was brave enough to renew his attempt, which had exactly the same results. This time he decided to leave well enough alone. The pen was finally wolf-escape-proof, at least until he figured something else out.

10

Spook

As Chakka approached adolescence, I was called away for a week. From the time I had brought him home as a pup, I had been with him every day. Although I hated to leave him, I wasn't really worried too much, because Jenny and Denny were still at home, keeping the bulk of his pack intact. I didn't want to consider what would happen if we all had to leave at the same time someday. How would Chakka react? Who would we find to take care of him? I could only hope it would never happen or that it would happen much later, when he was older and more secure.

There is a communication between Chakka and myself that, to this day, needs no words. Uncannily aware that I was leaving, he became extremely possessive about me; I couldn't move without having him under my feet at every step. Normally, he would doze off on the couch whether I was in the room or not, but for two whole days before I left, Chakka wouldn't let me out of his sight. Of course, it was all the unaccustomed packing activity that tipped him off, and he was trying to make sure that when I left he'd be along. But that was impossible. Imagine the pandemonium if I made a plane trip with a wolf perched in my lap. Some people just don't understand such things.

Eventually, the moment came. I took Chakka out to his pen with an especially juicy bone. I stayed inside with him, talked to him, and tried to assure him I would be back. His reaction broke my heart. He turned away, ignoring his bone, and walked slowly to the doghouse, dejection in every line of his body. Once inside, he laid his head on the door sill and watched me leave. I was almost in tears as I locked the gate behind me and looked into those beautiful golden eyes one last time. He turned his head away from me, and I fled. It really struck me then how devoted he was to us, and what a great responsibility we had accepted when we got him. We were his family, his pack, and the loss of any part of it was a blow to him. He was in our lifelong care, much like a dependent child. While a short trip by one or the other of us was traumatic for him, he could survive that; but it was clearly evident that if he were ever to lose his whole family, or be caged up in a strange zoo, most likely he would pine away. I made a silent promise he would never have to face that eventuality. Denny snapped me out of my morose reverie by reminding me that I was only going away for a week, but I still felt low as the car left for the airport.

While I was gone, Jenny assured me when I called that Chakka was rambunctious and full of vinegar as usual. He was eating heartily, acting normal, and apparently surviving my loss rather well, surrounded as he was by the rest of his pack. (It is interesting, however, that a year later, when Denny and I left for a week, we returned to find Chakka eleven pounds thinner and looking decidedly ratty, despite Jenny having stayed with him; clearly he needed the *bulk* of his pack on hand in order to function properly.)

Finally, I arrived home on the midnight flight, and Jenny and Denny met me at the airport. When we pulled into the yard and Chakka heard my voice, he let out a howl of welcome. I raced for the pen and had barely gotten the gate open when his furry form hurtled through the air and knocked me to the ground. I simply could not get up. He pinned me flat with kisses and wolf rubs, moaning and trilling happily. When Denny finally got me upright, Chakka leaped sideways, hitting me with the side of his body and nearly flattening me again. We let him work off most of his energy outside and then took him in the house. By this time my traveling clothes were in unspeakable condition but I didn't care. I was as happy to see that silly wolf as he was to see me. After roughing him up in play for several minutes, I bent to open my suitcase and retrieve a chewy toy I had brought him. As I knelt down, Chakka stood directly behind me. Suddenly, the back of my suit became very warm. It took a second to dawn on me what had happened. Chakka had lifted his leg, on me!

I couldn't believe it had happened. Not only had Chakka never raised his leg like that before, but he was housebroken. I was absolutely stunned. It was the kids' burst of laughter that finally got me in motion. As I tried to stand upright, Chakka rubbed against me in the most loving fashion. It suddenly occurred to me that what he had done was not a case of bad manners but an attempt to re-mark me and make me a member of his pack again. Jenny and Denny, weak from laughter, were shot the coldest of stares as I arose with what was left of my dignity and headed for the bathroom. Chakka padded happily along, well satisfied that I smelled familiar again. I couldn't punish him because he was so genuinely happy, but I made a mental note to teach him later that I needn't smell like a wolf to be a member of his pack. It would be a lesson offered at a more appropriate time.

Actually, I was almost as surprised by Chakka lifting his leg at all as I was at having been the recipient. Previously, he had squatted like a pup. This first truly male gesture indicated that he was approaching sexual maturity. He probably would not be fully mature until two and a half years of age, but he was getting there by stages, as he showed more dominance and a more possessive attitude toward what he considered his. Several times after this particular episode, he raised his leg and was reprimanded for it. Twice he did it after we had had a new dog in the house. The minute he came in the house and smelled the stranger, he commented by lifting his leg on a piece of furniture. It had nothing to do with forgetting his housebreaking; it was clearly a message for that other dog that this was definitely and unequivocally Chakka territory! The last time he marked something, it was another human being he was particularly fond of and had not seen for weeks. That time we had convinced him this was unacceptable behavior, and from that point on he contented himself by rubbing on people to mark them.

One thing, however, really puzzled Chakka. He was ready to accept the fact that he couldn't go around marking what he considered his, but if he couldn't do it why were we allowed to? Whenever anyone used the bathroom, Chakka padded in and sniffed around, wrinkles of concern furrowed between his brows. I know he was puzzled as to why we always marked the same spot, and why we put so much value on the bathroom that we continually had to leave our scent there. Twice he tried to leave his scent there among ours, and we stopped him. Finally, he accepted our rather peculiar behavior, but he clearly never understood it. How can you explain something like that to a wolf?

As the days grew longer and hotter, Chakka and Widget spent more and more time outside, lolling happily under the shade of the trees over the pen. Occasionally, Chakka became bored and needed a new toy to occupy him, but most of the time he was totally happy just playing with Widget. I grew accustomed to seeing Chakka stretched out on his side with Widget tucked under his chin like a white napkin. It is a truly unbelievable sight to see a wolf happily gnawing on one end of a bone while his tiny companion chews on the other. On certain occasions I would see Widget actually guard and hoard a whole bone for herself while Chakka stretched out beside her, waiting to be allowed a share as well. I never ceased to be amazed at his gentleness or wonder why he allowed her to bully him so. Somehow, Widget filled a need for him, but she remained the only animal Chakka ever submitted to constantly.

Toward the middle of the summer, when flowers were bursting with fragrance and nature was at her fulsome best, little Widget was lost to us. I had taken her with me to visit some friends on a farm. I never worried about her straying from my side or going near a road because she never had. That day she bounded directly across a road and was killed instantly.

The grief and agony of that moment cannot be described. She was so plucky and full of life that it didn't seem possible she was gone. We buried her at the farm, under a beautiful old apple tree, and I returned home, hours later, unbelievably saddened. The minute I saw Chakka, I realized I had made a terrible mistake. He was looking for his little companion, and pushed and sniffed repeatedly at my hands, asking me where she was. I should have brought her little body home with me for Chakka to see so that he would understand. It was cruel that he didn't know what happened, and I was powerless to explain it to him.

That night Chakka refused to come into the house, and when I checked on him in the pen later, he was lying with his head across his paws, staring into the corner of the fencing. In the small hours of the morning, he howled the most mournful wail I had ever heard him make. Somehow, then, he knew. Whether he blamed me for her death, I'll never know, but at least he never carried a grudge. He still loved me, but for weeks he was a subdued wolf. Three months later, when a tiny white pup was brought to me, Chakka almost tore down the pen to determine if it was Widget. When he found it wasn't, he turned his back on the puppy. No other dog could ever really take her place.

But life goes on and emotional scars heal, even for wolves. Although Chakka never really stopped looking for Widget, he did adjust gradually and return to his former self. One thing that helped immensely was Spook, the big black Great Dane who took up residence in the pen and kept Chakka company on his long lazy afternoons. She took the place of Muttley, who was spending the bulk of his time shadowing Jenny.

Spook was an old dog whose jet black coat was gradually graying around the muzzle. She'd been brought to us years before when she was found along a busy highway, a mass of cuts and bruises. We can only surmise that she had been hit or else fell from a car, but her owners never claimed her and she somehow managed to unobtrusively worm her way into the Gravlin household—a neat trick when you weigh close to 130 pounds.

Spook, like all Great Danes, was easygoing and well mannered. Danes have a quiet, dignified manner that can only be described as regal. Chakka liked Spook, as he liked all the animals he met, but she was no particular buddy or sparring partner. As far as he was concerned, she was simply there. But a few weeks after Widget's death, Spook came into a heat period, and Chakka's attitude underwent a remarkable change. Something new and interesting had been added.

I estimated Spook's age at that point to be somewhere around seven years. This is a rather ripe old age for Danes, who are shorter lived than most other breeds. In the five years we had had Spook, she had never come into a heat period, and I surmised she had been spayed. I had ceased to even think of her breeding until the unmistakable signs began to present themselves. I have no idea why she chose that particular time to come into heat, but I like to think she was waiting for the right man. Until Chakka came along, no one had really suited her fancy.

There is nothing more ludicrous or pathetic than a wolf who suddenly scents the odor of W-I-F-E and doesn't quite know what to do about it. Chakka was pathetic and majestic at the same time. He bore himself with a newfound dignity, strutting back and forth in front of Spook every chance he got, and then sashaying coyly before her while displaying the most engaging grin I've beheld in him. At the height of this engagement dance he'd usually fall all over his own feet, leaving a disgusted Spook gazing at him. Never daunted, he'd return immediately to his dance, hoping to really impress his entrancing lady. He nearly wore out his kidneys leaving love notes all over the pen. Spook was bored with the kid, but as her heat period proceeded she became a little more attentive. He might be young, but maybe he could learn.

It was the period of Chakka's life that I had been the most leery about. We had decided, long ago, after strenuous arguments both pro and con, not to have Chakka neutered. Bill suggested that perhaps it would make the wolf more amenable to handling. Wild animals are notoriously single-minded when it comes to sex. On the other hand, it would destroy something basic in him too. Also, we had talked about trying to breed Chakka to a Great Dane, which in itself presented problems. Andy had warned us about the pitfalls of crossbreeding a wolf with a dog. Some combinations brought out the very worst in both breeds, while others resulted in a congenital deformity called "seal-face." Pups born with this condition never develop properly and eventually die. This not only puts both animals through the stress of birth, but also disappoints the family-oriented wolf. After much debate, we decided to let Chakka make the decision and try to breed him to a Great Dane for one litter. If it didn't result in healthy pups, we would never try again.

Unknown to Chakka, this was his only chance, or so we thought. I had really geared myself up for a litter of half-wolf pups. We anxiously awaited the proper time in Spook's heat when she would stand for Chakka. Only one obstacle marred the marriage. Chakka was not really sexually mature. This became painfully evident as Spook progressed into her estrus.

Spook was obviously a lady of some experience. She knew exactly what to expect and how to go about the business of courtship. Chakka, on the other hand, bumbled his way through every phase of the operation except the last. *That* one had him completely buffaloed. He apparently had the right idea, but wasn't sure on which end he should apply the principle.

Spook suffered his advances for some time, bearing a look of injured dignity. After three days of the same useless maneuvers, Spook's look evolved to one of total disgust. Finally she told him, in rather unladylike terms, that he could take his advancing westward front and turn it toward the east. Two days later, Spook's heat period ended, and Chakka looked like a little boy who thinks, but is not sure, that his big chance in life has just gone by. I felt my hopes dashed and despaired of ever raising a litter, but consoled myself with the fact that Spook was probably too old to bear young comfortably anyway. Someday, later, we would find the proper mate for Chakka.

I had noticed very little change in Chakka's attitude when Spook came into heat. The only really evident behavior typical of breeding couples was Chakka's stepping between us and Spook. This was not done in any sort of threatening manner, but rather one of loving protection—both to Spook and to us. So far, all the dire warnings about staying away from breeding pairs had proved false. On the other hand, the episode had not been a true test, because Chakka was still immature. Someday in the future we would be better able to gauge how well we could handle the situation.

That summer we indulged in some wonderful times with Chakka. He went swimming with us, toting his people along on the end of a strong leash. Luckily, we are good swimmers. It is hard to imagine the strength of an almost full-grown wolf who decides to go downstream when the swimmer wants to go up. All in all, Chakka reacted like a wolf let out of school early. He chased frogs, rolled in dead, putrifying fish, ate seaweed, and swam with all of us. He was in his glory. The engaging adolescence that we had coped with so far was gradually being replaced by a more serious but loving adulthood. When Chakka approached people now, it was in a more dignified manner and with a bearing that demanded respect as well as affection. He was not aloof, but so wonderfully controlled and poised that people stood in awe of him. Just lying on the beach, he was a picture, but when he stood, I noticed that his chest was filling out and that he held his head more maturely. Far from being intimidated by the change, we welcomed and marveled at it.

But despite this, there were times during this period of new-found majesty that I wondered if Chakka would ever become a real adult. Just when he was displaying signs of graceful maturity, he would do something so goofy, charming, and unexpected that we'd be caught delightfully off guard—like the time he discovered earthworms.

Had he been a truly wild animal, Chakka would by now have

had some experience killing game, because adult members of the pack would have returned from the hunt with live prey. This they would place in front of the young wolf kits so that the essence of chase and kill might be practiced. But Chakka had had no such accommodating parents. I am myself the kind of coward who prefers to believe all my steaks are born in cellophane at the supermarket counters. Therefore, Chakka was not in the least skilled in the wolfly art of survival. All he had learned so far in that department was that cats, bunnies, raccoons, and so on made fine playmates and that it was impolitic to eat them. Had it been our plan to raise Chakka for eventual return to the wilds, we would have taught him the necessary hunting skills earlier, but being a house pet living amidst a variety of animals, his training was vastly different. That was probably why his reaction to the earthworm was so violent.

Chakka had been lying in the shade under a beautiful pine tree when a plain old earthworm dropped out of nowhere and landed on his nose. A bird must have fumbled it from an overhanging branch. Chakka, who had been lolling dreamily, suddenly froze. Both his eyes focused on the end of his nose where the worm was beginning to twist. Chakka bolted upright and shook his head. The slightly moist skin of the worm dangled down the side of Chakka's mouth. He snorted and pawed at his face, and somehow the worm ended up on Chakka's nose again, moving much more violently than before. Chakka's eyes focused on the worm once again before he reared backward and toppled into the trunk of the tree. He was on his feet in a second, snorting and vehemently shaking his head. The worm and Chakka parted company, with Chakka taking off in the opposite direction. Unfortunately, his leash had been attached to my ankle, and I skidded across the sand behind his terrified form. The only impediment was the forty pounds of sand that got scooped up in my bathing suit. We ended our day at the beach because Chakka adamantly refused to go near the tree again and I was feeling rather lumpy.

Luckily, Chakka's livelihood did not depend on hunting. It's also lucky he wasn't born a bird, with an obligation to develop a mastery over worms. As it was, the only hunting he did was for a place to lie down. But on one occasion he did hunt for the most improbable game of all: carrots.

If Chakka had his choice between a juicy bone and a fresh carrot, he would take the carrot. He could crunch a bone down in one minute flat, but give him a carrot and he would chew, chew, chew on it forever. Little orange crumbles would fall from his mouth while he blissfully crunched his way along the carrot. When the last tiny morsel disappeared down his throat, he daintily picked up every trace of the vegetable from the carpet. Nothing was wasted.

We discovered Chakka's penchant for carrots quite by accident. A friend had brought me a bag of fresh vegetables from her garden, and as usual Chakka had to investigate. He stuck his nose in the bag and very carefully pulled out a carrot by its leafy top. I had thought he would merely look it over, but he carried it to his "eating rug," where he took all his favorite food. He then proceeded to nip off the green top and begin demolishing the orange root with the most evident pleasure. We all laughed because we couldn't imagine why it took him so long to chew it. I think it had nothing to do with the flavor, but rather the firm texture and delight in something new. It took him a full fifteen minutes to eat the carrot, and when he was through he rolled on his rug in pure ecstasy. He would have eaten the whole bagful had I let him.

We tried him on other vegetables, with varying results. He chewed potatoes but spit out most of the pieces. He liked green beans in small quantities, but tomatoes were good only for grinding into the carpet. It took us one tomato to find that out, and thereafter he was denied that messy morsel. He also liked very firm apples, green pears, and an occasional green onion top, which we eliminated from his diet when we discovered that the gastric gas it gave him was well-nigh lethal to the humans who had to share the same house with him. I think we tried almost every known raw vegetable and fruit, but the closest we came to his love of carrots was with blueberries.

In the wilds, wolves eat quite a wide range of weeds, roots, and berries. Perhaps they enjoy the variety of flavors, aside from necessity. Some of these foods cleanse the system or act as a tonic, and a few are natural worm medicine. Bulk and fiber are needed to balance the high-protein diet of the carnivore; wild animals know what is good for them. Sometimes, however, they can and do get too much of a good thing. There have been reports of wolves getting drunk on fermented fruits and berries. Chakka never got drunk on any we had, because they were always fresh, but he once did overdo a good thing: He devoured the greater part of a crate of blueberries I'd set aside. I knew he'd gotten to them when I saw him trotting into the living room sporting a big blue grin. His face, ears, head, even shoulders were smeared in varying shades of blue. Clearly, when he had had his fill, he'd rolled and rubbed himself in what was left over. Anyone who has ever tried to wash out blueberry stains will sympathize with our plight. Absolutely nothing worked. I couldn't use soap on Chakka, so for two weeks he looked like a cheap toy whose colors had run. He rather seemed to think his new coloring fetching, by the way he carried himself, but I was less than pleased. Yet his smugness took a swift—if temporary—plunge when the predictable effects of the berries began to make themselves felt. He spent the afternoon doing what comes naturally in the yard, and even that evening his trips outside were hurried and frequent. He must have learned his lesson, because he never again ate more than a judicious few blueberries at a time.

Whatever it was his system required, Chakka would seek it out. I saw him eat the bark from certain trees, with an effect similar to that inspired by the blueberries, but on a much milder scale. I saw him eat corncobs for extra roughage. Violets growing in the garden were high on his list of delectables. He very carefully plucked every single bloom and ate it, never touching the stem or leaves, but what he didn't eat he rolled in or buried with his nose later. Either activity, you may imagine, works wonders on a flower garden. He was the only four-footed garden tiller in town.

That summer was a good learning time for Chakka. He investigated everything his nose would reach. He chased butterflies, but only if he was sure they were high enough so he wouldn't catch them. He wasn't about to have another accident like the earthworm episode. He dug great tunnels in the sandy banks when he was on his leash in the garden. It was a happy, strenuous activity that never failed to amuse him. Alert and inquisitive, he was forever expanding his horizons. It was a joy to watch. Had he been wild, this would have been his year to orient himself to his domain. His second year would be more geared to establishing his position in the pack and proving his hunting abilities. Every year after that would be spent guarding his position and proving his prowess. In our home situation, he had no need for such activities, but being an intelligent animal he practiced them for the sheer joy of it.

As Chakka began to fill out slightly, some of his lankiness disappeared. His head broadened, and when he turned to look at me I thrilled at the beautiful face and expression in his eyes—a truly magnificent animal. Just about the time I began thinking about what a king he was, he would fall all over his own feet and reveal himself to still be, despite his size, a youngster. It was hard to believe he yet had a lot of growing to do.

All spring and summer, the little orphaned or injured creatures that were brought to us never failed to delight Chakka. He could spend hours watching and listening to them. We'd keep the nest babies in the oven of our gas stove because the pilot light kept the oven at just the right temperature. Chakka glued himself to the glass-fronted oven door and stared into the lighted interior, where small boxes of birds chirped every time the little door was opened. Anyone who didn't know that the oven contained anything of interest might really wonder what was going on, watching Chakka and two or three cats sitting in silent absorption in front of it, their own animal TV.

One evening we humans were all sitting in the living room watching TV, while Chakka remained in the kitchen watching the oven door. The baby birds inside had long since tucked their heads under their wings and gone to sleep. As we watched a special program on wildlife, suddenly a scene of nestlings appeared on the screen, accompanied by chirpings. Chakka shot out of the kitchen and headed for our set in time to see the birds for himself. How long had we been hiding birds in there? He watched, tipping his head from side to side. He saw them, all right, but they didn't look like the ones in the oven. He pushed his nose against the glass and tried to sniff them. Suddenly, their chirping increased and Chakka raced to the back of the set to check whether he could see or smell them from there. We all sat with hands clamped over our mouths, stifling our laughter so as not to distract Chakka. Thoroughly mystified, he was more than a little determined to get to the bottom of the mystery. Once again he trotted to the front of the set and stared. The action was still on the screen, but somehow it didn't seem quite right. Ever so slowly Chakka leaned forward until his nose was on the set, and then with a sideways glance at me he licked the screen. If those birds didn't look right, sound right, or smell right, just maybe their taste would pass the test. The instant Chakka's tongue touched the set, however, he backed off. By golly, they even *tasted* flat! He left and returned to his kitchen unit. That one made a little more sense.

Often it seemed as if Chakka would never settle down, so busy was he learning and absorbing whatever came his way. If I brought an empty cardboard box into the house, he simply had to open it to make sure it really was empty. If a cupboard door was shut, he wanted it unlatched. He would sit square in the middle of whatever I was doing and make himself as pesky as possible. He once bit into an unopened coffee can, but dropped it in a hurry when it hissed at him. He made my life miserable and my dinners interesting when he tore the labels off all the canned goods. I was rapidly discovering that nothing was sacred—or even unassailable.

11

L'Amour

ONCE HE WAS OLDER AND HEAVIER, Chakka's diet became a bigger problem. When he was a pup, we kept up his protein level by supplementing his dry food with canned horse meat. But as his weight and size increased, we graduated from one to five cans of horse meat a day. At that rate, I began to think it would make more sense for us to eat the horse meat and offer him our suppers. Obviously, in order to both keep up his protein and keep a roof over our heads, alternatives were going to have to be found.

The dry dog-food portion of Chakka's diet contained 18 to 20 percent crude protein. Chakka's summer diet required at least 35 percent, and his winter diet, depending on the weather, needed 50 percent or more. Moreover, I was not happy with the "crude" protein, so I started looking for a way to supplement this necessary ingredient. A good friend came up with at least part of the solution.

A few miles away was an egg farm where young layers were set up assembly-line style to spend their lives doing nothing but laying eggs. As with any business, a portion of this produce was waste. Eggs were candled at the farm, and the number of rejects was phenomenal. If a dark spot showed anywhere in the egg during the candling process, it would be discarded. Most of the time the eggs were perfect, but a thick spot in the shell that threw a shadow could make the egg appear to have a blood spot inside and therefore render it unfit for human consumption. There were other reasons for rejection. Sometimes an egg would have a hairline crack or a weak, soft shell, which meant that it would not transport well. At other times, eggs that came off the line dirty and didn't clean up well in the first wash were discarded. These rejects were available as a case of over 600 for a dollar.

When I heard of this bonanza, I was delighted. I ordered three cases, 1,800 eggs in all, and confidently awaited their arrival. I planned to hard-boil them and then mash them into the food, but I hadn't taken into consideration just how much work that involved.

The day they arrived, I began setting large kettles on the stove for the processing. I started at ten in the morning, and by seven at night I was less than halfway through and thoroughly sick of the sight of eggs. Since the weather was beastly hot, there was no choice but to cook the eggs, mash them down thoroughly, and pack them in plastic bags in the freezer.

I also had not counted on another unforeseen problem. Some of the eggs hard-boiled fine, but the ones with cracked shells exploded, as they are wont, so that the minute all four huge kettles began to boil, every one of them bubbled astonishing masses of boiling water and cooked egg whites all over my stove. Before I could stop the action, I had a gooey mess flowing down the sides and front of the stove and all over the floor, much to the delight of the house animals. It took two hours to clean it up, and I went to bed well past midnight wishing I had never, ever seen an egg. At that point, I didn't care if the rest spoiled overnight. I was through for the day. By the next morning, rested and slightly more cheerful, I tackled the balance of over a thousand eggs in a different fashion.

I carefully separated the cracked eggs from the rest and

began scrambling them in a lumberjack-size frying pan. Even so, I had problems. I loaded the first pan almost to the top with eggs, which I discovered expanded considerably when they began to heat up. I soon had the same problem as the day before. I began frantically scooping half-cooked eggs into the other frying pans, trying to watch them all at once. Bill didn't make matters any better when he ambled into the kitchen that morning, eyed the stove mischievously, and said, "For me? You shouldn't have!" I hit him with a spatula.

We discovered that only about one in every fifty eggs had something really wrong with it. The rest were beautiful, freshly laid hen-fruit, perfect for human consumption. I put several dozen for family use in the refrigerator. Nonetheless, the stack of uncooked eggs beside me on the floor was not diminishing very rapidly. I sorted through more of them and set aside several cartons for friends of ours who were in about the same financial boat as we were. That still left me with over 800 eggs to cook before the day was over.

I have a four-burner stove, so the process was slow. I relegated the back burners to hard-boiled eggs and the front two units to frying pans. I was beginning to develop a system of sorts, and a false feeling of confidence flooded through me.

Lunch, during egg-cooking days, was a cold-sandwich-and-don't-ask-for-anything-else affair. I discovered my family trod softly and avoided the kitchen like the plague when they smelled cooking eggs. Our lives seemed to be dominated by those innocent-looking oval disasters. By eleven o'clock the second night, I was finally through cooking the abominable things. I had a rather unpleasant experience behind me and announced that to Bill. He walked into the kitchen, eyed three huge laundry tubs filled with hard-boiled eggs, and asked when I was going to shell and mash them. I let out a scream that could be heard for miles. I wasn't through at all! Bill suggested we put the tubs of eggs in the bathtub, run cold water over them, and call it quits for the night. It was the best idea I had heard all day, but it still left me facing eggs again the next day. I trudged wearily to bed, cursing chickens.

The next morning I was grimly determined to finish the egg chores, no matter what happened. I emptied one tubful of water, carried the eggs into the kitchen, and sat down to begin the peeling operation. By noon, I had one tubful finished and two hands of bleeding fingers, the shells being miniature stilettos that attacked my poor digits with a vengeance. I tried putting on leather gloves to ease the pain, but discovered that shelled eggs and leather gloves do not mix. Eggs have a mind of their own; just about the time one is almost shelled, it will slip from your hands and bounce like a slippery rubber ball across the floor and roll under the nearest piece of furniture. The cats and dogs were delighted with this unexpected treat, but after the first 400 eggs, their interest began to wane. Bill took pity on me and helped with the last two tubfuls. It was dark when we finished mashing and packaging the blasted things and had stored them in our freezer, full to the brim. Bill stared at the freezer for a moment and said, "With all those eggs on top, how are we going to get our food from the bottom?" He'd have been wiser to keep his observations to himself.

The battle of the bones was slightly less hectic than the egg situation had been. Ed, our local supermarket meat man, was a dear about supplying us with a huge case of meaty bones every week. He cut them into manageable portions after I discovered that a cow thigh was approximately seven inches longer than my largest pressure cooker is tall. Bone-cooking days smelled better than egg-cooking days by a long shot. In fact, the aroma was quite delicious. After an hour of cooking at twenty pounds' pressure, even the marrow fell out and was added to the rich, meaty broth. Out of each case of bones, we had about ten gallons of condensed broth to pour over the dry dog food, and the animals had so many bones to chew on that our yard began to look like a bulldozed graveyard. I can imagine an archaeologist a thousand years from now, digging up our property and wondering if ours had been a slaughterhouse or a sacrificial site.

Between the bone broth and the eggs, our animals' coats glistened and sparkled with the healthiest highlights imaginable. Chakka's weight was rapidly increasing, but he still had not attained the adult girth and proportions of which I knew he was capable. At times he acted older and more introspective, but only intermittently. Basically, he was a teenager at heart, capable of any prank to get our attention. It was disconcerting to see him looking so adult and acting so goofy.

He also seemed to have trouble remembering that he was no longer a small puppy. One day I took out a cardboard box that we had made for the cats to play in, with a hole cut in the side so they could dash in and out at their pleasure. When he'd been little, Chakka had delighted in playing with the cats and even squeezing into the box himself, which had been put up on a shelf and forgotten for several months. When I found it and dragged it down once again for the cats, Chakka bounded over to it in high spirits. Here was his beloved box again! He charged for the opening, ignoring the fact that although the box was the same as before, his own size had increased tenfold. Before I could stop him, he flew headlong into the small opening, which was only large enough for his head to fit through, leaving the rest of him hung outside in an ungainly sprawl. When he pushed harder to get inside, the box only moved forward. No more of Chakka would fit inside. Even though he could be very obtuse at times, he finally realized he and the box were now incompatible and began backing out. Unfortunately, his head was just a bit larger than the opening, so instead of getting out of the box, he found it following him around the room. When I called him, the box turned to look at me. Unsuccessfully stifling helpless laughter, I finally composed myself sufficiently to try to get the box, when Chakka turned around and ran into the wall. He shook his head violently, budging his cardboard headgear not one inch. What had started as a bit of fun now became a frightening reality: He was trapped. His lunges suddenly became frantic, and I was dodging about other animals to reach him before he demolished the living room. I managed to get my hands on the box just an instant before the TV set went crashing to the floor. I didn't have the time to save the set, but I did manage to extricate Chakka. His look of wild terror broke my heart, and I held him close, comforting him. Gradually, he calmed down and his shaking stopped. Finally, I released him and turned my attention to the TV on the floor. As I replaced it on the coffee table, the cardboard box whizzed by my head, missing me by inches.

Chakka had picked the box up by the cut-out hole and given it a tremendous shaking. A large chunk of corrugated paper stayed in his mouth, while the rest of the box became airborne. Chakka couldn't have cared less about the box. He directed his attention to the offending cardboard scrap, which he mauled and tore into small pieces to vent his anger. While he chastised the offending material, Scruffy, the cat, found the box on the other side of the room and crawled inside. When Chakka finished his lengthy abuse on the small piece of cardboard, he headed for its parent box. With the full force of his two front feet, he finessed a mighty leap and flattened it. Inside, Scruffy suddenly found himself plunged into darkness and borne down on by a steamroller. The exit hole had disappeared, and something was lifting the box into the air and shaking it. To Scruffy there was only one possible way out, and that was through the flaps on the top of the box, directly under Chakka's nose. Scruffy lost no time achieving his exit, more than indignant at what had transpired. Chakka stopped abruptly in midswing when the box exploded in his face and one angry cat roared out at him. Scruffy was partially stuck in the box, so he grabbed two pawsful of the nearest material: Chakka's muzzle. In effect, Chakka had a tiger by the tail. He couldn't even let go of the box, because part of Scruffy was still in it. Scruffy made all possible haste to remedy that situation. He grabbed more bunches of Chakka's face and finally broke clear of the box, leaping over Chakka's face and racing down his back before hitting the floor. A spitting, snarling ball of black fur disappeared upstairs.

Chakka had dropped the box on the floor and was pawing at his head. Aside from some rather painful punctures, he wasn't seriously hurt, but I began to wonder if he would hold Scruffy responsible for the attack. Apparently he wouldn't, or couldn't, blame his favorite cat for the experience, but he sure must have felt homicide in his heart for that box!

For the next half hour I sat and cheered Chakka's efforts to teach the box a lesson. The more he vented his anger on the object, the more I encouraged him. Finally, the box was reduced to a mass of wet pulp and Chakka was exhausted. He went happily outside on his leash, and in the last of his anger he marked every tree in the yard with venomous intent. Finally satisfied, he lay down in the sunshine and slept. Later that afternoon when Scruffy came downstairs, Chakka offered him an apologetic but cautious nose. Scruffy turned his face away and pointedly ignored him for the rest of the day. By bedtime they were once again on friendly terms.

Chakka didn't quite realize how big or strong he was. When he was a pup and we bent over to pet him, he leaped up and smothered our chins with wet kisses. When he was larger, he no longer needed to leap up to get to our faces, but that slipped his mind once in a while. At times we would bend over to pet Chakka only to have him leap up simultaneously. The connection between human chin and bony wolf's head can clap the human jaw shut quicker than a boxer's punch, and with about the same results. He knocked Denny completely out one night with just such a maneuver, and I have been hit so hard that I'm sure my teeth still don't mesh quite right. It never fazes Chakka, but he does get upset when we clamp our hands over our mouths and moan a lot. He kisses and whuffs in our ears until our agony subsides enough that we are able to push him away, get up, and assure him (through bleeding lips) that we are just fine, just fine. As hard as his grand slams are on the chin, they don't do any wonders for eyeglasses, either. Chakka hit Denny so hard one night that his specs were bent in the middle and the lenses left facing each other. Not a bad design if you have only an inch-thick head with an eye on each side, but Denny simply isn't built that way.

Chakka's increased size also meant that both of us could no longer get through a doorway at the same time, a fact he has never acknowledged. He still, on occasion, attempts the impossible. If he can't get through a door side by side, he tries to force his way through by walking between our legs. More than once I have ridden a very surprised wolf from one room to another before I could dismount.

If Chakka's largeness was a deterrent in some respects, it was an advantage in others. For example, he found that anything that came within six inches of the ceiling beams was within his reach when he stood on his hind legs. What little peace of mind I had left rapidly dissolved with that realization. There was, literally, no place to put anything where it would be safe. Finally, in desperation, we took to closing doors and restricting Chakka to the living room–kitchen area. This maneuver increased our chances of salvaging something for our old age, but it distressed Chakka immensely. Unhappy at there being places he couldn't investigate, he became adept at taking any and every advantage to sneak through an open door. If he saw one ajar, he threw his full weight against it. It never bothered him that someone might be on the other side. Bruises began appearing all over my body in some very suspicious places. Had it been necessary for me to visit a doctor during that period, I would have been hard-pressed to explain them to him. I once jokingly remarked to Bill that I was going to tell our friends he was beating me. His face took on a look of unholy glee as he said, "Go ahead. Then I'll tell them why!" I was left to mull that one over.

As summer edged past its zenith, Chakka's loving nature became, if anything, even more pronounced. He was so ecstatically happy when his "pack" of humans was home that he could hardly contain himself. He walked contentedly around the room, pushing his great head into our laps and rubbing against us with soft sighs and moans. There were times, of course, when one or the other of us had to leave to go into town. At such times, Chakka stood at the window and watched us leave. No matter who was in the house with him, he felt incomplete when any one of us was gone. He came to know the sound of our cars and would pick up on the approaching vehicle long before the rest of the family did. Often I'd see him wake from a sound sleep and rush to stand at the window, where he would hold his silent vigil until the car finally pulled into the drive. When he saw his packmate emerge, he'd place his big nose against the window and whuff energetically. The combination of wet nose and warm breath left (as my mother called them) "bark-prints" all over the windows. I could almost tell how long a person had been gone by the number of bark-prints a pane contained at any one time. If one of Chakka's loved ones happened to be working in the yard and had failed to take him along, he could fill six window panes with these decorations in two minutes flat.

Windows became a problem as Chakka's weight approached 120 pounds. I was afraid that someday he would push his way right through the glass and either hurt himself or escape. We had already discovered that the screen door could not withstand his assaults, so we left the bottom half of the Dutch door shut at all times. Even then, we dared not leave the room when he was in the house. He could go over the top of the door just as easily as he could step over a sleeping cat. We had long since constructed welded-wire-and-wood doors in various places throughout the house, to the point where Bill asked if they were there to keep Chakka out or us in. The family, however, was good-natured about the disadvantages of having to undo security doors before entering or leaving. Chakka thought it wonderful to stand with his nose pressed against the door as we fumbled with the locks, and then give a mighty push the instant he heard them click. This meant that the human had to scramble for his collar before he bolted outside. My exit was never graceful, and even Bill and Denny began experiencing difficulty in holding onto him.

The day did eventually come when Chakka actually went right through the heavy aluminum storm-screen door, scattering framework and glass all about him. I had just opened the Dutch door to take Chakka out when he spotted a strange dog in our yard. The dog was just approaching the pen where Spook, Chakka's mate, was lying. I had attached a leash to Chakka's collar, but I did not have hold of it. As soon as I saw the dog, I turned to grab for Chakka, but an instant too late. He was already in the middle of his leap, which knocked me flat. I managed to grab the end of the leash from my sitting position, but I couldn't get up fast enough to stand before the leash was stretched taut between us and I was skidding through broken glass and metal, yelling at the top of my lungs for Chakka to stop. I'm not sure if it was my screaming or Chakka's enraged growls that frightened the dog, but he took one look at what was coming in his direction and took off. Chakka was in a real rage, leaping and jerking me across the yard in three-foot jolts. Finally, Jenny came to my rescue and we managed to restrain Chakka.

I had never seen Chakka so angry or upset. He felt, somehow, that the strange dog was threatening his pack, or Spook in particular. As an ultimate insult, the dog had actually lifted his leg against the pen fencing! That was a challenge Chakka couldn't ignore, so he spent several minutes covering the spot with his own message and then scattering dirt and debris over the whole area and ruining a lot of lawn as well.

I am sure that if Chakka had not been restrained he would have made the strange dog submit in the strongest possible terms. Since the dog was a large one, it could have meant that one or the other might have lost more hide than pride. Generally speaking, a wolf will break off the engagement once an opponent submits, but dogs are prone to getting up and starting the fight all over again. Although I worried about what might have happened, I didn't think Chakka would kill him. In fact, in all the years we have owned Chakka, he has never inflicted even a puncture wound on a dog, despite all the terrible growling and muttering. But this dog was a stranger, he was in our yard, and he had dared to leave a love message to one of Chakka's pack—clear grounds for insane jealousy, at best. It was an object lesson that taught me that we could never relax our vigil, even though Chakka exhibited a friendly, dominant, inquisitive attitude toward dogs he encountered on our walks. Someday, it might happen that we would meet a dog who didn't feel friendly. If he started the fight, I was sure that Chakka would be capable of finishing it. We sadly decided to walk Chakka at night, when the neighborhood dogs were inside for the evening and two of us were present, one to hold Chakka and one to fend off any dogs. It was particularly frustrating to realize that even if a strange dog started a fight, Chakka, the "wild animal," would be blamed.

Summer's heat eventually reached its climax, and nights became cooler. More and more, Chakka decided that he preferred to sleep outside in the pen as long as Spook was with him. It pleased him to be able to get up and stretch his legs and sniff the breezes whenever he was moved to. Besides, the train went through the woods at about midnight, signaling Chakka's nightly howl. He enjoyed the occasion so much that he imparted some of his enthusiasm to Spook, who suddenly started raising her head to the sky and howling along with him. The difference between wolf and dog howl was immediately evident. Chakka's howl was soft, yet carried like a bell tone. Spook's howl was less mellifluous, harsher, and considerably louder, though the joy was still there. Chakka loved to harmonize with her strident bellowing. Much to my chagrin, dogs up and down the road found the howling an equally pleasant pastime and joined the chorus. Luckily for all of us, the howls were of short duration—usually a minute or two at most, and only occurred when the train went through or a siren sounded out on the highway. Once in a great while there would be a "happiness howl" for the sheer fun of it, but those were less of a problem. All in all, Chakka and his penmates were more quiet than the average dogs, because they did no barking. The most noise Chakka made when he was agitated was his whuff or a low growl, and he wouldn't tolerate any senseless barking in the pen around him. *He* would decide what barking or howling was appropriate, thank you.

The days were growing steadily shorter and the trees began to flame with autumn colors when the schools opened once again. Chakka loved this time, because a crowd of children gathered across the street every day to meet the school bus. Early in the morning Chakka began watching faithfully for his little friends. He stood at the edge of the fence with his muzzle pushed through the wire and wagged furiously at each new arrival. He gazed with such yearning at their games and scuffles that I felt truly sorry that he wasn't able to run free and play. We made sure that when friends who had children came to visit, the kids were allowed to go into Chakka's pen to greet him. He always pranced and pawed and submitted to them in the most winning, endearing fashion possible. We had to teach him not to jump up, so he usually approached them with head and shoulders lowered to the ground and a silly grin on his face, hindquarters swaying from side to side to keep up with the tail. If the children were very small, he rolled over and invited them to scratch his tummy while he wiggled and moaned happily. He was always dejected and disconsolate when the children left, and it would take him several hours to find something else worth his attention. Bill suggested we get him a Hertz Rent-a-Kid, but none were available that year.

We did everything we could that fall to keep Chakka's life as varied and full as possible. We took him on long walks down deserted, wide sand beaches that rim the bay. He always brought home a trophy or two to puzzle over in the security of his pen. Some were rather less than pleasant. His particular pride was the dried wing of a dead sea gull. We were lucky that all he found was the wing, for he was particularly reluctant to part with it. He had it in his pen for weeks, and when things got boring he rolled on it to remind himself what a wonderful day he'd had. Everything was all right as long as the wing remained dry and virtually odorless, but a rain brought out its worst qualities. The more it smelled, the more Chakka loved it. I finally had Bill take him for a walk, and while they were gone I buried the evidence. When Chakka came back, he tore all the straw bedding from the houses in search of his smelly toy, and for three days Chakka and I argued about where the bedding belonged. He finally gave up, but he was in a sulk until we found him a new toy.

We had tried all manner of rubber balls for Chakka to play with, but no matter how well constructed they were, they'd be reduced to shreds in a matter of minutes. When we were shopping one day, Denny spied a large beach ball on sale—the kind that is filled with compressed air like a basketball. It was very nearly the size of a basketball. I felt that ball might last longer because it was large enough that Chakka couldn't get the whole thing in his mouth to bite down on. We decided it was worth a try.

When we got home and tossed Chakka's new toy over the fence, he immediately leaped into the air and landed on it, after which it zipped across the pen and bounced into the fencing. Chakka was two pounces behind it. For several minutes we stood and watched a majestic animal (who should have been chasing a moose) cavort with a multicolored sphere. Spook stood at the entrance to the doghouse and eyed Chakka with something like pity. She was far too dignified to resort to such inane activity. We finally left Chakka to his entrancing game and turned to go into the house.

I had just reached the door and was glancing in Chakka's direction when I saw him catch the ball in midair. I still don't know how he did it, but somehow he managed to get enough of the ball into his mouth to clamp down on it. A sudden muffled *bang!* and the cheeks of Chakka's muzzle blew outward and flapped in the breeze for a minute. Pieces of rubber flew through the air and landed all over the pen. Chakka had done a backward somersault trying to dodge back from the toy that had suddenly turned into a bomb, and Spook had bolted into the doghouse. I ran for the pen to see if Chakka was hurt, but by that time he had recovered and was sneaking up on several pieces of the ball.

Chakka used the same technique to "kill" the rubber remnants as he would have to kill a mouse in the wilds. He approached them ever so slowly, hunkered down, and then leaped into the air and brought all four feet down on the pieces. Had they been a live mouse, they wouldn't have lasted for long. Chakka grabbed the bright-colored bits and tossed them into the air. The minute they landed, he pounced on them again, growling and punishing them into submission. It was even better sport than playing with the inflated ball. Spook poked one eye around the corner of the doghouse door and watched her crazy friend, but she wouldn't come anywhere near where that thing might explode again. Chakka played all afternoon until the pen was strewn with rubber confetti.

Chakka's mature winter coat was beginning to respond to

subtle hints of colder weather around the corner. For the first time he was building up a magnificent ruff of fur, which encircled his head and extended down the front of his chest. The fur was incredibly thick, so thick that I found it impossible to wriggle my fingers down through it to get anywhere near the skin. Before I could touch the base of the guard hairs, the downy pelage—or underfur—formed a thick, impenetrable second coat at least two inches deep. I could feel the heat radiating from Chakka's body and becoming entrapped in this undercoat, which was in turn protected from rain and snow by six-inch-long outer fur. Even the pads of Chakka's feet were covered with velvety, springy fur that could take on the attributes of giant snowshoes. His new coat made him look twice his usual size. He ate prodigious amounts of food and gained more weight every day, but it was the fur that made Chakka look like the adult wolf he was becoming.

I had noticed Chakka's increased appetite for fats, which is normal in an animal preparing for winter. Where Chakka used to chew on the knuckle-ends of bones we gave him before he attacked anything else, now he cracked huge thigh bones neatly in half and licked up every vestige of marrow he could find. We increased his fat intake in the broth we poured over the food every night, and found he licked the platter clean. His coat was glossy, his teeth were perfectly clean, and he radiated health. In fact, he was in such good shape and so well prepared for winter that he was really uncomfortable before the last warm day or two of summer finally gave way to cold rains and sleet.

Gray clouds scudded across the sky every day, and that fall we had sixty straight days in which it either rained or sleeted at least part of the day. Chakka lay in front of the fireplace, happy to be inside but panting because of his winter coat. He could take it for only an hour or so before he asked to be let out to the pen to cool off. As he stood in the drizzle we could see steamy vapors rising off his fur. He panted huge clouds of steam until his body temperature was reduced to a comfortable level; then he would lie on the protected porch of the doghouse and watch Spook. Although Spook stayed inside our house with Chakka, he usually refused to leave without her, so she had to suffer the cold weather along with him when he went into the pen. Because a Dane's coat is short, Spook was not as equipped as Chakka to endure winter's blasts, so we installed radiant floor heating in Spook's side of the doghouse. The heat, plus two feet of thick, golden straw, afforded her comfortable accommodations. Chakka slept in the other doghouse across the porch and lay inside with his head resting on the doorsill so he could watch Spook's every move across the way.

One day early in October, I went out to the pen to let the animals in. Spook came out of the house and started toward me, but Chakka repeatedly pushed against her, keeping her from me. He approached me and gave me loving kisses, but the minute Spook made a move, he pushed her away. Puzzled at his actions, I finally reprimanded him as I got hold of Spook's collar to lead her into the house. When I returned to get Chakka, he was hurling his full weight against the gate, only too happy to follow into the house.

Muttley was in the living room when Chakka entered, and instead of running to play with his friend, Chakka leaped on Muttley and made him submit. Muttley, as surprised as we were, submitted gracefully. He had little choice, since Chakka was double Muttley's weight. As soon as Chakka was satisfied that Muttley understood whatever rules he was trying to impose, the wolf sauntered over to the fireplace and lay down next to Spook. Chakka allowed the cats to wander up and down his back and rub against Spook, but if Muttley approached, he laid his head across Spook's back and glared. Muttley gathered up his dignity and lay down on the couch.

I began to wonder if Spook was coming into heat. Over Chakka's protests, I examined her, but no sign of a heat period was evident. Nonetheless, Chakka's attitude indicated something unusual. We had decided to prevent Spook having any litters because of her age, but the decision was not without its complications.

I had contacted several vets about having Spook spayed. None of them would agree to the operation because of Spook's age and the fact that, since she shared all of Chakka's meals, she was grossly overweight. When I inquired about putting her on contraceptive pills, they again demurred. She was old, and the pills would have several adverse effects that could even result in death. We were left with a dilemma.

I knew better than to try to separate Chakka from Spook if she was coming into a heat period. He would have torn the pen and house into shreds in order to get to her. Whether or not he was successful in breeding her was beside the point. She was *his,* and our interference would really upset him. I finally hit upon what I thought was a solution, but I decided I wouldn't enforce it unless I really knew she was coming into heat.

Within three days, it was no longer a question. Chakka was in an amorous mood, and this time he knew what he was about. It was only Spook's reluctance to "stand" for him that prevented her being bred, but I knew now it was only a matter of time for that to happen. Now was the time to put my plan into action. I had decided we could avoid the breeding by using contraceptive foam on Spook. That would prevent conception, and yet leave Chakka with his husbandly rights. The solution seemed perfect.

Denny and I dashed to the big discount store on the other side of town, where I picked up six tubes of foam. I approached the checkout counter with nothing in my basket but the obvious. I had been standing in line for several minutes before it occurred to me that people were staring. I left the line and went searching for Denny, who was in another part of the store. When I found him, I thrust three of the packages into his hands and asked him to go through another line while I went through my own checkout. He dropped the boxes like hot potatoes. "I am not going through checkout with those things!" he muttered, outraged and blushing, "not even if you *pay* me!" He stalked off to wait for me in the front of the store, well beyond the checkout point. I was forced to get in line again, on my own.

Managing an air of insouciance, I whistled softly under my breath while coolly staring down anyone presuming to glance at my basket a moment too long. Finally, the cashier began ringing up my purchases, but her flying fingers paused over the keys after the third box of foam. She glanced at me under lowered lashes and quietly rang up the other three boxes. Not one word was spoken, but I felt every eye in the store on me as I fled toward Denny, who was out the door long before I got there. He wouldn't even be seen walking with me until we got to the far end of the parking lot.

On the way home, a new thought struck me. What if Chakka resented our interference? Although he'd behaved like a gentleman during Spook's first heat period, he was only a youngster then. This time he was a full-grown, 140-pound animal who knew his own mind. Any altercations we had had with Chakka in the past would certainly be nothing compared with what he might consider an infringement on his conjugal and pack rights. At this point, I gave myself a mental shake. I was doing exactly what I had condemned other people for doing: I was judging Chakka on the basis of his being a wolf. Certainly, if I used care and consideration, there was no reason to believe we would not succeed. Part of being a wolf owner is reading the signs correctly, and I felt we had done that in the past. As long as we continued to take Chakka's feelings into consideration, he would continue to interact with us as he always had. This time I would use all the care and compassion possible, and if the situation was stressful for Chakka, I would have Denny take him for a walk while I made the necessary arrangements.

The next morning, it was obvious that Spook was progressing into the heat rapidly. I knew within the next day or so she would be standing for Chakka. In order to prevent mishaps, I decided that starting her on the foam immediately was the only remedy. Denny and I gathered the necessary materials and went into the pen.

Chakka immediately forced Spook into the doghouse, then came running to greet us. He was as affectionate as he had ever been, lavishing us with kisses and licking our ears with happy noises. Finally, when he had properly greeted me and was intent on doing the same for Denny, I walked quietly to the doghouse and bent over to reach in. I heard Denny yell behind me, but before I could move Chakka had bolted onto the porch area, sending me sprawling. I got up immediately and knelt in front of him, rubbing his head and talking as if he understood every word I said. Spook poked her nose around the door but made no move to leave the doghouse when Chakka growled at her.

Chakka's reaction to my activity was gentle but firm. He was not going to budge a bit, nor was Spook. When I pulled on Chakka's collar, he licked my hand but remained adamantly anchored. Finally, I backed out of the close quarters and called Chakka to me. He came, but only after warning Spook to stay where she was. I attached a leash to Chakka's collar and told Denny to take him for a walk. That was the worst thing I could have done. The second Denny began pulling on the leash to take Chakka from the pen, there was a swirl of angry gray fur. Chakka turned with lightning speed, snarling—not at Denny, but at the leash! Though he made no threatening gesture to Denny, I heard his teeth snap shut on the leash as it fell apart in Denny's hand. Spook had partly left the doghouse and I had her by the collar when Chakka rushed toward us.

I was so surprised at the suddenness of the move that I hadn't even let go of Spook when Chakka reached us. Mouth open, he was headed straight for my hand. I had no fear that he would bite me, but I was reasonably sure he would take my arm and force me to let go, albeit gently. Instead, he took Spook by the neck and forced her to lie down in submission, dragging my hand with her. That brought my head right down by Chakka's ear, and I said "No!" in the most forceful terms. Chakka held onto Spook for a moment, but my second *no* startled him. He let go and sat down looking at us. I patted his head, telling him he was a fine wolf. Denny had not budged on the other side of the pen, knowing full well that another person in the melee might provoke Chakka into making a move alien to his nature. Finally, after I'd talked to Chakka for a while, Denny approached quietly and took Spook's collar from my hand. While I spoke soothingly to Chakka, I removed the paraphernalia from my pocket and walked toward Spook's tail end. Chakka followed every move, inquisitive and reproving. Despite his disapproval, I began doing what needed to be done while Chakka sniffed and whuffed. It took only a minute, and when it was over I sank down in front of Chakka and held his face in my hands, rubbing his nose with my nose. He accepted my apology, then turned to inspect Spook.

The crisis was over. He certainly didn't care for the odor of the foam or our interference, but he had behaved admirably in spite of it all. We played with him for a moment, then turned to leave the pen. Just as I reached the gate, I felt a small tug on my jacket. Before I could stop him, Chakka had pulled the tube from my pocket and bitten into it. As the foam squirted out, he dropped the container and pounced on it. Suddenly we were covered with the stuff, and so was Chakka, but it seemed to satisfy some need in him. He continued to "kill" the tube until it was empty, then he rolled on it, picked it up, and flung it expertly over the fence. I couldn't be mad at him. All I could do was laugh.

Once the first session was over, Chakka knew that what we did was not harmful to himself or Spook, so he suffered further ministrations to his spouse without interference. The instant we were through, he would attend to his husbandly duties with a vengeance.

The day finally came when Chakka successfully bred Spook. I had been cleaning the pen and had my back to them both when I turned and almost fell over Chakka's back. The act of breeding is a personal thing, and here I was stumbling all over them. Slipping on the snow that had fallen the night before, I couldn't stand upright without steadying myself on Chakka's back. I can give Chakka no greater credit than to report how he exhibited restraint. He simply turned his head, delivered a small kiss, and then turned away. I was clearly being dismissed. I gave his head a pat and left the pen. There are some boundaries of decency over which it is impolitic to tread, even for a wolf owner.

Over the next few days, Chakka courted Spook with a wonderful display of affection. He groomed her constantly, strayed only inches from her side, and nudged her toward the food and water dishes constantly. When we took out the evening suppers with broth, Chakka stood with his head over Spook's back and waited patiently until she had eaten her fill. He seldom ate his own supper and lost several pounds during the courting period. Spook accepted this attention as her due, and lorded it over Chakka every chance she got. As her heat period came to a close she became peevish and snapped at Chakka. Her estrus and amorous instincts both being over, she made it clear to Chakka that he could forget that silly kid stuff. Far from being abashed, Chakka doubled his efforts to be solicitous. There was a new dimension to his life, and he delighted in the role.

I decided we had come through a difficult period with excellent results. Equilibrium was maintained, and Chakka loved us as much as he ever did, even if he had become suddenly aware that there was more to life than just people. We were still his "pack leaders," his head wolves. His dual role suited him.

We weren't sure the contraceptive foam had worked, so I marked the breeding days on our calendar and counted off sixty. If, heaven forbid, Spook were pregnant, the pups would be born in early December. Her normally rotund form gave us no clue, and efforts on my part to see if I could feel the developing fetuses through the abdominal wall were frustrated by layers of fat and solid muscle. It was like feeling through the walls of a fifty-gallon oil drum. Our only choice was to watch and wait.

When the sixth week rolled around and Spook showed no signs of pregnancy, we heaved collective sighs of relief. We congratulated ourselves on preventing pregnancy with little or no stress to Spook, and certainly not the dire consequences of either a spay or contraceptive pills.

But by the time Bill came home the next weekend, we knew our efforts had been confounded. Spook began making nests in the straw, forming a clean circle right down to the heating pad on the bottom. She had begun to look like a barrel on four very inadequate legs. Chakka was happier than I had ever seen him. He pranced around, head held high and tail wagging. He fawned over Spook every second, bringing her bones in the doghouse that she immediately put outside again. When Spook was not inside the pen, he lay on the porch area guarding her door or resting his head at the opening. The normally placid Spook began to get querulous and snappish at him, not realizing that a wolf father has as much to do with the birthing and raising of the pups as the mother does. In fact, he took his new duties so seriously that he stopped coming into the house, preferring to remain by Spook's side. Since the day she'd made the nest, Spook was loath to leave it for a moment. Her time was drawing near, and instinct told her to stay in the place she had prepared, just in case.

Three times every day we inspected the nursery, but no pups appeared. Spook's day of delivery came and went, and I began to wonder if it was a false pregnancy or if she was unable to bear pups. Time and again I cursed myself for this stupid predicament. Finally, on a Friday night, two days after I had estimated her pups should be born, I made an appointment with the vet for the next morning. I went to bed depressed. I knew that if I took Spook from the pen at this stage, Chakka would never forgive me.

12

Fatherhood

AT TWO-THIRTY IN THE MORNING, I awoke to Chakka's howl. No sirens were sounding or trains passing, and I knew it was a happiness howl. I was just drifting back to sleep, listening to the quavering, soft notes, when it hit me. The pups! I hurried out of bed, sliding into my slippers and tying my bathrobe so fast that I tied part of the blankets to myself. When I got disentangled I hurried downstairs and grabbed the flashlight.

As I stepped outside a numbing cold hit me, almost taking my breath away. It was a clear, starlit night, and as I made my way toward the pen I could see Chakka clearly. He was standing just outside the doghouse door, head and tail up, while his howling cut through the crisp air. He spotted me and wagged furiously, but did not move from the pen. When I reached him and got down on all fours to crawl inside, he placed one paw on my shoulder and looked me full in the face. His expression radiated excitement, expectation, and happiness. Finally, he moved to one side and allowed me in. While I flicked on the flashlight and crawled closer to the doorway, Chakka resumed his paternal serenade outside.

Spook was lying heavily on her side, panting. The doghouse was exceptionally warm, and little straw motes danced in the light beam. I forced my head and shoulders inside for a better look. Just behind Spook's elbow two squat, fat little legs and a tiny fur ball protruded. Gently I reached in and lifted the little pup in my hands. The eyes were shut, and the ears were two pink flaps barely half an inch long. The little muzzle was already making sucking noises as the pup nuzzled my fingers. It was a strong, fat, jet black female, still slightly damp from being born. Spook lifted her head and gave the pup a lick and nearly toppled it from my hands. I placed her back at Spook's side, guiding her gently to Spook's breast. In two seconds the pup was firmly attached and drinking noisily. I watched for a few more minutes before I began to back out and let Spook get back to work. As I was turning to leave, the beam of the flashlight caught something just under the straw in the corner. It was another, very still pup. I reached in, but the minute my hand touched the little body I knew the pup was a stillborn.

As I sat in the cold looking at the pup, Chakka put his muzzle into my hands. The pup was still in its fetal sack. Spook had not bothered to clean it up, knowing it was useless. She had simply nudged it out of the way. Chakka gently put his mouth over the pup and lifted it from my hands; then he took it outside on the snow. There he proceeded to clean off the sack and afterbirth, and lick the pup in an effort to revive it. I decided that if he was going to try, I would also. I went outside and sat in the snow with the pup on my lap and began artificial respiration after cleaning out the mouth and nasal passages with my handkerchief. Chakka and I worked together for several minutes. I pressed the tiny rib cage, while Chakka licked with his warm tongue, but our efforts were in vain. When I stopped my ministrations, Chakka removed the pup from my lap and laid it once again on the snow. Then he lay down himself, cradling the pup between his two great legs and lowering his head protectively over it. Since I

FATHERHOOD **207**

was beginning to lose feeling in my feet from the cold, I rose to leave. Chakka reluctantly allowed me to remove the pup, but he followed me to the gate. He pushed it once more with his nose, then turned away and returned to the doghouse, where he stationed himself on the porch. I was glad Chakka knew the pup was dead, and that he *did* have a live one in the doghouse.

I woke Denny and Jenny with the news. Both were upset about the dead pup but elated that at least one had been born alive. If the healthy pup was free of deformities and lived beyond the critical ten-day period, its chances of surviving were excellent. Also, there was a good chance that Spook would give birth to more pups before morning. We could only wait and see. I wrapped the dead pup in a small blanket and laid it aside to bury in the morning.

Saturday morning, December 7, dawned to gray skies and snow flurries. We all got up early and dressed warmly, then hurried outside to see Spook. Chakka was in his accustomed place, guarding, but he rose to greet us warmly. He looked every inch the father, strutting proudly and not at all averse to letting us see his handiwork. Jenny climbed in first. There was a long silence, after which she emerged with another dead pup. There was no sense trying any resuscitation. The pup was still in the sack, cold and deformed. Chakka nosed it briefly, then turned away.

Tears rimmed Jenny's eyelids, but she tried bravely to hold them back. I took the tiny body from her and asked if she had checked for others. She brushed back the tears and scrambled back into the doghouse. A muffled voice quavered through the door. "Mom! There are two pups in here!" She rummaged through the straw, then backed her way out again. "There's one boy and one girl," she announced excitedly, "and they both look just fine!" Denny ducked under the roof and crawled onto the porch so he could peer inside, as I kept tugging at his pantleg, wanting my turn too.

Spook was relaxing on her side in deep contentment while two black bodies attacked her nipples with fierce determination. Little paws pushed and kneaded at her to encourage the milk flow. This time I took a few moments to look the pups over as they fed. Both appeared normal and were eating lustily. I was surprised at how small they seemed. I had imagined because they were part wolf they would be much larger, but they were actually slightly smaller than a purebred Great Dane pup. Perhaps, in a way, it was better that only two had survived. They would have full benefit of plenty of food and mother love. As I emerged from the doghouse, Chakka slurped me in the face, then pranced around with his chest out and his head held high. He was so proud of himself we all laughed at him. First-time fathers are all alike.

If Chakka's efforts had seemed solicitous during her estrus, his display of affection later was almost overwhelming; Spook had not one moment to herself. Even when she was in the house with the pups, Chakka dangled his head over the doorway in slavish devotion. She couldn't look sideways without seeing his attentive grin, and every time the pups so much as whimpered, Chakka rose and put the whole front half of his body through the door to see what was happening.

When Spook emerged from the doghouse the afternoon of the pups' birth, she was intent on relieving herself and having a stretch. Chakka was so delighted to see her that he pounced all over, licking her head and ears so enthusiastically she couldn't see where she was going. When she tried to squat, Chakka knocked her off balance and pushed her normally sanguine nature to the breaking point. Spook turned and bit Chakka right on the nose just as he was coming in for another happy kiss. He was so startled by her actions he fled back to his porch in unhappy confusion. Spook, pleased by that reaction, took her time sauntering around the pen and limbering up. Later when we went out to visit with her, I noticed that Chakka was still keeping close to the doghouse. Finally, Spook decided that it was time to return to her pups.

Because of Spook's enormous girth, it was hard enough for her to get into the doorway at any time, but I was surprised to see her stuck half in and half out. I went to see what was wrong and offer a little shove, but instead of going in she backed out, dumping us both in the snow. I got up and peeked into the interior of the nursery. There was Chakka, curled around the two pups, cleaning and loving them with all the paternal instinct possible. I had expected Spook to be terribly nervous over this unseemly, undoglike behavior, but instead she simply retired to the other side of the duplex, crawled in, and went to sleep. Chakka stayed with the pups until early evening, when we took the new parents their super supper.

Spook and Chakka both came out into the pen, but Spook was not interested in eating. She drank long, refreshing gulps of cool water and returned to her side of the house. Chakka made several trips to the door, trying to encourage her to eat, but she ignored him.

Chakka ate his fill of supper and then did something normal to a wolf but terribly rude to a dog. He went straight to the door of her house, stuck his head in, and regurgitated the meal so that she and the pups could eat. It is how a male wolf tends to the female in the den when she is unable to hunt or go outside. It may have been a kindly and touching thing as far as Chakka was concerned, but Spook was put out. When I glanced in, she was recoiling in horror and pulling the pups after her, while nosing fresh straw over the offending mess. I cleaned the offering up with a small hand shovel and carried it out of the pen while Chakka tried to nudge Denny toward the doghouse. His pride in his new pack and his fatherly duties was quite evident.

Over the next few days, we had several such repeat episodes, but each time I was able to straighten things out before Chakka's feelings were hurt. He became accustomed to us viewing his babies, and he greeted us at the gate and led us to the nursery with obvious pride. Spook began getting sick and tired of his activities and became totally unpleasant about him sticking his nose in where it wasn't wanted. Instead of being abashed, Chakka took to approaching Spook in a wholly submissive manner, head and shoulders lowered to the ground while he whined happily. Anything, anything at all to please his mate! Denny made some disparaging remarks about fatherhood, but Chakka ignored him with a "Wait till you're a father" look. We resigned ourselves to the fact that Chakka would probably keep this up for some time.

At the end of one week the pups, which previously fit well into one hand, now took two hands to hold. They were growing prodigiously. There was no end to their hunger, and the instant they sensed Spook's presence, they greedily went after their next meal. Spook was now not entirely happy about feeding them. Her udders were a welter of cross-hatched lines and tender to the touch. Using a pair of toenail clippers, I clipped the pups' sharp little claws, and this seemed to give Spook some relief. But two days later Spook was reluctant to feed again. The pups had extremely sharp, wolfie teeth, and their meals consisted of as much chewing as nursing. Spook, red and raw, refused to let her milk down. We decided to relieve her by supplementing the pups' feedings with bottles, and gave her a rest every other meal.

Cow's milk may be fine for some wild animals, but I had been warned that it was not good fare for a wolf. Luckily, we had two wonderful friends who raise goats, and they came to our rescue with enough milk to cover the extra feedings. Goat's milk is well tolerated by wolf pups because the fat globules are finer and more easily assimilated. Very little stomach distress is ever experienced from this nutritious product, and the pups seemed to thrive. In the meantime, we treated Spook's sore breasts with old-fashioned bag balm from our local farm supplier.

The minute I am lulled into complacency, something happens. This time it was almost a disaster. The night of December 17, a blizzard struck and the temperatures plummeted to below zero. Spook and her pups were cozy in their side of the house. I checked all the other animals, bedded everyone down warmly for the night, and retired to the sound of the howling wind. If it hadn't been for the fact that the doghouse was against the outside of Jenny's bedroom wall, we would have lost the male pup that night.

At about 4:30 A.M., Jenny was awakened by a strange sound. Over the howl of the wind was a peculiar, quavery, high-pitched wail, intermittent but insistent. Jenny is an extremely heavy sleeper, but something in the urgency of that small tone woke her. She slipped on her robe and opened her door, which was next to the pen. At first, all she could hear was the storm; then the sound came again. She was sure it must be one of the pups, and equally sure that the sound hadn't come from inside the doghouse. Pulling her door shut against the wind, she plowed her way through the deepening snowdrifts. Chakka and Spook were both in their houses, but about five feet in front of the porch area, almost covered with snow, was a small black shape. Jenny hurried into the pen and scooped up the pup. He was so cold, he was almost stiff. The only sign of life was the small wailing sound that came with every breath. She decided he was too far gone to put back in with Spook, so she tucked him inside her robe, took a second to make sure that the female pup was inside with Spook, and then hurried into the house. When she woke me up and laid the pup in my arms, I had little hope it would survive.

I threw a couple of heavy towels in the dryer to warm them up, and then prepared a mixture of honey, whiskey, and warm water for the pup in the meantime. He was so weak he had trouble swallowing more than a drop at a time. Finally, we wrapped him in toasty warm towels, gave him a shot of penicillin to counteract pneumonia, and got two whole dropperfuls of whiskey water down him. The alcohol would increase his circulation, and the honey would give him immediate energy. For the next hour we alternated warm towels, rubbing his tiny body. When finally he began breathing normally, I took him to bed with me, laying him on my chest and covering him with warm blankets. I firmly believe that an animal lying near a heartbeat has a much stronger will to survive. It also meant that if he stopped breathing, I would know it immediately. For two hours he lay still. At seven o'clock, he began nuzzling my neck, looking for breakfast. I took him downstairs to fix a bottle.

Chakka's attitude toward the stricken pup both puzzled and worried me. He was so proud of them and such a caring father that it didn't seem possible he could have stayed in his house and ignored the crying pup outside. I knew that he had heard it. If we could hear it inside, he could certainly have heard it five feet from his door. The only plausible explanation is that in the harsh rules of the wild, only the fittest survive. Probably Spook pushed the pup outside because she didn't want to nurse them both anymore, and Chakka, relying on her wisdom, failed to protect the pup. Sometimes it is better to let one starve than to lose the litter. To test my assumption, Jenny brought the other pup into the house. There was a good chance that Spook might push that one out in the cold also. She couldn't be blamed, for nursing them was a painful experience—so painful, in fact, that she wasn't producing her normal amount of milk. We concluded we would have to take over the feeding entirely.

Chakka was upset when the pups were brought inside, but not in a fury. We decided to allow him in at any time to see the pups. I also decided that although we would feed the pups, Spook should continue to groom and clean them. A mother's licking accomplishes two things. First, it cleans the pups and prevents uric acid burns and chronic skin conditions. Second, it is the cleaning by the mother's tongue that stimulates proper elimination of the pup's bladder and bowels. I could substitute by cleaning the pups with cotton soaked in warm water, but I felt Spook should participate in raising her babies. That was the least she could do!

By midmorning, Chakka wanted to come inside, so Denny brought him and Spook into the house. Chakka headed immediately for the box containing the pups and nosed around, snuffling and whuffing happily. By that time the little male was moving around and acting normal, despite his brush with death. In fact, he never did display any complications at all, not even a cold. Chakka was overjoyed to see them both, and began licking and grooming them. Spook wouldn't even look at them. Finally, I had to force Spook to lie down on the floor so I could place the pups in front of her. Perhaps she would have been content to groom them if they hadn't headed repeatedly and unerringly toward the nearest dairy bar. The minute they moved in that direction, she refused to have anything else to do with them. After half an hour of trying to coax her to perform her motherly duties, I put the pups back in the box. Spook retired to the opposite side of the room, but Chakka headed straight for them. He lifted them out so gently that they never even whimpered, and then set about cleaning up his clan. A few minutes later, both pups were glistening and ready for another bottle.

Chakka simply couldn't understand the bottle routine. He kept pushing it out of my hand and away from the pups' mouths. Finally, I turned the plastic bottle toward his nose and gave it a squirt. The stream of warm milk hit Chakka dead on the nose and made him shake his head in surprise. Then, as he hesitantly licked at the droplets, he decided it was all right and allowed me to finish feeding his babies. When I was through, he again groomed both pups and then allowed me to return them to their heated box. From that point on, Chakka seemed to accept me as surrogate mother. The grooming of the pups, however, remained his job.

Chakka probably would have stayed in the house with the pups if he hadn't suffered so much from the heat. His coat was so thick he simply couldn't stand more than an hour at a time inside. Spook wanted to remain where it was warm, but Chakka nosed her toward the door and refused to leave without her. Once they were outside, he was more than content. He had his mate, his warm house, and an area to stretch and run in. We kept him well supplied with bones for his amusement, but his greatest delight was playing with Spook. After the removal of her litter, she had become much more companionable. It was ludicrous to see her lumbering toward Chakka like a bulldozer, only to have him step out of the way at the last second and watch her smash her way into the fence. It never stopped her, and the game would continue indefinitely.

At two weeks of age, the pups began eating solid food, a necessity since they began chewing off the ends of the rubber nipples from the bottles before they were finished feeding. Afraid they would swallow one and choke, I tried to feed them out of a Pyrex pie plate. It would be heavy enough so that they couldn't tip it, yet shallow enough for them to drink without burying their heads in the milk. I was only half right. They leaped into the dish with all four feet and guzzled so ravenously that milk went flying in all directions. By the time they were through, the pups and my carpet were all the same milky color.

The next feeding went slightly better. I added half a can of horse meat to the milk until it was soupy. They chowed down until their tummies were hard, round balls. Still, however, they managed to cover themselves liberally with their supper, to Chakka's delight. I was afraid he'd eat them instead of grooming them, so enthusiastically did he attack the chore. Only one point worried me about the pups' diet. I was afraid, since they were half wolf, that they wouldn't digest their food properly without the enzymes the mother adds from her stomach when she regurgitates their food. These pups, however, apparently never read that book, for they continued to eat and gain weight at an unbelievable rate. They tripled their weight and size in one month's time, and from the size of their feet, it looked as if they were going to do a lot more growing before they fit into those furry snowshoes. (The male pup, at one year of age, weighed 215 pounds, larger than either parent.)

The wolf nature of the pups began to become evident when I found them out of the box and exploring everything within range at three weeks of age. We switched to a larger box, but once they'd had a taste of freedom they were not content to remain confined. We were back in the same dilemma we'd had with Chakka, and the only answer was to put up the gates on the porch hallway where Chakka had spent his baby days. This seemed to satisfy the pups, but since one of the gates separated porch from kitchen, they developed into terrible moochers. The instant they smelled anything cooking, they scrambled at the gate for handouts. Because of the competition, they were not gentle about eating from fingers, as Chakka had been. Not wanting to be permanently mutilated, I developed a training system. When we handed them tidbits, we held the scrap in our fists. If they bit in their haste, they were soundly and firmly tapped on the nose. Once they settled down, the hand was opened and they got their treat. Eventually, they learned to accept their food in a gentle manner. I also learned exactly how many BandAids come to a box, but all told, it worked out well.

After the problems we had with Chakka on the porch, I was a little wiser with the pups. All chewable items were once again removed, and my plants found themselves hanging once more from the ceiling. One pup, in a fit of resisting confinement, chewed half the windowsill off, but other than that the porch sufficed. When Chakka was in the house, the pups were allowed into the living room to visit Dad and learn the fine art of stealing shoes and pouncing on cats. The feline representatives of the household began to make themselves scarce when visiting hours approached. They had been amazingly patient while they were helping to raise Chakka, but two pups spelled double trouble, and they tired of protecting their front lines only to be destroyed by a flank attack. The pups were little wizards at coordinating their efforts, and even I didn't have enough hands to protect myself. Sometimes the only way to get any peace was to give the hellions a cooked beef bone and let them attack it for a half hour. It was amazing what they could do to solid bone with those baby teeth, but better a beef bone than my ankle.

At about this time my mother bought me a steam cleaner for my carpets. It wasn't a necessity; it was a sanity saver. Denny referred to it as a piece of furniture because it sat in the living room constantly, there never being an opportunity to put it away. Between housebreaking, greasy bones, and slopped milk, the machine accumulated more mileage than a ten-year-old car, but it kept our home clean and livable.

The pups' personalities developed as rapidly as their bodies. The male assumed the dominant role and spent many happy hours hanging on his sister's neck to make her submit. She, in turn, used every available opportunity to destroy his image. If she caught him unaware, she flew into his side and sent him sprawling. That wasn't too bad unless he had his head in the milk dish; then things became more complicated. That meant that the hated steam cleaner was going to be turned on, and they would have to scurry for the security of the couch. Both the steamer and the vacuum cleaner sent them into small terrors, and every effort to show them that the appliances were harmless was met with utter resistance. Even sitting in my lap when the machines were on gave them no security. I finally gave up, allowing them to whuff from their hidey-hole under the couch at whatever I was using. After half an hour of cleaning, they were so whuffed out they invariably went to sleep.

At one month of age, the pups were characters who were rapidly imprinting with our household. This presented a problem. We had decided that they needed individual attention. If they were left in a pack situation with Chakka, they would be less amiable as pets.

When their birth had been imminent, several family friends had expressed an interest in having a pup. Much as I liked the people involved, I felt that owning a half-wolf pup might prove more than most people could handle. It is a full-time job and requires a great deal of patience. I finally picked two people I thought could handle the challenge. One was Becky, the young lady whom Chakka loved almost as much as he loved us. When she saw the pups, she fell in love with the female and dubbed her Molly, a name I felt was mundane and lacking in dignity, but the pup didn't seem to mind. The other pup was christened Nitcha, meaning "leader" in Eskimo. Both learned their names easily, but it was amazing how Molly attached herself to Becky and began imprinting even during Becky's few visits. I could see the bond strengthening between the two of them, and it was finally decided that Molly would go to her new home the following week.

Placing Molly with Becky had many advantages, but the main one was that since Becky lived nearby, we'd be able to visit our pup often. For a period while Becky worked, Molly spent afternoons with us. That made the adjustment easier on her, but I also worried about the effect on Chakka and how he would take the adoption. We decided on a trial period to see if both the pup and her new owner were really happy, and if Chakka could make the adjustment. Otherwise, we might find ourselves with two more pups to rear. This prospect dampened my spirits somewhat. Feeding a penful of huge animals was not cheap, and besides, I wanted the pups to grow up as Chakka had, surrounded by attention and human love.

I didn't have to make any decisions about Nitcha. Jenny stated quite firmly that she and her fiance wanted Nitcha as their pup. They planned to work with him every day, and when they were married the following year he and Muttley would be ready to go with them. Meantime, it meant that Chakka would have a youngster to fawn over.

Chakka, endlessly surprising, took Molly's adoption in stride. The night she left, he didn't see her go. When he came into the house the next morning, he sniffed around for a while and settled down to playing with Nitcha, but Chakka knew Molly was missing. Two days later, Molly spent the day with us and Chakka gave her a thorough bath and loving, which she just barely tolerated. She wanted to play.

It was wonderful what the pups could do with impunity. They literally tore the edges of Chakka's tender ears ragged, pounced on him every chance they got, grabbed his tail, and walked all over him when he tried to lie down for a rest. He did not lose his patience or retaliate with anything but loving reproof, a role model for most human mothers. He did, however, reinstitute his domination by forcing both pups to "submit" as many as three or four times an hour. It never seemed to have anything to do with their behavior; it was simply a strategy to remind them that he was top wolf and they had better remember it.

It was Molly who rebelled most at having to submit. Nitcha seemed to respect Chakka and accord his father the proper honors due a man of the household. Molly, however, who had learned the fine art of subterfuge in her battles with Nitcha, was prone to applying the same tactics to Chakka. When Chakka approached Nitcha, growling, and put his muzzle over him, Nitcha immediately rolled over in delicious terror. Molly did the same, but once on her feet took a stand quite different from her brother's. Nitcha would be up and away like a shot, prancing and seeking love from his human family. But Molly never missed an opportunity to inflict a small nip on Chakka's nose or a ram charge at his legs. Dad may have coerced her to submit, but winning one battle didn't mean the war was over. It was exactly like seeing a chastised child leave the room while sticking her tongue out at her father behind his back, and about as effective. Chakka ignored her sassiness but continued to drill her on who was boss every quarter hour.

Several weeks later, when Molly had been with Becky and imprinted properly, things changed. When submission time rolled around, all Chakka had to do to Nitcha was look and growl, and his son would roll over like a wounded bull, round tummy protruding in the air. Molly, however, was becoming more used to submitting to Becky, and she began to resent having two large bodies dominating her life. Instead of submitting to Chakka immediately, she would stand her ground for three or four seconds before rolling over, and when she did submit, it was never gracefully. Far from being the weaker of the species, she showed more spunk and courage in facing the old man than Nitcha did. Chakka was as loving as ever in his ministrations, but he firmly insisted upon Molly remembering that her adoption did not make him one whit less her father.

Finally, the day arrived when Molly decided to test Chakka. At four months, she was full of zip and vinegar. Her visits with us were not as frequent, now that Becky was no longer working and did not need regular babysitting services. Nitcha, however, remained under Chakka's constant yet benevolent control. Molly, feeling that her eighteen-inch height gave her some sort of superiority, sadly underestimated Chakka's determination when she decided to test her obstinacy against her father's good nature. Once again, as he tried to make her submit she stood her ground and growled. But now there was no hesitation on Chakka's part. He pushed her down with his nose, she standing her ground defiantly until her pudgy little legs splayed at odd angles and wobbled with her effort to remain upright. Chakka seemed to realize that rebellion was best nipped in the bud, so that's where he nipped her. Molly squealed in outrage and humiliation. Nothing was hurt but her pride, and that had suffered horribly. Her knees buckled and she rolled over immediately, urinating a small stream signifying total submission.

Chakka, mindful that she was a stubborn child, decided that perhaps the lesson was not quite over. With his muzzle firmly gripping her chest, he settled down on his elbows in leisurely fashion and stretched out, still holding her. Molly was thoroughly abashed and slightly terrified. It was like a public spanking that never ends. Since she was not being hurt in the slightest, I allowed Chakka to show her who was boss. Her squeals subsided to whimpers, then to sobbing hiccups. Suddenly it occurred to me that there was a matching set of nervous hiccups directly behind my feet, under the couch. Nitcha was peering out, so upset that his little chest was heaving with sympathetic convulsions.

At last, Chakka released his toothy grip on Molly, but when she attempted to get up he once more pinned her to the floor. Each time he let up, she stayed put a little longer. Finally, she lay upside down between his paws with no more threat from him than a low growl. After she remained immobile for a while, Chakka felt she had learned her lesson. He got up, stretched, and retired to his food dish. Molly didn't budge until she was sure he was out of the room, then fled to the safety of her hideyhole.

It may have seemed like an unnecessary lesson, until you consider a wild pack of wolves. Only the strongest are allowed to lead the pack, and in order to do so they must constantly assert their dominance. A son, or even more likely a daughter to the pack leader, will constantly test the superiority of the head wolf. If they find him lacking, they will drive him from the leadership position or even the pack itself. If that happens, they must be strong enough to lead themselves. To this end, all manner of "tests" are conducted each day to see if there is any weakness in the leader, or if any stronger leadership can be found in a subordinate. It is an ongoing process that is essential to the well-being of the pack. A moment's hesitation on the part of the head wolf will be construed as weakness. Love and leadership are equated with firmness, and only strength is tolerated and respected. Molly learned her lesson for the day, but she would continue to test her father. Much to his credit, he continued to meet each act of resistance with the same resolve, despite Molly's persistence in trying to upset his applecart.

Nitcha, on the other hand, a much more gentle-natured animal, abhorred violence or confrontation of any sort. He tended to lean more toward the Great Dane side of his nature. A simple look from Chakka could send him rolling over on his back in abject submission. That is not to say that he didn't do his share of teasing where his father was concerned, but it was never done with the determination of purpose his sister exhibited. Nitcha's testing play was pure deviltry; Molly's was hopeful insubordination.

Molly took her submission lessons much more gracefully from Becky than she did from Chakka. In her young experience, Becky became the real dominating figure. Becky admitted, once, that it took every ounce of determination on her part to get down and bite Molly's ear the first time. She had found biting the muzzle near the nose to work even better, but this put one's nose in direct proximity to a full set of formidable teeth. On occasion, however, it was done because the effect was much longer lasting.

When Molly reached four months of age, we reluctantly decided to discontinue her visits with Chakka. She still went to the mesh sides of the pen and greeted him, and he showed every consideration toward her, but our decision was not based on Chakka's attitude. Molly was adjusting so well to Becky that having two "masters" might eventually be upsetting to her. The more she viewed Becky as her only leader, the better she would behave. I didn't want to turn her into a "scapegoat"—the lowest wolf in the pack whose spirit is broken by having to submit to every individual above him. Molly had too much vitality and was too happy with Becky to chance that.

As it was, Nitcha almost turned into the scapegoat because of his normally placid nature. Somehow, after Molly left, Nitcha lost interest in being dominant. Perhaps it was because he had no one to pick upon. Or, more likely, it was because as he got older he found it easier to slide through life being placid. He never bore a grudge about anything and was a hail-fellow-well-met kind of guy. If Nitcha had a bone and someone else took it, he'd find delight in playing with a leaf, or a sock, or whatever else caught his attention. It just wasn't in him to be a fighter. Although he was visited frequently by Chakka, he was not under complete domination because he didn't live with his father in the pen; his life was more centered with his human family. Then, one fine spring day when he was six months old, Nitcha's life took a new turn.

It was one of those false spring days when snow lies heavily on the ground, ice coats the trees, and the southern breeze is balmy. We had taken Nitcha outside for a stroll, and although he pulled against his restraining leash like all wolves, his attitude conveyed more than the usual nerve. Perhaps it was the unaccustomed warmth, or maybe the delicious odors that hint at summer, but whatever it was, Nitcha began acting odd. Even at his age, I was having problems restraining him and keeping my footing on the slippery ground. Finally, I decided it was more prudent to return home and put Nitcha in the pen with Chakka to work off his excess energy. It would be Nitcha's first foray into the realm of Chakka's world.

The two were ecstatic at seeing each other, and Nitcha bounded from one side of the pen to the other, cheerfully submitting every time Chakka demanded it. Nitcha's exuberance at being unfettered was beautiful to watch. It was the first time he had ever been able to run any distance without a human attached to him. It gave him maneuverability and a chance to test his prowess. He and Chakka bounded and leaped about like two deer, for the joy of it. Sometimes he succeeded in besting Chakka by simply plunking down his ample hind-end and forcing the chasing wolf to fall over his good-sized bulk. Spook stood to one side, eyeing the antics. Her attachment for her pups had never been as great as Chakka's. She preferred to watch rather than participate. Participation might have meant a loss of some dignity.

For two hours Chakka played with Nitcha, giving him instructions on how to "kill" a leaf. Nitcha imitated his father with clumsy but well-intentioned motions. Finally the pup began to tire, and the once balmy afternoon breezes turned chill. We took Nitcha back inside.

After having Nitcha in the pen with him, Chakka kept encouraging an encore. On his next visit to the house, Chakka attempted to force Nitcha to return to the pen with him. It was a nasty, sleety day, and I felt that Nitcha would be better off not to go outside for any length of time, but Chakka was so insistent that I finally brought Nitcha out. I had planned on leaving him for no more than fifteen minutes. Ten minutes later, when I glanced out through the window, I discovered that Spook had Nitcha pinned to the ground and was making the pup submit. It puzzled me because I had never seen her use such tactics before. The reason, however, became clear several minutes later when Nitcha tried to go into the doghouse. Spook would not permit him to get to the entrance. She defended both her heated side and Chakka's den, making it clear to Nitcha that he was not welcome. The more the pup tried to gain access to the pens, the more she made him submit. Finally, Nitcha turned to Chakka to play, but his father was busy grooming himself. When Nitcha insisted, Chakka turned and made the pup submit to him! That was almost too much. Nitcha sat in the snow and stared at the house window, waiting for rescue.

Fortunately, things eventually settled themselves. After Nitcha began going out to the pen on a daily basis, Spook more or less accepted his presence and stopped making him submit. This left Chakka in the role of lesson giver, and Nitcha never minded submitting to Chakka. Chakka was also careful to alternate submissions with fun times, so Nitcha knew that even if Chakka was a strict disciplinarian, he was also a playful father. They kept each other occupied for hours playing tug-a-dog or hunter-stalker. Nitcha learned to move like a shadow and how to slink up to his prey, belly down, until he was only inches high. He imitated Chakka's four-paw pounce to perfection. He managed to look lordly while standing stiffly at attention, sniffing breezes. His greatest accomplishment, however, was still to come.

It was the first really warm evening of the spring, and Nitcha had been playing with Chakka in the pen all day. Because it was so lovely out, I decided to leave him there until we went to bed. It was Nitcha's first time out after dark, and although it hadn't occurred to me until it happened, it was also the first time that Nitcha was with Chakka when the train went through. Chakka waited for the train every night as a signal for his evening howl. Nitcha had heard Chakka howl, but only from inside the house. This time he was sitting right next to his father when the sound reached them.

I had just gone outside to get the pup when I saw Chakka lift his nose high and purse his lips on the gentle introduction to his song. Nitcha watched him intently, then leaned against his father and lifted his head also. The first notes were soprano, quivering, a little uncertain, and then he took a deep breath and really got into the duet. The two of them leaned compatibly against each other, howling to the dark skies in harmony. Spook stood in the doorway of her house and added her voice as the music swelled. Down the road, several dogs joined as the train roared through the wood, blowing its whistle.

I watched for a moment with tears in my eyes. Chakka was in great form, well content as patriarch of his pack, happy with the world around him. I hesitated just a moment before going into the pen, when I knelt in front of them, putting my arms around both and adding my howl to theirs. Suddenly, the back door opened, Jenny stuck her head out and laughingly howled along with us. The upstairs window opened and Denny poked his head out to join the chorus. Between laughter and tears we all howled together until the train's caboose disappeared around the bend. We had howled our unity and happiness to the world, and we could sleep with the firm conviction that we were the best wolf pack around.

13

Family Business

CHAKKA CHOSE MORE AND MORE TO stay in the pen with his "pack." Although he seemed to love to visit us inside after a good walk, he needed more room and less heat than the house afforded. There was also always a danger that he might go through the windows if something outside caught his fancy. Twice before I had found it necessary to replace windows and wooden mullions, all because he thought he'd seen a mouse outside. Luckily, neither time was Chakka hurt, but he could have done real damage to himself on the jagged glass. His decision to remain in the pen was really rather a relief to us, but to Spook and Nitcha, it meant that they must undergo constant lessons in wolf protocol.

Spook did her best to ignore Chakka, and refused to roll over every time he wanted to establish supremacy. She was simply not going to tolerate this constant submission test! Eventually, poor Chakka was reduced to being content with placing his head over her shoulders and telling the world that he was lord and master of all he surveyed. Sometimes he had to sidestep rapidly alongside Spook when she walked, just so his head could continue to rest on her shoulders. Although it detracted from the dignity he earned at the moment, it was all he could do, under the circumstances; some women are just more difficult than others. Nitcha, however, began taking clues from Spook, and would put off submitting for as many seconds of rebellion as he dared before rolling over on his back. The intervals became longer and longer, but Chakka held the upper paw and persisted. The time was coming when we felt that Nitcha would openly challenge Chakka, and it would probably be because of Nitcha's rapidly approaching sexual maturity.

After many long discussions regarding solutions to the problem, it was finally decided that we would neuter Nitcha. This meant that Chakka could still have his full pack in the same pen with himself, without having to duel with Nitcha over Spook's favors, or even the scents of any neighborhood dogs in heat. Once that decision was made, I called a veterinary friend and asked her if she would please do the surgery here at home, so that Nitcha might return to the pen with Chakka as soon as possible. She agreed, and we set the date for the next week. It was to prove none too soon.

It was spring, and many female dogs were allowed to run free, even if they were in heat. They came into our yard near Chakka's pen, tantalizing his mating instincts, but oddly enough, even though he became aroused by their pheromones, his only real mating gestures were directed toward Spook. I think even if Chakka had had access to the other females, his wolf nature would have dictated that he remain faithful to his alpha female. All this should have been immensely flattering to Spook, but her own absent heat periods and her advanced age made her a mite peckish when the old man got amorous. She told him where to take it in no uncertain terms, and retreated to the doghouse in a snit. Chakka would sit outside the porch area, leaning heavily against the wall and guarding her privacy as well as his own conjugal rights. Nitcha, however, was becoming more aroused and less social. He possessed no such fine distinctions as fidelity to any one female. He would gladly have given in to the dog side of his ancestry and bred anything that came his way. He was simultaneously frustrated and feeling his oats. I felt that we were getting him fixed in the nick of time, before he challenged Chakka beyond the point of propriety.

The vet arrived one beautiful sunny morning, and we set up the surgery area in the dining room. Jenny and her fiance, Dave, took Chakka on a leash for a very long walk, while the vet and I brought Nitcha into the house. We were using a very short-term anesthetic, so that Nitcha would be on his feet within a half hour of his surgery. That, along with a shot to keep him comfortable after the surgery, would enable him to return to the pen before Chakka returned. We hoped that this would upset Chakka less and keep things more normalized.

Nitcha was very good about getting his shot. He had other things on his mind, and kept looking back over his shoulder at the screen door, hoping to catch a glimpse of some alluring female. A few minutes later, he was sliding slowly to the floor in a snoring heap. We struggled to lift his heavy frame onto the surgery table we had prepared, and ten minutes later the almost bloodless operation was over. We carried the sleeping Nitcha back to the pen and laid him on the warm cement. Before Chakka and the kids returned, Nitcha was up and walking around, albeit a little unsteadily, but in control for the most part.

The one thing I had feared was that Chakka might have a bad reaction to the smell of blood on Nitcha. I had the kids open the pen door and return Chakka while I remained inside the pen to protect Nitcha if necessary. I stayed at Nitcha's side, between him and Chakka, ready for anything. Chakka knew instantly that something was wrong, and he repeatedly pushed me out of the way with his nose while he edged in to investigate the few stitches and smell of anesthetic. Nitcha was still slightly groggy and totally noncombative. I was more afraid of Chakka trying to make Nitcha submit, and hurting him unwittingly in the process, or perhaps trying to clean Nitcha and tearing out the stitches, than I was afraid of outright conflict. Chakka did neither. He turned and approached Nitcha on the other side, standing shoulder to shoulder with him in silent commiseration. When Nitcha moved quietly on, Chakka supported his slightly shaky stride with his own body, lying down beside Nitcha when Nitcha lay down and assisting him in his attempts to rise. Only later in the day when Nitcha was once again totally in control did Chakka turn his attention to other wolfly matters, and even then he returned frequently to check things out. The next day, it was as if nothing had happened. Nitcha was once again expected to perform his submission routine, and Chakka was master of his pack.

We had very carefully watched Spook for any signs of heat periods, but none were forthcoming. I did not intend to have her bred again, because although the pups were beautiful and a joy to behold, finding homes that were good enough for them was a monumental task; many people who would love to have one are not really able to comprehend what it takes to own a wolf, or even a part wolf. So we watched Spook with an eagle eye, ready to intervene should she show even the slightest signs. Otherwise, at her age, I would not subject her to surgery. Two possible estrus cycles passed with no indication that she would ever come into heat again, and when the third period was due and we had her tested, it appeared that she was truly beyond her breeding age. We heaved a collective sigh of relief.

Chakka and his pack seemed to be the only constant in my life. Other things around me were changing rapidly. Jenny was planning a wedding for the following summer. My son Kim and his wife and two children had been living just a few doors down the road, but a new job offer in another state had beckoned irresistibly, and so they would be moving in short order. Bill had been traveling farther and farther afield in his work, and all the foster children who had lived with us over the years were now adults pursuing their own lives and careers. Only Denny remained, but even his work demanded much time away. Chakka missed the boisterous activities as much as I did. He was used to the door banging in and out with a steady stream of people.

Kim had decided that my humble home needed a new roof.

Small leaks had been appearing, and before they became a real problem, he decided to tackle the project for me. Kim and some of the kids spent days on the roof, much to Chakka's delight. He loved new activities, and this certainly was an area he hadn't hitherto explored. He wanted to join the fun and knock down shingles while he played tag with anyone trying to work. In silent industry, Chakka jumped at the wall that made up one end of his cage. There were times when I wasn't quite sure that he wouldn't scale it after all. He certainly gave it his best. Time after time, he would race from the far end of the pen and hurtle at top speed toward the wall end. Most times he tried to scale the roof of the doghouse, but the metal roof defied his attempts and shot him back to the ground in a disgruntled heap. His only joy was in catching (and keeping) any stray pieces of construction detritus that fell into his pen. He terrorized shingles, demolished scrap lumber and—joy of joys—totally removed the vinyl cover on a hammer handle before Kim could retrieve the "indestructible" tool. His whole day was spent in happy anticipation of the next gift from heaven, but he almost met his maker when a can of pop dropped to the cement in front of him. It didn't break open, but in the heat of a summer day, after its thorough shaking up, it was a time bomb. Chakka pounced on it immediately as I winced, expecting the worst. I was scrambling to open the lock on his cage door when he picked it up in his mouth and shook it. I was yelling at him to quit. He paid as much attention to me as he usually does when he knows he has a scant few seconds more to do whatever it is I don't want him doing. The can was still, miraculously, intact as I pushed open the pen door and started toward him. He dropped it once again at his feet and grinned at me—and then all hell broke loose. Spook was three or four feet away, sitting down lazily scratching her neck with her hind foot when a weak spot or tooth dent in the can gave way. There was an ominous, muffled boom, and a jet of brown spray shot with unerring accuracy straight into poor Spook's raised ear. She was filled to overflowing before she could get her foot down and scramble out of the way. Even worse, the can began to spin, and the stream followed her terrified flight across the pen. Chakka suddenly found the jet aimed at him and literally danced trying to lift all four feet into the air at once. Both dogs nearly killed each other trying to get into the doghouse at once, and I was helpless with laughter until I got hit with the spray myself. I had really underestimated the force of the spray, which felt like sticky needles as it hit my skin, and by the time I got the pen door open again, the can had made three more turns and doused me thoroughly. An hour later, after a shower, I returned to the pen, where I could still hear Chakka and Spook licking the horrid stuff off their fur. Nitcha, who had been on the other side of the doghouse when the commotion hit, was still peeking timidly around the corner, waiting for the next barrage.

After this, Chakka became much more cautious about what fell from the roof. It had to lie still for several minutes before he would even approach it, and then he would glide up to it, practically on his belly. Any little noise made while he was sneaking up on the object would cause him to leap straight into the air. He remained gun-shy for several days, after which he seemed to regain his confidence. Besides having the men on the roof to watch, he was overseeing my project at the other end of his pen. I was busy trying to plant a small vegetable garden, and Chakka was busy trying to grab whatever came close to his fence. Twice I suffered amputated garden hose and watched in dismay as nothing but a dribble appeared from the working end. It became a game between us to see if I could divert Chakka long enough to toss the hose around the corner, turn on the water, and race to pull it out of his reach before he noticed. He was getting better and quicker each time, and I was racing harder to beat him to it, when I rounded the corner at extra speed and overshot my mark. I hadn't noticed a wicked-looking small steel beam that had been laid on the other side of Chakka's pen. Originally propped against the wire, it had somehow become dislodged and dropped part of the way down until it snagged on a tree branch. When I ran into the jagged end of it at full blast, I was jerked off my feet as it ripped through my scalp, laying my head wide open. I remember my neck snapping back, and then dropping to my knees while blood flooded over my face. Dimly I heard Kim on the roof calling, "Mom! Mom!" He had seen me go down, and was already sliding down the ladder to my rescue. Chakka, in the meantime, had been diverted by his easy victory over the garden hose and hadn't noticed me sinking slowly into the west. He did, however, see Kim come bolting across the yard, and something in Kim's demeanor spelled haste and trouble. In seconds, Kim was at my side, lifting me and leading me into the house as I moaned out loud. When we turned and walked alongside Chakka's pen, I was shocked to see him lunge repeatedly at the wire, growling and tearing at the mesh. I didn't stop to contemplate the meaning of his actions, but went straight into the house to treat my head wound. It wasn't until the next day that we discovered what had happened.

Kim and Chakka had always gotten along famously, but the day after my accident, whenever Kim got near the pen, Chakka's fur rose in threatening waves. Somehow, in his wolf thoughts, he had connected Kim running at me with my injury. He had been frantic to protect me, and still hadn't forgiven Kim for hurting me. Despite all my attempts to get Chakka to understand, he was never friendly with Kim after that. Although he was not threatening, he steadfastly refused any friendly overtures. Kim, who dearly loves animals, was crushed.

As winter approached, I automatically increased the amount of protein and fats in the animals' diets to build up their body weight. Every fall when Chakka shed his fur in preparation for the wonderfully heavy winter coat coming in, he lost a considerable amount of weight as well as fur. Most of his body energy was going into forming new fur, and he needed assistance. I added extra vitamins and chopped vegetable treats, picked berries for him, supplied herbs, and cooked tons of meaty bones donated by the markets. I even rolled acorns into the cage, because I had read that the tannin in acorns is a natural vermifuge that would rid Chakka of worms that stubbornly resisted modern medicine.

Wolves have extremely tender stomachs, but luckily they seldom eat anything truly harmful. Chakka loved the acorns as far as crunch goes, but he would stand there and salivate for ten minutes after eating one. When I finally tried one myself I found it extremely bitter. They are fit for human consumption only after boiling in three or four successive water changes. That's fine for flavor, but it defeats the worming purpose. The tannic acid, a vermifuge, is boiled out in the process. I did, however, find a natural vermifuge that did not distress his system, was flavorful, and turned the trick: raw garlic. We tried with a clove or two at first, then increased the dosage gradually, even adding fresh raw onions. His fur began to fill in with a shiny bounce that denoted exuberant good health. I remarked to Bill that I had never seen Chakka's eyes so shiny. Bill's caustic reply was that they weren't shining, they were watering! We stood at the edge of the fence and watched Chakka play and bounce, calling and encouraging him as he shook an old knotted sock to death and pounced on it in mock ferocity. He was having a wonderful time, but we had to back away from the fence when he bounded over to share his toy and breathed on us. He could knock over a moose without touching it. Unexpectedly, a bonus to the worming herbs we were giving him was that he was not troubled with flies or fleas while his diet was rich in those aromatics. When I remarked to Bill that we should give our house dogs the same treatment, his eyes widened in disbelief. As he walked back into the cabin to pack for his next trip, he was mumbling about my having a long, cold, lonely winter.

Actually, I might really have tried it during the time that Bill was away, but I knew that if the dogs' breath didn't get me, the resulting flatulence would. Chakka had enough gas to fly out of the pen. I didn't need that in the house. I was already blessed with a dear little orphan dog who had been abandoned several weeks before. I couldn't understand how anyone could dump such a precious creature, but a few days in an enclosed area with her pinpointed the problem. She couldn't move without making rude noises, and she smelled like burning rubberbands. We finally gave her a thorough medicinal worming and eliminated all dog food containing red dye. Her intestines settled down and the lining of my nose gradually returned to normal. We found her a wonderful home before Christmas.

By the time snow began falling, I made Chakka's seasonal health checkup, taking stool and blood samples to the vet and examining his ears for mites. For the first few years that he'd been with us, his ears had been clear, but this time the look of dirty sand (digested blood from mites' excreta) told me Chakka had an infestation of mites. That meant I had to treat all three animals, putting a special oil in the ears and swabbing them clean daily. This would probably go on for weeks until all signs of infestation vanished. But I anticipated no problems at all. In fact, Spook absolutely loved having her ears done, and would roll and stretch with happy groans as I dug deep into the ear canal to clean it. Often Nitcha would interfere, pushing his head between us in expectation of his turn. It must have felt extremely good to them both, because the minute I produced the bottle of oil, they both weaseled happily at my feet. And Chakka—well, he'd been so good about even having his blood sample taken with a syringe, a simple ear check or treatment was sure to go smoothly. Right?

The maneuver started out well enough, except for Chakka's inquisitiveness. No matter what I was doing, he had to have his nose in it. He would grab things out of my hands and flip them in the air, and while I was scrambling to retrieve them he would raid my pockets. Cotton swabs and cotton balls sailed merrily in the air, and the plastic oil bottle was crunched under his foot until the contents sprayed all over, after which he would rub in it. I had a devil of a time until I hit upon the idea of making Chakka submit. When I first tried it, he looked at me as if I had lost my marbles. Then he decided that it was beneath his dignity, but since I persisted, he would humor me. He rolled over onto his back, huge feet in the way, and grinned at me upside down. The ears were no more accessible that way than they had been before. I finally had to straddle him before I could get out the supplies and begin my ministrations. It was then that I discovered the truth. Chakka's ears were extremely ticklish!

The minute I poured in the oil and began swabbing, Chakka's eyes squinted up, his nose wiggled, his lips quivered, and he exploded in gigantic sneezes. The sneezes continued the whole time I worked in the ears, sometimes becoming so violent that he banged his head repeatedly on the cement. The minute I was through, he would snap upright and shake his head until the medication sprayed all over the dogs and myself. A few more powerful sneezes, a roll on the ground, and he was set to take on the world. Chakka's aversion to having his ears done was so powerful that, at the end of two weeks of treatment, all I had to do was pull out cotton balls and he'd begin sneezing and acting goofy.

The last day of treatment was the first truly cold day of the winter season. I was working in a hurry to get the ears finished before my fingers fell off. I tackled Chakka first, getting both him and his sneezes out of the way while I still had some mobility in my frozen digits. Then I tried blowing on my fingers to warm them enough to work on Nitcha's ears. Luckily, Nitcha was very cooperative, and I moved right on to Spook. In spite of the cold and the dusting of snow on the ground, she rolled over in ecstasy while I worked on her. I was just putting away the medication and standing up when I looked down and saw something that made me do a double take. Spook's breasts were swollen down both sides, and there was a suspiciously ominous swelling to her tummy. Without a doubt, Spook was once again pregnant—with no warning signs whatsoever—and she was too far along for surgical intervention. We had a problem.

14

Separations

Spook had a perfect affinity for giving birth in the worst storm of the season. Once again it was Jenny who heard the pups' first whimpers through her bedroom wall and alerted us to their birth. Light was just beginning to appear on the horizon when I pulled the heavy jacket on and trudged through the snow to the pen. Chakka was parading importantly back and forth in front of the doghouse, eager that I should see what wonders he had wrought. The minute I got down on my hands and knees and crawled into the porch area to peek around the corner of the door, Chakka pushed his way in also, poking and snuffling over my shoulder. The two of us were jammed in so tightly that it was hard to see anything, but I finally managed to get out my pocket flashlight and count noses. Three jet black pups were already firmly attached to Spook's nipples, and one gorgeous wolf-colored pup was wobbling around in the straw, mewling pathetically. Spook paid no interest to any of them and acted thoroughly blasé about the whole affair. When I laid my hand on her side, I could feel an occasional contraction rippling the muscles beneath, but she didn't seem to be straining. I checked the heating mat under the straw to make sure it was working, looked the pups over as best I could, and backed out the entrance while Chakka stepped all over me in his attempt to get back in and see the pups.

I cannot kill anything. I even built my house around a tree because I didn't want it cut, so the option of putting away any pups was never even considered. I began to wonder how we would provide space and food for a full-sized wolf pack, and decided that I would still try to find each pup a perfect home. If that was impossible, then we owed them the right to the best life we could provide right here. Somehow we would manage. I did, however, decide that Spook would be spayed as soon as the litter was weaned. If I, with my veterinary assistant background, had been unable to detect any heat signs from Spook, the only sensible alternative was sterilization. We could not bring any more little lives into the world without making provisions for their total welfare.

Several more times that morning, I checked into the doghouse, but no new pups were forthcoming. At 2:00 in the afternoon, I was just headed out to the pen when I saw Chakka emerge from the doghouse with something in his mouth. He deposited it in the snow in the corner of the pen and mounded more snow over it with his nose. I knew what I would find as I hurried through the pen door and went straight to the corner. Chakka had turned and walked away, disinterested and remote. Under the snow, I found not one but two pups still in their birth sacks. Both pups were malformed and had quite obviously been born dead. There would have been no hope. Chakka did not waste parental grief on either of them. In the wilds, all energy goes to preserving the babies that have the best chance of surviving. If extra energy is expended on imperfect pups, the healthy ones suffer, and the imperfect ones never survive in the harsh realities of the big world anyway. Nature's economy dictates that only the strongest survive. Chakka never learned that lesson in the wild, but he proved that it is an inborn trait. He was aloof as I removed the pups from the pen. He went straight to Spook's side in the doghouse and lay in the doorway.

The porch area of the doghouse, lying between the two apartments and designed to protect the occupants inside from winds and weather, was where Chakka curled up instead of retiring to the apartment on either side. Poor Nitcha sat outside with a thoroughly hang-dog expression. Chakka not only paid no attention to him, but he also wouldn't allow Nitcha access to the house. Nitcha's thick fur was keeping him warm for the moment, but come evening he wouldn't be comfortable lying outside in the snow and howling wind. As the day wore on and it began to get dark, Chakka showed no signs of relenting. On my final check of the pups (which still numbered four), I decided that we would have to bring Nitcha inside. Here I was, expecting the whole family home for a ten-day Christmas holiday, and I was going to have to cope with a klutzy, oversized, rambunctious Dane-wolf pup, but there you have it. Fate doesn't cater to all our expectations.

Sometimes when you expect the worst, your fears are amazingly not borne out. Aside from knocking ornaments off the tree in his wagging enthusiasm, Nitcha was very little trouble. In fact, he had a wonderful time. He didn't have to submit every fifteen minutes, he didn't have to ask permission to get into the doghouse, and he could spend hours playing with Scruffy the cat and Muttley the dog. Luckily, Nitcha had been inside enough to be housebroken before this emergency arose. He loved everything except the temperature. To counteract the combined effect of heat and a heavy coat, he practically took up residence on the floor in front of the door. Any cold air that might have snaked into the house under the edge of the door was firmly trapped by a 140-pound black cold-baffle. When he would get up and stretch, we could actually feel one side of his body significantly colder than the other, but it was the warmest the house had been in years. It did, however, make any access to the outside a considerable problem. Nitcha was loath to move just because someone wanted in or out (which, with our amount of company, could occur at five-minute intervals). He would groan and stretch, taking his time about arising and moving as if he were anchored in mud. In fact, there were times when he had just plain had it and refused to move. Talking to him—even yelling at him—evoked no response. He liked to pretend that he was so sound asleep that he couldn't hear us. We would end up having to slide him across the floor by grabbing all four feet and pulling. At that point, he would "wake up" and scramble back to his post by the door. Depending on who was quicker, Nitcha or us, we would either get outside or we would have to repeat the whole maneuver all over again. I stayed inside more than usual over those holidays.

During the most hectic part of the holidays, we would put Nitcha outside in the pen for the better part of the day, bringing him back inside if the weather was bad or evening was coming on. Chakka was a little less dominant in the porch area, having moved into Spook's house to be with the pups. Spook hated this and grumbled excessively about pushy mates, but she seemed glad enough of Chakka's protection of the pups while she meandered outside in the pen, or else came into the cabin to join us for a few hours. As much as Chakka loved coming inside to visit us, he would never leave the pups alone. If Spook left, Chakka remained curled around them, offering full protection and extra warmth. On occasion I even tried to coax him out so I could get in and examine the pups more thoroughly, but he refused to budge. I was reduced to sitting cramped up on the porch area and lifting the pups out one by one to check them over. When I put them back, Chakka would push them under his fur and legs, nudging until they were all but hidden from view. During the examination, I found that all four were healthy, fat, sleek little creatures. One was a pudgy black female with a tiny white tip on her tail; one was a much larger black male with a hint of gray-brown coloring showing through; and two were jet black males.

It was astounding how fast the pups grew. By the end of the holidays, they were more than twice their birth weight. Poor Spook's tummy was laced with cross-hatched scratches from the pups' nails. We trimmed the little daggers at least once a week to keep the old girl comfortable, but we couldn't do anything about the needle-sharp teeth. She was getting less and less enthusiastic about feeding, but I didn't dare start them eating from a dish. I knew they would thoroughly soak themselves, and that would spell disaster in this cold weather. I started treating Spook's nipples with old-fashioned bag balm from the farm supply store, and actually took a nail file to the needle ends of the puppy teeth. Just blunting the sharpest points helped immensely and didn't hurt the teeth themselves. Spook seemed to settle down to motherhood with a little renewed enthusiasm. Before spring rolled around, we placed discreet ads in some downstate newspapers and began interviewing possible new owners for the pups. The long winnowing process had begun.

Many nice people answered the ads, but sadly, not many of them had the right facilities or the amount of time needed to raise a partly wild animal. One large male pup, the most beautiful Chakka had ever sired, went to a family that proved to be ideal. As we followed the progress he made in his new home, I was thrilled at how they handled him and what accommodations they made in their lives to assure his happiness. Periodically we talked and kept tabs on his progress, until they left a year later with the pup to live in Alaska. Before their departure, we had a good many laughs over their exercise routine for "Bing."

Bing and his new family lived on a river with a large amount of acreage surrounding them. I had warned them not to let him run free, as it only encouraged bad habits of running away and getting into mischief. They were careful to exercise him twice daily by running him through the fields on a long leash and letting him snuffle and investigate to his heart's content. This worked fine as long as the pup was small, but with his phenomenal growth rate, it wasn't long before he was going faster than a healthy human male is designed to run. The owner thought he had this problem solved: He hauled out a small motorcycle, set the pup in a box on the back, and rode out to the fields with his hand on Bing to reassure him that it was all right. When they reached a large, flat area, he put Bing on a very long leash and rode behind him as Bing romped and raced. At the end of an hour, the pup was panting and tired, not at all reluctant to be put back into the bike box for his ride home. Over the months, the pup grew, the sessions became longer, and a new twist resulted. As the owner drove his wide circles around the field, Bing would run ahead, flatten himself in the grass, and lie in wait for the bike to come by. Luckily, the man was an excellent rider and could keep the small bike under control when Bing launched his attacks from the grass. He would come sailing out in a high arc, leap into his box on the back, ride for a circle's worth, then leap off again and rush ahead to another ambush area. It must have looked like a circus routine, with the bike going in circles and Bing leaping on and off like a well-trained dog. But Bing was no dog, and he leaped on and off only when he jolly well felt like it. I wonder if the game continues to this day in Alaska.

Chakka did not seem to mind when Bing left. He still had plenty to keep him occupied, and the pups were getting large enough to venture out of the doghouse on milder days. This meant that Chakka got no respite from their teasing. There was no place to run. He bore all their bullying with placid good humor, and by the time that they were old enough to begin eating from a dish, Chakka was the one who cleaned them up and nuzzled them back into the doghouse for a nap with Spook. We began to have a few mild days when Spook and the pups were able to lie out in the sunshine for a few hours. She was still nursing intermittently, but not happy about it. It was with a sigh of relief that we found an ideal home for the second male pup, who looked the "wolfiest."

The owners, a biologist and his physician wife, had the space, the money, and the time in their collective schedules to raise the pup properly. They took the second-largest male home with them with a promise to maintain contact with us about his progress. All pups that we placed went only after the new owners had signed a paper that if they were unable to keep the animal at any time, we would be notified and the wolf returned to us. I didn't want any of our progeny to end up in unsuitable homes or dog pounds. Their welfare would always be our concern.

The second pup was adjusting very well to his new home, making wonderful progress in his bonding with the new family, when disaster struck. He suddenly stopped eating and lost weight. They X-rayed him at once and discovered an abnormal thickening in the kidney area. Exploratory surgery revealed an unusual form of cancer that had spread throughout the renal system. Because of the massive involvement, he was allowed to sleep away without waking from the operation. Devastated, they called me that evening with the news. That was our first loss of one of these wonderful animals, and we cried together. I suggested they come up the next weekend and look again at the last male. They had been torn between the two, and I offered to replace their loss with Toby. When they left our home that next Sunday, they were carrying little black Toby in their arms, and we were left with only Tippy, the female runt of the litter.

For the most part, Tippy (whose name was shortened from The One Who Has the White Tip on Her Tail) appeared normal, albeit smaller than her siblings. She ate well, grew within an acceptable norm of growth, and appeared alert. But something was different. Tippy was unusually timid, shying from hands or any proximity to humans. She was never outwardly rambunctious like the other pups had been, nor was she inquisitive enough to approach us on her own. Hiding behind her mother or father, she chose to view the world from the security of their protection. Even food would not entice her into stroking distance, and the few times I physically caught her and held her for petting and bonding, she squirmed constantly to evade my touch. She wasn't mean or aggressive, but seemed clearly frightened and overly cautious. I performed several experiments to see if her vision or hearing were affected, causing her to be unnecessarily startled, but all faculties seemed normal.

For a whole month, I forcibly cornered Tippy so I could pick her up. I rewarded her with food, with love, with stroking, even toys, in order to provide a stimulus strong enough to break through her barriers. As I sat in the pen one day grooming Chakka, who was stretched on his side in the sunshine, I watched Tippy out of the corner of my eye. No matter where she moved, she kept a line of retreat open, and yet the rest of her behavior strongly reminded me of a family friend's autistic daughter's. There were inappropriate, repetitive movements such as pacing, rocking, and swinging the head. But any movement on my part toward her arrested her own, and she was all watchfulness. Something was obviously wrong, but I couldn't find the key. I decided to take her into the cabin and try to work with her there, away from her parents.

After a half hour inside, I was ready to admit defeat. I had only made matters much worse by isolating her from the only security she knew. It was a cruel thing to do, because her immediate reaction was to fling herself repeatedly into the walls and scramble her feet against the door in a pathetic attempt to escape. My soothing words and gentle strokings only served to increase her panic, and her breathing became rapid and labored. She was salivating profusely, trembling in every limb, and a good candidate for nervous collapse or a heart attack. I decided to return her to the pen before irreparable damage was done.

For the next few weeks, I decided to try to get through to Tippy via Chakka. I spent extra time sitting down in the pen, grooming Chakka and pretending not to notice her. If she got anywhere close, I deliberately turned away from her, letting her inch nearer for a sniff. I kept my movements slow and obvious and my stature low to the ground so that she felt less threatened. The rewards were minimal but significant. She finally got close enough to the back of my arm for me to feel her warm breath as she sniffed at my skin. I stayed perfectly still, hoping she would make further advances, but the sound of a car door slamming across the street sent her flying away from me and into the doghouse. She refused to come back out, and I finally left.

It was almost two months later that I got so far as to induce Tippy to put her nose against my fingers, but even then it was only through the wire mesh of the pen. If I curled my fingers gently upward, she moved her muzzle so I couldn't touch so much as a hair. I had to content myself with small gains and hope that over time she would learn to trust. One thing was clearly evident: We could not place Tippy in a home. Not only would she not bond properly, she would lose the only security she knew—her pack. It seemed that she would be with us the rest of her life.

Time had passed so rapidly that Jenny's wedding was upon us before I was ready for it. In the swirl of activities that surround these happy events, I had to quit working with Tippy and concentrate on the upcoming nuptials. With the family all converging from various parts of the country, it was once again like old times. Chakka was in his element, monitoring the proceedings from his pen and weaseling and cavorting at the slightest attention from any of the children. Nitcha, however, was not quite so happy with the social turn. To him, it only meant more submission lessons inflicted on him. He was now much larger than Chakka, and it must somehow have occurred to him that it was ridiculous to bend to the will of someone smaller than himself. He grumbled and tested the limits of Chakka's patience more frequently than usual, but Chakka kept the upper paw with firm determination. In spite of the growls that always accompanied these lessons, no blood was ever shed, and only egos suffered.

Bill was home for the proceedings, and even he tried to entice Tippy into friendly activities, but she seemed more fearful than ever. The slight improvements were barely noticeable. True, she had stopped the head swinging and mindless pacing (unless she was nervous), but she remained aloof. Strangers sent her into the doghouse immediately, so we saw very little of her during this time. One evening, shortly before the wedding, I was standing outside the pen, talking to Chakka as the sun passed down behind the line of trees. In the quiet shadows, Tippy inched forward and, wonder of wonders, flipped her tongue through the wire fence and lightly touched my hand. I was so shocked that I stood stock-still. Jenny, just out the back door, had seen what happened. She walked over and we quietly talked about the animals and their various personalities. Then she surprised me with her next comment. "Mom," she said, "would you let us take Nitcha with us as soon as we move? Chakka is always making him submit anyway, and we would love to have him now. Maybe Tippy would quiet down with less competition. Besides, Nitcha wouldn't be alone. We would have Scruffy the cat and Muttley the dog to keep him company."

I had known that Jenny and Dave wanted the animals, but had assumed they would wait until their home was built instead of making the transition while living in a small rented trailer. However, it appeared that my furry population was going to diminish rapidly. But the more I thought about it, the more sense it made. Jenny and Dave would be living just a few miles away, so animals and people would be visiting back and forth anyway. Perhaps it was for the best. But before Nitcha left, we bought a good-sized pen and installed it outside their trailer. It would be ready when they returned from their Florida honeymoon, and Nitcha could spend days when they were at work in a world of his own making, king of all he surveyed.

Jenny's wedding passed in a blur. It seemed that all manner of problems were encountered—things forgotten, caterers fouling up, the weather *hot*. The only good thing to come out of the affair was that I inherited the most wonderful son-in-law possible. My daughter was not totally lost to me, and she would be living close enough to continue to be part of my life. I counted my blessings one evening as I sat in the quiet cabin after everyone had left. I had a loving, supportive family and animals that meant so much to me. What more could one need?

When Jenny and Dave returned from their honeymoon, looking tan and fit, they were ready to settle happily into their small home. The trailer they'd rented was situated on the edge of a dense woods on a gravel road—rather a remote location, but peaceful. The animals were moved, and they adjusted beautifully, especially Nitcha. He began to fill out in girth and walked with a more sure and purposeful step. Nitcha and Muttley roughhoused together, sending the cat into a spike-furred dither when they got too rambunctious. Scruffy could be found clinging to the top of the curtains when Dave started rolling around on the floor with the dogs. On top of all that confusion, a small kitten was dumped off near their home, and soft-hearted Jenny took that one in also.

Nitcha was fascinated. He didn't know cats came in that size. Scruffy was a huge cat that tolerated no guff from anyone, but the kitten was about the size of Nitcha's nose. The first time he met this little bundle of fur, the kitten was sitting behind a throw pillow on the couch, cleaning itself. Nitcha caught its scent and went hunting to locate this fascinating new arrival. Hail-fellow-well-met Nitcha, like the partygoer who slaps you on the back and sends you flying into the nearest stationary object, swiftly thrust his nose beneath the pillow and sent it sailing as he poked and snuffed at what was behind it. He met a miniature virago of spiky fur and incensed temper. Ten little needle nails whipped forward and attached themselves to that offending nose, while the hind feet flipped forward and attacked with ten more equally painful scimitars. Nitcha whipped his head backward, but the kitten remained firmly lodged and dug in deeper. Things were not going well at all. Nitcha was ready to charge through the first wall he came to when Dave rushed in and plucked the kitten away. A sound like separating velcro fasteners filled the air, rapidly drowned out by an outraged kitten scream and Nitcha's whine, which had reached a very unhappy pitch. He could take most punishment, but his nose was his Achilles' heel. For days afterward, he walked a wide arc around the cat, whether it was sleeping or awake, and the cat, sensing a victory of sorts, played its advantage to the hilt. If Nitcha came within sniffing range, he was told off and swatted at for his impudence. Eventually, things did quiet down to the point where they could both sleep side by side, but it was an armed truce. Nitcha was careful which way he moved.

Meanwhile, back at the ranch, Chakka seemed content. Oddly, I noticed, he never once attempted to make Tippy submit. Not even in the smallest way. I could understand when he didn't press his advantage with Spook, because she was his alpha female, but Chakka had always maintained total and constant control over the remainder of the pack as he would have done in the wild. It was his position and bound duty to do so, or anarchy among the strong-willed animals would have broken the cohesiveness of the pack. Their pecking order determined their role in the work of hunting, patroling, guarding, and breeding. Chakka was the word and the law. So why wasn't he keeping Tippy in line and telling her what her place was? He neither ignored her nor reminded her who was boss. He just seemed to look at her with the same perplexity I felt when I tried to gain her trust. Neither of us could quite break through her barrier of remoteness. It was like dealing with a disturbed or mistreated child, but Tippy had never been hurt or threatened by anyone. Some small piece of the puzzle was missing, and all I could do was protect Tippy from a world that wouldn't understand her. Perhaps when she grew up, she would feel more secure.

It was time to spay old Spook. I hated to do it at her age, but I couldn't risk any more pups. Her next estrus was rapidly approaching, so I called our vet and made arrangements to have her come out the following Monday to perform surgery. That afternoon, when I went into the pen to feed and water the animals, I sat down to pet Chakka. Spook came over and plopped down on the other side, rolling over on her back for her usual tummy scratch. As I absently ran my hands up and down their sleek bodies, a chill went through my fingers. All along the left side of Spook's breasts, ominous swellings had appeared, and further palpations revealed other ragged lumps in the groin and neck areas. I knew what I was feeling, but I went straight into the house and called the vet immediately anyway.

Her examination confirmed my worst fears. Even without a biopsy she was sure that Spook had a massive invasion of cancer cells, and at her age treatment was not a viable option. It would have been painful and hopeless to make her last days a misery. I made the decision for Spook that I would have made for myself. We would keep her comfortable and at home as long as she didn't suffer. I would not let her end her days in pain. In the meantime, we would do our best to make her life happy.

We began by bringing Spook into the house without Chakka in the evenings and giving her special attention. She got meaty treats and rubdowns, both of which left her in a state of moaning ecstasy. At first, Chakka was upset to be left behind, but Denny took it upon himself to take Chakka for long walks to compensate. Some evenings, they both came in and relaxed, but Chakka was ready to return to the pen much sooner than Spook. Toward the last, when Spook's energy was waning, Chakka would return to the pen without her, and she would settle on her crib mattress in front of the fire, warming her back and snoring loudly. Fall had come, and the weather had cooled quite rapidly. Spook's energy was needed just to keep going. She needn't expend it on trying to keep warm also.

I can't explain Chakka's change in attitude. I like to think that he realized that she was unwell and needed to stay inside, but I don't think that was it. He simply seemed to be more content going back to the pen with Tippy than he was staying with Spook in her state of diminished response. Some days she went outside for an hour or so in a short burst of energy, but she elected to return at dark and take up her position in front of the fireplace. We used to laugh and say that the last thing to go would be her appetite. She could always eat and was a terrible mooch, but her weight slowly dropped nonetheless, and she began having trouble going upstairs at night to sleep in her bed next to mine. For several weeks we had to carry her upstairs, even though she was ambulatory on a flat surface and seemed to enjoy everything around her. Snow was falling on Christmas Eve when she shared a big turkey dinner with the family, wolfing down huge portions of meat and polishing off the potatoes and gravy. Bill remarked that she seemed much better and certainly had a healthy appetite. We carried her upstairs after Chakka had returned outside, and covered her with her favorite blanket. At four o'clock Christmas morning, I awoke to the sound of her whining and thrashing. The cancer had hit the painful level, and it was time. An hour later, she was sleeping peacefully after an overdose of sodium pentathol. I was there holding her, sobbing, losing a dear and valued friend, but grateful her end could be painless and in the security of her own home. Because of our wonderful vet, she hadn't had to go to a sterile hospital with unfamiliar people to end her days. She was with her family.

We performed the one final service we could in her memory. We wrapped her in a blanket and took her outside to Chakka's pen. There we allowed him to sniff her all over and recognize that she was dead. I didn't want him looking for her, not understanding what had happened. Chakka pawed at her several times, pushing her with his nose, but she didn't move. Finally we wrapped her in the blanket and took her out of the pen. As we were loading her in the car, Chakka's mournful howl, reminiscent of the time Widget died, floated on the bitter cold air. It was soft, sustained, and a totally flat monotone. Again and again he repeated the sound, and I heard it all the way down the road as we took Spook's body to the crematory at the vet's.

15

Tippy

CHAKKA'S GRIEF MANIFESTED ITSELF IN A way I hardly expected. Instead of continued howling or refusing to eat or pacing endlessly, as one might have expected, he simply grew quiet and introspective. He was always glad to go for walks or to lie stretched out across my lap while I groomed him. He'd come into the house and visit with the other animals, but there was no overt playing. He was more content to just lean back against my legs and stare into the fireplace. If I put the tug-a-dog sock in his mouth, he would just hold it a moment, then spit it out. I could entice him to eat just fine, even though he had lost a noticeable amount of weight. But he didn't seem interested or enthusiastic about anything, and his interaction with Tippy was as it had always been—casual. At my wit's end, I even desperately considered getting another female for him, but I held off—luckily. Time has a way of healing things, and Chakka's zest for life returned to some extent over the next two months, and by spring he was feeling quite a bit better. Even though I know he missed his pack, he was doing goofy things like clowning around for the school-children who waited for the bus.

Those children were the source of amusement for another animal at our house also. Beaky (short for Mr. Be Caws) was a crow who lived on the screened-in porch just off the kitchen. He had only one wing, so he was unable to function in the wilds. We took him along with us to schools when we visited to show the children the animals. Beaky, who adored kids, was such a showoff that he continually embarrassed us by screaming out inappropriate words and phrases. Some words were picked up from the older school kids when they congregated across the road, waiting for the bus in the morning. Beaky loved their chatter and could easily pick up on it, especially those words and phrases uttered with conviction or vehemence. One particular phrase, repeated often, soon became his favorite because as soon as it was uttered, things got lively.

It would start the same way every morning, with children in bright coats headed down both sides of the road toward the bus stop. Beaky always eagerly awaited them, whistling, calling, and mimicking their laughter with eerie accuracy. It was like having the whole kindergarten on our porch. On rainy, windy, or cold days, the children sought the shelter of the recessed doorway of the little store. They jammed into that area like so many colored jelly beans. They were protected all right, but packed in so tightly that they were unable to see around the corner to watch for the bus. One poor, luckless little individual was always appointed to stand out by the road in the cold and wait to see the bus pull around the corner from the highway. He would then yell in a very important voice that the bus was coming. The jelly beans would spill out of the doorway and rush to jostle into position to board. It didn't take Beaky long to get that phrase down pat. Within a week, he could yell across the road, "The bus is coming!" after which the children would rush out in the rain to form their lines, little faces turned expectantly toward an empty road. Beaky would cackle and chortle with absolute glee, and while his "hee, hee, hee" echoed into the kitchen, it didn't quite drown out some of the unkinder comments children can make. Beaky learned the phrase "Damn crow!" rather easily also.

Although he still wasn't himself, Chakka was showing definite signs of making an adjustment. He and Tippy would lounge side by side in the pen, apparently quite comfortable with each other and enjoying some sort of companionship short of normal pack relationships. Tippy herself was no more warm or trusting with me than she ever had been, but certain signs of curiosity were evident when she would sneak behind me for a sniff as I fed or groomed Chakka. Without turning, I would put my hand gently behind me, but nothing more than her warm breath ever touched my skin. When she was in front of me, she seldom looked me directly in the face unless I was looking away. Her whole demeanor perplexed me, and even Chakka's attitude toward her indicated that she was, indeed, different. It seemed nothing would ever improve, but about the time I think all is lost, the animals prove me wrong.

It was one of those glorious, balmy mornings that herald the approach of true summer. I had decided to go out and work in the yard before the day got too hot, and I was raking the grass along the edge of Chakka's pen. Chakka would reach under the wire and try to grab the rake when it got close enough. He was having a grand time when Tippy emerged from the doghouse and stretched and yawned in the sunlight. Chakka sat watching her, tipping his nose into the air and sniffing. Suddenly he lost interest in playing with the rake and walked over to Tippy's side. He licked her face and put his muzzle across her shoulders, the way he had with Spook. He didn't attempt to make her submit, but simply seemed content to stand that way for a minute or two. He was treating her like alpha female. *Alpha female?!* Tippy was not yet six months old, but the cold reality was that she just might be coming into heat. Pups are not supposed to be spayed until they are at least six months of age because they haven't put enough growth and maturity behind them. Besides that, Tippy should not have been coming into heat until at least eight months of age, and even then, being part wolf she might skip the first one or two heats. That was the wolf side of her. The dog side seemed to be winning. I ran inside to call the vet. No more puppies!

After our vet examined Tippy, she decided to put her on birth control pills, an option we had not considered earlier. It was worth a try, but I extracted the promise that if they didn't work, she would come and spay Tippy before the pregnancy barely had a chance to start. She promised and left the pills. It should have been an easy manner of administration, hiding the pills in a small mound of dog food and giving it to Tippy every day. It was easy, all right. Chakka had his nose in the treat before Tippy—cautious beast that she was—was through nosing it over. Twice Chakka got the dose meant for Tippy. The vet assured me that it wouldn't hurt him, but he would probably never give birth. Very funny! The third time I tried, I gave Chakka a big bone, which he grabbed and took to the far end of the pen while I gave Tippy yet another mound of food with its concealed pill. She took it in her mouth like a hot tamale, barely touching it with her teeth, lips drawn back in suspicious disgust. She backed up several steps, placed it carefully on the cement, and proceeded to lick all the canned food away, leaving the offending pill, which she nosed way under the doghouse.

The battle lines were drawn. I went back into the house and cooked up some pieces of beef, searing them just enough to brown the meat and get the juices running. Even my mouth was watering. Then I very carefully sliced a tiny pocket in one cube, put in the pill, and took a plateful of about ten pieces out to the pen. I tossed a plain one over the fence, which Tippy caught expertly and swallowed without hesitation. By the time the second plain one was sailing over the fence, Chakka was dancing on his toenails, making an expert catch. The third and fourth, no matter where they were tossed, ended up in Chakka's mouth. I tossed one into the far corner of the pen, and when Chakka wheeled to retrieve it, I poked another plain one through the wire to Tippy. She took it. Good! I tossed another one into the far corner for Chakka, and he turned just as I gave Tippy the loaded cube. Chakka nosed in, grabbed Tippy's cube, and then raced once again for his own before anyone else got it. The score was wolves eight, humans nothing.

Things were definitely not going my way. I went back into the house, loaded one of the last cubes, and returned. Chakka was ready. What a wonderful game this was, and the rewards were so tasty! This time I was sneaky. I moved my arm as if tossing a treat into the corner for Chakka. He turned, I slipped one quickly through the wire for Tippy, and when Chakka spun back to take hers, I had one all ready for him. Victory! It worked that once, and never worked again. I was reduced to waiting for Denny to get home from work and take Chakka for walks before I could give Tippy her medication.

At nine months of age, Tippy appeared to be ready for her surgery. We planned it for a weekend morning when the kids would be home and could keep Chakka out on an extended walk while Denny and I somehow got Tippy immobilized for her tranquilizer shot. I had worried excessively that cornering her and pinning her down would ruin even the small bit of trust she had placed in me. I would probably never gain her trust after this, but the alternative was more pups. The decision was irrevocable. Saturday morning at ten o'clock, on a beautiful, warm, sunny day, the vet arrived with her equipment. Dave took Chakka for a long walk along the beach, and Denny and I went into the pen while the vet waited outside the wire with a syringe.

Tippy was no one's fool. Sensing instantly that something was wrong, she headed straight for the doghouse. If she got inside, we would have to wait all day, because pulling her out would be nearly impossible. Denny ran to head her off, while I rushed to the doghouse to slap a piece of plywood up across the porch entry. It worked! I put in two nails to hold it, and then Denny and I started toward Tippy. She backed warily into the corner, facing us with lowered head. I fully expected to get bitten; it would have been understandable. Even dogs don't like being cornered. I approached Tippy talking quietly to her, hiding the choke-chain collar I held in my hand. Denny backed me up, arms out, moving whichever way Tippy seemed about to bolt. I was almost up to Tippy when she swung her head past my legs to see where Denny was. It was more by accident than plan that I made a lucky move and slipped the choke chain over her head. I held the end in my hand as she skittered backward against the fence corner. Denny was there in a second, pressing her hindquarters against the wire while the vet slipped the needle into her hind leg. Tippy never bit, or even tried to. She was more intent on getting away, and she bolted as soon as the vet yelled, "Done!" and we'd released our hold on her. She raced to the other end of the pen and stood panting in fear and confusion, eyeing us warily, ready to flee if we should approach her again. For a couple of minutes she eyed us with lowered head, then her legs began to splay out from under her. As she was going down, I rushed in to support her fall, and Tippy and I went down together, her head resting across my legs. I petted and talked to her as the vet and Denny came forward with a blanket. Ten minutes later, Tippy had received her anesthetic I.V. and was sleeping soundly, undergoing a successful and rapid surgery.

This time, we had once again planned to have the animal back in the pen before Chakka's return. However, unlike the short-term anesthetic that Nitcha had received, Tippy's surgery required much longer-acting medication. She would probably sleep for a couple of hours, so I prepared to stay in the pen most of the day. We laid her on the warm cement in the sun, and I went back inside to help the vet clean up and to get a dish of water for Tippy when she woke up. I was just starting out the door when I looked up to see Dave coming in, without Chakka. Seeing Tippy in the pen, he had assumed that it was all right to place Chakka in there also. I went back out at a dead run.

Chakka was standing over Tippy, pushing her with his nose, when I entered the pen. As soon as he heard the latch click, Chakka turned to face me, then dropped to all fours and placed his head and shoulders across Tippy's sleeping body. It was the most touchingly protective gesture I had ever seen Chakka make, and I watched his expression intently as I crossed the space between us. When I knelt down by Tippy's side, Chakka pushed his head tighter against her body. As I reached to check her breathing and pulse, Chakka nosed my hand. He wasn't exactly pushing me away, but it was as if he were telling me to be careful because something was wrong. I stroked his head as well as Tippy's, and sat down with my arm across Chakka's back, resting against the fence. For two hours we stayed there, and twice I had to roll Tippy over so fluid wouldn't settle in her lungs. Chakka monitored the situation carefully, pushing with his own nose and settling once again with his head across her neck.

Finally Tippy moaned and raised her head. Chakka rose at once, moaning along with her and attempting to push her up with his nose. Tippy tried once, but fell back in dizzy confusion. Her feet wouldn't do what she wanted them to do, and here she was with her head across the legs of that human! She looked directly into my eyes, then sighed and went back to sleep. I laid her head on the pavement and tried to get up, but I was so stiff that even Chakka became concerned and tried to nose me upright also. Chakka was certainly having a busy day of it taking care of his pack! I went into the house for a quick cup of coffee and to get that bowl of water for Tippy, and by the time I returned to the pen half an hour later, Tippy was wobbling on her feet but standing with Chakka's help. I went in with the water and laid it in front of Tippy, but Chakka pushed her roughly aside and sniffed at the bowl. He wasn't taking any chances that she would get something else that wasn't good for her, and he wouldn't allow her to touch it until he'd ascertained that it was safe. I knew that after her drink of water, Tippy would go back to sleep for a while, so Chakka and I supported Tippy on each side and helped her return to the doghouse, which Denny had reopened. Once inside she slumped down and snoozed off. I backed my way out of the porch area, and Chakka settled down against the door to guard her against any further harm. He was still there the next morning when Tippy finally emerged, slightly unsteady but more like her old self.

That protective episode seemed to trigger something in Chakka, and his attitude toward Tippy changed. He seemed to feel that there was an affirmation of his leadership. She needed him. His overt protectiveness was just what Chakka needed, and it seemed to give Tippy a slightly different view of the world. She did not appear to be as frightened as before, but she was still a nervous and retiring animal. It took her several weeks before she would come anywhere near me again, and then she only approached from the back. We were back where we started, but at least I hadn't lost any ground because of her surgery. I just hadn't gained any, either.

I had thought that Nitcha would be coming home to visit more often, but Jenny and Dave had staggered work schedules that made it difficult. If Jenny was at work, she had the car and Dave couldn't come over, and vice versa. The summer came and went like the wind. Nitcha, Scruffy, and Muttley had settled into their home as if they'd lived there forever. Nitcha didn't even have to miss his howls. At first, without Chakka's leadership, things were pretty silent, but before long the animals realized that the woods behind their home, and the swamp below, harbored some pretty interesting wildlife.

The first night that Nitcha heard the bobcat scream somewhere near the trailer, he had been sleeping on the floor at the end of Jenny and Dave's bed. When the first screaming notes hit the air, Nitcha was already two feet off the floor and pulling covers from the bed in his haste to get to the safety of the family bosom. It is really pathetic to see such a huge animal cowering in fear and showing the whites of his eyes. Jenny had to sit up with him to quiet him down, and she only succeeded when she encouraged him to howl. It was tentative at first, but like a little boy whistling as he goes by the graveyard, Nitcha lifted his nose to the sky and warbled a few notes. The screams outside stopped, and Nitcha gathered a little bravado from that. His howls became louder and more sure until Muttley felt constrained to join in. Yes, sir, things were going better! The two of them harmonized for several minutes and were taking a vocal break when Nitcha's ears picked up another sound. Deep in the swamp, another chorus was playing back their song. A pack of wild dogs that were known to run in that densely packed wooded area were answering a call they had never heard before. By listening carefully, Jenny could pick out the baying of a hound or two, the barks of several medium-sized dogs, and the deep, mellow tones of much larger dogs, probably the shepherds that had been seen running the farmers' fields in the moonlight. Over the years, the pack had fended for itself, assimilating extra dogs that had been dropped off by uncaring owners and hunting dogs that had become lost. The animals stayed mostly out of sight, slipping like shadows across corn stubble and wheat fields only after dark. But after hearing Nitcha's howl, they began coming much closer to the trailer. Nitcha's evening serenade was joined by his own chorus hidden behind the shadows under the trees. Moonlight never revealed their faces, but their voices became quite well known to Jenny and Dave.

One evening, Jenny came home from work and noticed that Dave was not in the trailer. She walked around outside in case he was at the pen, but there was no sign of either Dave or the animals. Jenny, surmising they were all out for a walk, went in to fix supper. An hour later, she began to worry. Still no sign of Dave or the dogs. By the time Dave returned, shortly after dark, Jenny was frantic with worry, and the look on Dave's face did nothing to alleviate her fears.

Dave had wakened from his nap and taken the dogs outside to the pen to do their thing. While they were playing and stretching, Dave went back into the trailer and took a shower. Almost an hour later he returned to the pen and discovered that the latch had not been properly secured. Both Muttley and Nitcha were gone. Dave set out immediately and tried to follow their tracks in the soft sand, but he lost all trace as soon as they entered the woods. He pushed ahead anyway, calling and searching as far as the swamp, but the approaching twilight forced him to give up and return to the trailer. Dave and Jenny had a quick supper, got in the car, and began driving the miles of country roads surrounding the woods and swamps. By ten o'clock, they'd given up in dismay and returned home. It wasn't until nearly morning that both animals turned up on their doorstep—tired, muddy, and grinning from their adventure. Jenny and Dave let them in, scolding in determined tones.

The next evening, Jenny and Dave were both home and had the dogs inside while they watched TV. Suddenly someone pounded violently on the door. Both dogs raced to the door, and Nitcha, shocked by the sudden sound, growled menacingly as Dave opened it. There stood a neighbor from down the road, brandishing a loaded shotgun in their faces, telling them he was there to shoot their dogs. He especially hated the big black one, and as he pushed his way into the trailer, Dave had all he could do to restrain Nitcha. Over the man's shouted threats, Dave had to try to cope with the dogs and the fact that the gun could go off at any time. He finally made sense of what the man was saying.

He raised goats, and they were allowed to roam outside with their kids, nibbling on the grass. They never strayed far and were usually home in the small barn at dark. That last evening, when the man went down to close the barn door, he discovered that both the does and their kids had been viciously mauled and killed. No, he hadn't seen it happen, but he knew that Nitcha and Muttley had been out because he had seen them farther down the road beyond Jenny and Dave's house. Now he was going to kill them.

Somehow, Dave managed to get the man out of the trailer, and they both went down the road to his home to view the carnage. Dave was sick at heart, and helped bury what was left of the poor animals, but the welter of tracks around the pen area gave no clue because of the nature of the soft sand. Whether Nitcha and Muttley had done such a terrible thing was something that could never be proved, but because they were loose at the time, Jenny and Dave paid to replace the goats. In view of the man's threats, Nitcha was sent home to me. Because he could easily go through a window, he was the only animal that had to stay outside in the pen if no one was home at Jenny and Dave's, and his safety was definitely in question now. Muttley and Scruffy, on the other hand, were confined to the trailer. And yet despite all their plans and precautions, both Muttley and Scruffy disappeared within a month and were never seen again. Once more, nothing was ever proved.

The evening they brought Nitcha home, Chakka was ecstatic. When we put Nitcha into the pen, they greeted each other effusively, wagging and pushing in a delighted greeting. Tippy nosed tentatively at Nitcha, but would not join in any of the wolf rituals. She simply retired to the doghouse and stayed there until all the boisterous excitement had subsided. Shortly after dark, Nitcha and Chakka raised their muzzles to the moon and harmonized in happiness. Tippy silently moved to an area behind them and joined their chorus. It was soft, harmonious, and blended naturally with the sound of frogs in the woods. That night I let them howl for three minutes, and even joined in to the best of my human ability.

16

Change

CHAKKA'S WHOLE DEMEANOR CHANGED. Somehow, having his pack back seemed to validate him. There was order to his world, an order that was his duty to maintain, being head wolf. Nitcha submitted, but not really gracefully. He was older now, wiser, and had had some freedom away from the discipline. But the loss of Muttley had permanently altered Nitcha. He seemed slightly disoriented, more withdrawn from other animals, and perhaps a bit touchy. I should have taken warning from these signs, but I thought that eventually he would stop looking for Muttley and settle down. I was wrong.

Taking Chakka for a walk made Nitcha jealous, so we began taking both of them whenever the situation permitted. Tippy refused to budge from the security of the pen and set up a terrible fuss if we so much as approached her with a leash. Eventually, we gave up even trying, and contented ourselves with walking Nitcha and Chakka only.

I use the term "walking" euphemistically. I knew what to expect with Chakka. After years of flying behind him, I'd developed the winged heels of Mercury. I knew that hitting every third step was cause for celebration, and staying on one's feet warranted a medal. Anyone accompanying us on our walk usually insisted I take Nitcha, because common wisdom had it I couldn't keep up with Chakka's speed anymore. Both Dave and Denny were tall, long-legged men whose jogging left my short frame in the dust. Therefore, Nitcha and I were paired up. A not illogical decision, since Nitcha was less interested in keeping up with Chakka than he was in exploring the world around him. That was fine with me, but I began to find his sudden stops to sniff something interesting were injurious to my physique. We would be trotting at a brisk pace when Nitcha would stop instantly, head down, investigating the trail of some chipmunk that had gone by two weeks before. I did some very interesting cartwheels and headstands over his crouched form before I began extending the length of the leash so that a little slack was available before my gymnastics became inevitable. But as usual, the minute I find a solution, the animals find a problem.

Nitcha discovered that the extra slack on the leash meant some excess of freedom for him. He was not the least interested, at that point, in keeping up with Chakka. He would much rather whip from side to side, whuffing his nose up and down along the road, covering as much ground as possible. This was fine as long as he stayed in front of me. However, going forward at a good clip meant that he was reading the ground scents in rapid form. Once in a while he would double back for a clarification. That meant that I had a leash whipped around me, front to back, before I knew what was happening. Even that was no particular problem as long as Nitcha continued on the same route. Nitcha probably knew this, because he elected to run around me three or four times before leaping forward on another quest. The very predictable effect of having him pull energetically on a leash wrapped around my middle was that of a human yo-yo completely out of control and falling all over the road. Nitcha loved that. I was reduced to yelling for help while four huge black feet stomped about my curled-up body.

The easiest way to walk both animals was to take them down to the sandy beach and let them pull to their hearts' content. Their leverage diminished in the sand, and the obstacles were fewer and lower. Of course, the occasional sharp stone in the bottom of a human foot made an interesting spectacle of the leash holder—much to the delight of the animals. Chakka especially loved the beach because of its exotic, wonderful odors. Rotting fish left in the wave froth was just too enticing to leave alone. The minute he found anything like this, despite our efforts to avoid all manner of such things, he would roll his shoulder and neck to the ground and rub enthusiastically. Perfume of the natural gods! Even a minnow would afford him ten minutes of rolling and rubbing. Somewhere in Chakka's memory, there lingered visions of the sea gull wing that he had taken home and treasured for so long. Although he never seemed to connect its disappearance with anything I did, he nevertheless had searched diligently for it for months after it had met its fate in the burn barrel. Not one to be left out of any fun, Nitcha picked up this lovely habit the first day he ever hit the beach and refused to be dissuaded by any tugging on my part. We finally gave up, let them have their fun, and then tried to stay upwind the rest of the trip.

Ahead of me, I could see Chakka and Dave weaving back and forth between the shoreline and the beach grasses on the hillocks. Chakka's nose was glued to the ground as he approached a thick tussock of tall beach grass, and he had almost passed by it, dragging his human behind him, when the grass exploded. There was a large flurry of sand, a blur of movement, and Chakka backed into Dave so fast that he sent them both flying. A sound like thunder issued from the center of all this activity, and Chakka did his best to regain his feet and get the heck out of there. Before any real progress was made, a white virago barreled down on poor luckless Chakka, who barely escaped by rolling over Dave and seeking sanctuary on the other side. A huge white swan, who had been placidly sitting on her nest, was now lauching attacks on those who chose to come too close to her babies. I'll tell you right now, if it came to a choice between facing a pride of lions or one incensed mother swan, I'd pick the lions any day.

Adult swans are quite able to break a human's leg with one bash of their powerful wing, and I can attest to the grinding, smashing power of those big beaks when they connect with flesh. Chakka had been completely overcome by the element of surprise. Oddly enough, he did not seem to defend himself. I have often wondered if there is not some unwritten rule of nature that says "Thou shalt not tangle with angry mothers." Or perhaps it was the fluffed-up wings-spread size of the swan that intimidated him. Whatever, Chakka wasn't in the mood to fight. All he could see were flailing wings, snapping beaks, and angry red eyes. And he wanted O-U-T! Dave seemed to agree, because contrary to the laws of nature and gravity they both levitated upward and shot outward at the same time, making some truly astonishing speeds. Nitcha and I were far enough away from the swan to be safe, but Nitcha didn't think there was any such thing as "far enough away." Before I was aware that Nitcha had turned, I was whipped around, my head snapped back, my jaw jerked open, and I was leaving a trough as wide as my body in the beach. Undeterred, Nitcha headed for safety in the next town while I played anchor. Somehow, we all stopped before we were run off the map, but I ate enough "sand"-wiches to last quite a while. We were careful on all our other walks to avoid that area—in fact, the animals headed resolutely down the beach in the opposite direction every time we walked there.

Chakka was becoming more invigorated every day, while the long-term effect of being a puppet on the other end of his leash was becoming more than I could handle. Several times I attempted to take Chakka for walks by myself, but found to my dismay that I had little if any control. Joints that used to do my bidding were now in rebellion. Years of picking myself up off the road and peeling myself off stop signs and walls had taken their toll. Chakka was in his prime, while I was rapidly slipping past mine, with his help. Even getting into Chakka's pen was becoming a challenge. If I tried to slip through the gate with anything in my hands, Chakka would push my knees with his nose, trying to get out for a run. The only time that Chakka left me alone was if he had something more interesting commanding his attention. Tossing a bone or a tug-a-dog in ahead of me was a surefire method of diverting him, and it lasted a whole week. Clearly, I had to come up with something better. Like a beleaguered general, I began to plan my campaigns with more covert cunning than frontal attacks.

Dragging in a twenty-five-pound bag of dog food was difficult enough, what with getting it in the gate while keeping Chakka away, but that was only half the battle. Even though Chakka had a big bucket of dog food on the house porch, he simply *had* to have a wee nip of the food fresh from the bag. That meant that while I was fumbling around with the top of the bag, trying to undo those nasty little strings that say PULL HERE (and then crochet themselves into the Gordian knot), Chakka was expertly ripping the bottom strip out with one swift pull. Probably one out of every twenty bags made it to the porch in one piece. The rest got lighter with each progressive pull across the pen as they spilled their contents over the cement. Chakka and Tippy had a delightful time skating through the kibble, while I desperately tried to sweep up enough to put in the bucket. Things were not going well, and I wracked my brain trying to come up with a method to keep Chakka at bay while the chores were performed.

Chakka loved a challenge, which is why he got into so much mischief and made such a nuisance of himself. If it was something he shouldn't have, that's what he wanted. The solution was so simple, I wondered why it had taken me so long to come up with it. The next time I entered the pen to feed, I purposely worked in the yard near the pen and garnered Chakka's interest. Then I laid an old shirt of mine on the ground near the pen, tied one sleeve to a sapling, and left a tantalizing sleeve near the pen wire. The minute my back was turned, Chakka began working his paw under the wire, lying on his side to do so. While he edged the fabric closer to his mouth, I entered the pen and filled the dog dish in record time, with no interference. I managed to fill the water buckets, shovel up the messes, and hose down the whole thing undisturbed. Chakka was still working on the sleeve, getting larger and larger shreds coaxed into the pen, when I left. I knew it would only be a matter of minutes before he had the whole shirt, and I left smiling. He could have it! An hour later, as I went out the back door on the way to my car, I glanced at the pen, and then stood still in shock. It was a mess! The cement was littered with shreds of shirt, mounds of black dirt . . . and what was left of a very nice maple sapling. Chakka was sleeping soundly in the sun, content with a job well done.

Keeping Chakka's world interesting was a challenge that had unexpected turns. Nothing is sadder than an animal left on a leash or in a pen with nothing to do. It's bad enough with a dog, but disastrous with a wolf. In order to pique Chakka's interest and amuse him, we went through a variety of "toys," such as the rubber beach ball and assorted rawhide bones, plus cooked bones, tug-a-dogs, and cardboard boxes. Although he loved bones and chewed happily on them for quite a while, Chakka really found more fun in an empty cardboard box. He could stick his head inside, roll it over, toss it in the air, attack it from every angle, rip off the flaps, and pounce on it for a final kill. He was always disappointed when, like some humans, it flattened out in final defeat. I had tried for years to come up with an indestructible toy for Chakka, and came to the conclusion there was no such thing until someone suggested a bowling ball.

Of all the items that seemed to be suited for rough play, this was it! It was round, offered no corners to chew, was heavy, made of tough material, and could roll all over while Chakka chased it. I went immediately to the nearest bowling alley and asked for an old used bowling ball, condition unimportant. When I was asked about size, weight, and so on, I knew what was coming. Age makes one smarter. Instead of being dragged into an explanation about how it was going to be used, I simply pointed to a ball, paid the price, and left. I grinned all the way home.

I saved that ball for the next time I had to go in and clean the pen. But I pulled a real sneaky. I put the ball out in the yard near the pen, in full sight under the tree. It was nowhere close enough for Chakka to get at it, so he had to sit and stare holes through it for a couple of days before I decided I needed its diversion while I cleaned the pen again.

Chakka saw me come out, and when I approached the bowling ball, he knew something good was coming. The minute I picked it up, he began pacing the length of the pen, whuffing happily as I approached. As I opened the gate, he pushed at me insistently, eager to get at this new toy. I put it just inside the gate, gave it a shove, and Chakka leapt immediately on it. It rolled away and he chased it, tail wagging, trying to get his mouth over the top of it to pick it up. Not only was it too large for his jaws, but it was also too heavy for him, even if he had managed to get it into his mouth in the first place. He had to resort to pushing it with his nose and chasing it while it rolled an erratic path across the cement. When it rolled slowly into the fence and stopped, Chakka hooked both front feet over the ball and sent it flying through his legs, backward. Things were going so well that I turned to the hose and began washing down the pen when I heard a startled *whuff!*

Chakka had pulled the ball back between his feet again, but this time it hit a small depression in the concrete and skidded sideways, rolling over Chakka's toes. He lifted one foot and danced aside, grumbling a little while he licked his wounded digits. As he was easing the pain in his foot, the ball rolled a few more feet, hit the wire wall, and came ricocheting back at a rather good clip. Chakka looked up just as the ball rolled over his front foot. Wolves on only two legs do not stand up well. Chakka went down, rolled over, and got to his feet just as the ball came rolling lazily toward him once again. This time he was taking no chances. He danced aside, favoring two sore feet, and retreated until the ball quit rolling and ended up in the corner. Cautiously Chakka approached, ready to leap backward at the least sign of aggression. The ball lay still while he touched it with his nose. Finally, assured that it was dead, he lifted his leg and gave it a final salute. He never played with it again, and I finally removed it the next spring.

Chakka really enjoyed watching the world outside his pen.

The country store across the street had blossomed and grown into a small neighborhood market that carried everything from groceries to fresh pizza and submarine sandwiches. The odors wafting across the street on a hot summer day were enough to keep anyone's mouth watering for hours. Business was brisk, and Chakka could whuff at people to his heart's content. The more people who walked across the street to see him, the happier he was, especially if they were children. Seldom was anyone ill-mannered toward Chakka, and if this happened, he'd turn away and retire to his doghouse. I always felt sorry for him at those times, because his trust was so great that anything that eroded it was unwarranted and cruel.

One hot July Fourth holiday, Chakka was happily watching the steady stream of cars across the road. It was a day much to his liking, with all sorts of activity. It started out with the normal holiday traffic, people shouting back and forth about places to meet, and which beach was best for swimming. The sounds were happy, upbeat, and excited. Chakka felt the mood and pranced around his pen, showing off. He made Nitcha submit whenever someone came close to the fence, both to show his superiority and to make sure that Nitcha behaved appropriately. As the day wore on, however, the mood began to change. It became hotter, and people were in more of a hurry to reach their destinations. Some of the loud voices were slurred in an obvious excess of drink. Car motors were gunned, tires spun, and an altercation between two young men even resulted in a fistfight. All this served to upset Chakka. He was not used to humans behaving this way, and I began to worry that a speeding car might even miss the stop sign and slam into my little home. Everyone's nerves were getting taut, but the worst was yet to come.

In spite of laws to the contrary, people began setting off firecrackers in the store's parking lot. They were lighting them, throwing them into the air, and laughing, but Chakka was terrified. It was no fun for him, and his nervousness carried to Nitcha and Tippy. Chakka herded his pack into the doghouse, but Nitcha refused to stay, rushing out to bark at the noise and confusion while the odor of gunpowder floated in the air. He was salivating with nervousness, panting, pacing, tense. I had finally had enough, and I walked across the street to ask them, please, to desist. They were just drunk enough to be loud and obnoxious, but I persisted. They piled into their car and tore down the road as I returned to the house and headed for the pen. I had just gotten around the corner approaching the pen when I heard the car coming back. Before I reached the gate, the car pulled over close to the fence, and firecrackers sailed over and into the pen. Chakka and Nitcha were both standing outside when the explosions took place and the car sped away.

Chakka was frantic, trying to make Nitcha get into the dog-house. Nitcha refused, terror driving him to previously un-known actions. He wheeled on Chakka, and the most terrible fight I have ever seen erupted. Chakka struggled to maintain his status as head wolf the way he always had, but Nitcha was bigger, heavier, and more frightened than he had ever been in his life. The tables were turned before I could get into the pen, and Chakka was thrown to the ground by Nitcha who had him by the back of the neck. Now that Nitcha had the upper hand, Chakka was so severely defeated that he submitted for the first time in his life. He stopped fighting and lay still, urinating helplessly. Had Nitcha been a wolf, that would have signaled the end of the fight, but Nitcha was half dog. He wanted to fight to the death.

I rushed forward and grabbed Nitcha by the collar, trying to pull him back away from Chakka, but he was mindless in the darkest meaning of the word. He neither saw nor felt me, and continued the attack with a ferocity that was primal. I attempted to force my legs between them, but could not gain any ground whatsoever. I pulled Nitcha's head backward by straddling him, reaching on both sides of his head and pulling the corners of his mouth, the only handhold I could get. It was useless. I grabbed him by the throat as I saw the flesh begin to tear from the back of Chakka's head. Nitcha was killing him. As Chakka's flesh gave way, Nitcha lifted his head and thrust for another bite. When he did, I slid over his shoulders and got between them, one hand under Nitcha's chin, clutching his collar and forcing him back. Even in his aggravated state, he never attempted to bite, but he lunged repeatedly at Chakka, who was lying wounded on the cement. I stiff-armed Nitcha until I could get up, then backed him across the pen and out the gate, which I slammed behind me. I tied Nitcha quickly with the walking leash we left by the door, and then returned to Chakka.

It is hard to describe the horror I felt as I knelt by the wolf, lifting his head gently. Blood was everywhere, a huge flap of flesh was torn from his skull, and one ear dangled by less than an inch of skin. Chakka was in shock, staring sightlessly, each pant ending in a groan. I left him to dash into the house and call the vet, but it was a holiday and no one was available. I grabbed some supplies and raced back out to the pen. Chakka lay where I'd left him, and during the next half hour that I worked on him, he never moved.

I was able to clean and disinfect the wound and actually take four quick stitches to hold the scalp and ear in place. The open edges were sealed with antiseptic powder and pulled as close together as possible. Under the circumstances, it was all I could do until we could reach a vet. With the wound closed, Chakka would not suffer as much shock. I sat in the pen, holding Chakka's head on a clean towel, talking to him and sobbing uncontrollably. By the time someone arrived home (I'm still not certain who it was), I was brought fresh supplies, warm milk, and a blanket. Chakka and I lay on the warm cement until well after dark, when he finally struggled to his feet and wobbled to the doghouse. The most immediate crisis was over.

The next day we found a used dog pen, small but necessary, and put it next to Chakka's pen. Nitcha was put inside. He hated it and paced the sides, glowering at Chakka when he came out—but it was necessary. Never again would I put them together. It was not the best solution, just an expedient one, and the only one I could make. I yearned with a red-eyed vehemence to get hold of the young men who had tossed those firecrackers and show them what an awful thing they had done. Their moment of wild insolence had very nearly cost me a big part of my life, and things would never be the same again. Chakka would, and did, recover, and Nitcha was just as loving with us as ever.

But the pack was broken, and Chakka's spirit very nearly broke with it.

We worked for weeks getting Chakka back into shape. He received daily penicillin shots for a week and never complained. His wounds were cleaned twice daily to prevent flies from laying eggs on the raw edges. He submitted with dull eyes and then returned to the doghouse. At the end of the second week, he grumbled a bit when I pulled a leaf from the wound edge. It was his first sign of displeasure, and I welcomed it, giving him a big hug. He licked my face, assuring me he hadn't meant it personally. From then on, he healed in body and spirit, but his beautiful, proud head bore the signs of his defeat. One ear hung uselessly down, while the other stood proud and tall. It gave him a lop-eared insouciance that was both pathetic and comical. It would mark him for life.

Chakka made a full recovery, resumed a lot of his old bounce, and even played occasionally the way he used to do, but he was now quieter. He dared to grumble back at Nitcha through the wire as they paced each other, and even acted smug when he got his bones one minute ahead of Nitcha, who had to wait his turn. Tippy was no challenge to Chakka in his role as pack leader to her oneness, because the minute he looked at her she dropped in submission, much to his disgust. The fight had done something to her also, making her more timid than usual, but somehow she seemed a small comfort. She was all he had.

By fall, things had assumed a semblance of normalcy. Chakka was losing some weight, as he normally would have during the shedding process. We increased his intake of protein and fats and offered him treats of fruits and nuts. His coat completed its fall shedding, and as the winter coat began to appear, I noticed something unusual. Chakka was going gray! His coat definitely showed a lighter tone than usual, and his muzzle was much more gray than it had been. He was showing the first real signs of age (the same ones I recognized every time I looked in the mirror). But in spite of the color change he was healthy, active, and still prone to pulling pranks, as we discovered.

We had a visitor who'd come to see Chakka, and as we talked the man turned to face me and leaned against the fencing. The pocket of his jacket just happened to be pressed against the open area of the edge of the gate and the beginning of the fence. In the blink of an eye, Chakka grabbed at the pocket of the man's jacket and pulled it expertly with one swift tug. Jacket and pocket parted company, and out fell a packet of trail mix, a confection of nuts, fruits, oats, and coconut. Chakka had never encountered this exotic blend before, but he found it very much to his liking. He tossed the jacket pocket farther into the pen for later examination, then turned his attention to the trail mix itself. Something in that blend affected him deeply. He sniffed big lungfuls of air, then raised his nose slowly, until it pointed directly upward. I watched this maneuver in amazement, noticing that his eyes looked glazed and watery and his nose was quivering. As I leaned forward for a closer look, he took one more deep breath and then exploded in a wonderful wolf sneeze. We both laughed, but before I could reach under the fence to retrieve the packet, Chakka was repeating his exploration with the same results. We later discovered that coconut has the same effect on Chakka that catnip has on a cat. He began to act goofy, tipping his head sideways and dancing on a diagonal toward Tippy, who viewed this behavior with grave concentration. If he wasn't coming at her to nuzzle or growl, what on earth did this all mean? Her ears were pulled forward, making wrinkles all along her face as she waited for Chakka to reach her face. She was leaning backward as far as she could when Chakka got in front of her and bounced straight up. Tippy was so alarmed that she fell backward into the fence and then scrambled upright in a dash to the doghouse. There she remained, poking one eye around the corner, watching Chakka roll, weasel, shake, and sneeze his way across the pen. He ate some of the trail mix and rolled in the rest for another half hour before prancing around the pen and tossing leaves and sticks in the air. I had never seen him act this way before, but any time after that, trail mix could be counted on to inspire the same behavior. It did not seem to harm him, but we still restricted its use

CHANGE 273

to the occasional treat. I didn't want his dignity to suffer too much.

That fall one cold and windy day, Bill came home from his job downstate, and we sat talking in front of the fire. We usually used these times to catch up on our various bits of news, but this time we talked about buried problems that ought to have been discussed years before. Too late, we discovered that we had grown in different ways and taken different paths. There was no animosity. Bill was a man of intelligence and gentleness who encouraged anyone pursuing a worthwhile goal. He had been a support and confidant to me, and a very good friend. Now, in the parting, there was only sadness coupled with goodwill and genuine caring. We went our different ways, keeping in touch and visiting often. It is a lasting credit to this good man that we remain friends to this day, and that he and his new wife visit often and share my joys as well as sorrows. I have been doubly blessed.

It seems that everything happens in threes. In very short order, my mother died and my father developed Alzheimer's. Dad came to live with me, and although I didn't understand it at the time, my days would be severely restricted timewise. Chakka amazed me during the three years that Dad lived with us until his death. Chakka seemed to know that something was indeed very wrong but that this person was a valued part of my pack, and so he treated Dad with a gentleness that was reserved for children alone. Instead of grabbing at Dad's clothing in a playful way when he leaned against the fence, Chakka simply rubbed his head against the wire and licked Dad's frail hands. They communicated on a nonverbal level at a time when Dad's speech had deserted him. They understood each other perfectly, and drew comfort from each other's presence. During the last year of Dad's life, he was restricted to a wheelchair and then his bed. Chakka, of course, did not see him at all, but the bond somehow remained intact. The night the hearse came to the house in the final ritual of death, Chakka howled the monotone, mournful note that he had not uttered since Spook's death, and later that night, Chakka and I sat in the pen leaning against each other in a communion older than civilization. I realized then how much strength and happiness I drew from that animal, and how very much he had taught me.

Time and life go on. Denny, the last one home, has left to live in his own apartment nearby. Jenny and Dave and my three wonderful new grandchildren are a scant few miles away and a big part of my life. Kim and his wife, Bev, and my two exuberant teenage grandkids live far away, but make it home for holidays. A whole new generation is learning about the animals we take care of, and a wolf in particular. They think that young people who don't have a wolf in their backyard are underprivileged, and I agree. I wish more people knew the beauty, courage, and love this animal has. Then, perhaps, the world would learn that wildlife has a lot to teach us.

Chakka died in the spring of 1992. He left this pack of one, me, to grieve for the best animal I have ever known. I hope this story helps protect the rest of his species.